Ryan Butta's first book, *The Ballad of Abdul Wade*, was longlisted for the Indie Book Awards nonfiction book of the year for 2023. His feature writing has appeared in the *Good Weekend* magazine and he is a regular contributor to Galah Press. Ryan's works of historical nonfiction look to reveal and understand the hidden and forgotten stories of Australia and the Australians who came across the seas to make their home here. Ryan now lives on Dharawal country on the New South Wales South Coast.

THE BRAVEST SCOUT AT GALLIPOLI

RYAN BUTTA

For you, Carolina. Always for you.

First published by Affirm Press in 2024
Bunurong/Boon Wurrung Country
28 Thistlethwaite Street
South Melbourne VIC 3205
affirmpress.com.au

Affirm Press is located on the unceded land of the Bunurong/Boon Wurrung peoples of the Kulin Nation. Affirm Press pays respect to their Elders past and present.

10 9 8 7 6 5 4 3 2 1

Text copyright © Ryan Butta, 2024
All rights reserved. No part of this publication may be reproduced without prior written permission from the publisher.

 A catalogue record for this book is available from the National Library of Australia

ISBN: 9781922992086 (paperback)

Cover design by Luke Causby/Blue Cork © Affirm Press
Typeset in Garamond Premier Pro by J&M Typesetting
Proudly printed in Australia by the Opus Group

'A truly brave man is ever serene; he is never taken by surprise; nothing ruffles the equanimity of his spirit. In the heat of battle he remains cool; in the midst of catastrophes he keeps level his mind. Earthquakes do not shake him, he laughs at storms.'
Inazō Nitobe, *Bushido: The Soul of Japan*

'At the going down of the sun
and in the morning
We will remember them.'
Laurence Binyon, 'For the Fallen'

Contents

Prologue … 1

Part I **Fight, Fight, Bullets and Shells**
Chapter 1 Hell on Earth … 7
Chapter 2 Born Between Worlds … 17
Chapter 3 The 'Mexican' Scout … 35
Chapter 4 In Search of a Commission … 52
Chapter 5 A Hero's Return … 73

Part II **Bread and Jam and a Cup of Water**
Chapter 6 Japan and Australia … 81
Chapter 7 A Mis-start at Montavella … 92
Chapter 8 'Repugnant Restrictions' and Corruption at Kentucky … 106
Chapter 9 Slim Pickings … 125
Chapter 10 Goodwill Mission … 154

Part III **They Got Me**
Chapter 11 An Agent Revealed … 175
Chapter 12 Undercover Operations and an Underhand Attack … 197
Chapter 13 Deathbed Whispers … 208
Chapter 14 Young Harry … 231

| Chapter 15 | A Hero Forgotten | 238 |
| Chapter 16 | Answers in the Archives | 246 |

Epilogue	260
Acknowledgements	265
References	267

Prologue

'Freame. Harry Freame, 0007,' I said to the lady behind the counter when she asked who I was there to see.

The name made no impression on her. 'How do you spell that last name?' she asked.

Around us the routines of death went on uninterrupted. People in tracksuits arrived to pick up ashes, others in suits and long dresses held bunches of brightly coloured flowers. Like me they had come to the Macquarie Park Cemetery and Crematorium to visit graves. Some freshly dug, others long settled. The man standing beside me had mislaid his mother. 'I've come once before,' he said in apology. 'Maybe if you can just point me in the direction of the Jewish sector, I'll remember where she is.'

After locating Freame on her database, the lady looked up proudly at me. 'Got him,' she said. 'Harry Freame, Church of England Section D, grave plot 0007.'

'That's him,' I said, then came to the reason I was there: 'I thought the grave was unmarked.'

The lady turned her eyes back to her screen. 'Yep. Unmarked. That's right, love'.

'But it's not,' I said. 'There's a small engraved stone laid on his grave. It looks like black marble.'

She studied her screen again. 'Harry Freame, plot 0007. No, it's definitely an unmarked grave. It says so right here,' she said, and tapped the screen with a red fingernail, producing a little clicking sound.

'I was just standing at the grave. It's marked with a headstone. And the details on the stone are wrong. His birth year is wrong and the date of death for his daughter is out by thirty years. Is there any record on your computer of who may have laid the stone? Or when?'

But all she could tell me was that the records showed it as being an unmarked grave despite the rock-hard physical evidence to the contrary less than 300 metres away from where we stood. There was no record of who had laid the stone or when.

I should not have been surprised to find that Harry Freame had one more mystery for me. His whole life was a riddle wrapped in a mystery, inside an enigma and soaked in intrigue. From his remarkable feats of courage at the Anzac landing at Gallipoli that made him a hero of the First Australian Imperial Force (AIF) to his recruitment into the Australian intelligence service at the outbreak of World War II, the record of his life and deeds is a battle between oral history and written documents, each as unclear and as unreliable as the other. Sometimes the discrepancies were created by Harry himself, a deliberate muddying of the trail; at other times they are the fault of others, hyperbole, bad reporting or patriotic embellishments. It was the case then and still is that the distance between fact and fiction is often no more than the length of a journalist's pen. Unravelling it eighty years after his death was like walking through a thicket of lantana at night. But of all the intrigues and mysteries of Harry's life, there were two that came to dominate my thinking, two that drove me on to find answers.

Prologue

The first was the circumstances of his death. On 11 October 1940 Harry Freame boarded the SS *Tanda* at Sydney Harbour bound for Tokyo, where he would take up his position as interpreter for the first Australian legation to Japan. Harry was aware that the Japanese knew his role as interpreter was a cover for his real work in Australian military intelligence. The Japanese consulate in Sydney had had their spies tailing him for weeks. He knew how the feared Japanese secret police, the Kempeitai, a law unto themselves, had dealt with another British spy, James Cox. Cox had been thrown out of a fourth-storey window a few months earlier, a short but fatal journey. In short Freame knew before he left Australian shores that his cover was blown, his life in danger, and yet on that Sydney morning in the flush of spring he boarded that ship. Six months later he would be back in Sydney, choking on his own mucus, dying in a small bedsit, unable to eat or swallow and gasping for breath, surrounded by his wife and a few close friends. 'They got me,' he whispered in a painful rasp of a voice. Why had he gone there, even when he knew he was in so much danger? And why wasn't his death as a spy in the line of duty acknowledged by the Australian Government?

The second question also centred on the lack of acknowledgement of Harry's life. In the years after World War I, Harry Freame had a legitimate claim to be considered the most famous Anzac soldier to have landed at Gallipoli. The recipient of the first Distinguished Conduct Medal to be awarded to an Australian soldier for his efforts in those first bloody days of Gallipoli, his name was legend among the Australian troops who had fought that tragic battle. And as the landing turned into trench warfare, the troops knew that Harry Freame risked his neck each night to venture out into no-man's-land and map the Turkish defences.

Harry was on personal terms with the key Anzac commanders, and in the postwar years generals would visit him and reminisce about the war. Australia's official war historian for World War I, Charles Bean, who first met Harry in June 1915, was another fascinated by Harry and would continue to be so for his whole life. The Australian public came to know Harry through the newspapers of the day that splashed his wartime exploits of courage and daring across their pages.

When I set out to write this book, I wanted to discover why we had forgotten Harry Freame. Why, when our schoolchildren learn of the history of the Anzacs, do they learn more about a donkey than a man who was known at the time as the 'Marvel of Gallipoli'?

And I wanted to know why the Australian Government covered up their role in the death of Harry Freame, why the man Charles Bean described as probably the most trusted scout at Gallipoli was never believed when he said, 'They got me.'

Part I
Fight, Fight, Bullets and Shells

Chapter 1

Hell on Earth

Harry Freame's boots hit the sands of Anzac Cove at around 7.40am on 25 April 1915. He was part of D Company, 1st Battalion. By the time they landed, Anzac Beach, as it came to be known, was already strewn with the broken and bloodied bodies of the men and pack animals that had come before them on that infamous morning. It wasn't Harry's first sight of the region – he had sailed this way before – and it wasn't his first taste of war.

There is a picture of Harry taken before the landing, most likely in Egypt. In it he is in full uniform, flat-brimmed hat, a bandana tied around his neck, wire clippers and binoculars attached to his belt. He holds his Lee–Enfield full wood .303 rifle by the barrel, the butt resting on the ground. He is looking slightly downwards at the camera. There is none of the naive merriment so often seen in the pictures of young Australian soldiers who had mistaken war for a great boys' own adventure. But nor is there any fear in those eyes. Harry knew what he was in for, and he was ready for it.

As he waded through the waist-high water towards the sand, Harry carried in his pack three days' rations and an extra 150 rounds of ammunition. He would have heeded the warning of Lieutenant General William Birdwood, the British officer in overall command of the ANZAC (Australian and New Zealand Army Corps) forces, who had advised the troops prior to landing to drink as much water as they could, as once ashore supply of food and water could not be guaranteed for at least three days. Birdwood had signed off his missive to the troops with four final bits of advice:

> Concealment whenever possible,
> Covering fire always,
> Control of fire and control of your men,
> Communications never to be neglected.[1]

The landing itself had been rehearsed as much as possible on the nearby Greek islands, under conditions nothing like what Harry and the rest of the Anzacs would soon face, but as the 1st Battalion's official war diary records, 'we knew very little of the actual plans for the attack. In fact, the whole thing seemed to be rather in the air, and so it proved.'[2]

All that the officers of the 1st Battalion knew was that the 3rd Brigade was to land first and rush the enemy positions. When Harry and D Company landed on Anzac Beach, they had no idea what success, if any, 3rd Brigade had had. Judging by the dead and dying who littered the beach, staining the Aegean waters red, and the enemy bullets and shells that whistled around their heads and whipped the waves to foam, it could be easily believed that none of the 3rd Brigade had survived that hellfire of a dawn.

Harry's battalion formed up just north of Anzac Beach, in the shadow of Ari Burnu, sheltered from the murderous fire being poured down upon the landing from the peaks of Gaba Tepe, and waited for orders. When the orders came, they 'were very vague', alluding to nothing more than the need for the battalion to reinforce the firing line.[3] But to reinforce a firing line, you needed to first find the firing line, and when the men looked up towards the imposing ridges and valleys that confronted them, there was no firing line.

The ridges above the beaches were crawling with pockets of men, some engaged in isolated fights, hand-to-hand combat wherein they lived or died by the thrust of their bayonets or the quickness of their wits. Recalling that bloody morning, poet John Masefield wrote:

> All over the broken hills there were isolated fights to the death, men falling into gullies and being bayoneted, sudden duels, point blank, where men crawling through the scrub met each other and life went to the quicker finger, heroic deaths, where some half section which had lost touch were caught by ten times their strength and charged and died. No man of our side knew that cracked and fissured jungle. Men broke through it on to machine guns, or showed up on a crest and were blown to pieces, or leaped down from it into some sap or trench, to catch the bombs flung at them and hurl them at the thrower. Going as they did, up cliffs, through scrub, over ground ... they passed many hidden Turks, who were thus left to shoot them in the back or to fire down at the boats, from perhaps only fifty yards away.[4]

The firing line, a concept easily imagined in the safety of an officer's headquarters, was non-existent on the actual field of battle. On that first morning there was just a mad rush for high ground, up the forbidding slopes and into the ridges and valleys that held not only Turkish and German and Syrian troops and gunners but also the hope of cover and survival. A primeval need to push further and further inland gripped the soldiers, in the hope that there, beyond the next valley, the next ridge, lay safety.

By 10am with clothes still heavy with sea water after the landing and many of their rifles jammed with sand, now useful only for bayonet thrusts and charges, Harry and what elements of D Company were able to be formed up left the beach and set off for the ridges. Coming upon officers from the 3rd Battalion, D Company was redirected to the hill known as Baby 700, where reinforcements were urgently needed.

Through dense, waist-high scrub of gorse-like bushes and along the dried-up water courses littered with boulders, the men forged ahead uphill, legs heavy but the words of the commanding officers to advance, advance, advance running through their heads. Many of the men of D Company who fought their way up towards Baby 700 that clear bright morning would etch their names into the history of the Anzacs and the 1st Battalion: Major FJ Kindon, second-in-command of 1st Battalion; Major Blair Swannell, commanding officer of D Company; Captain Harold Jacobs, second-in-command of D Company; Lieutenant Geoffrey Street; and Captain Alfred Shout, the man who would leave Gallipoli the most decorated soldier of all, though sadly not with his life. And beside Shout, as was so often the case in the blood-soaked months that followed, in lock step, there was Lance Corporal Harry Freame.

Strategically important, Baby 700 had been the focus of intense fighting all morning, with remnants of the Australian 9th, 11th and 12th battalions all joining the battle as the Turkish troops advanced and retreated in a series of intense skirmishes conducted under the continuous hail of shrapnel fire from unseen Turkish positions. The approaches to Baby 700 were complicated by folds of ridges and valleys, and in these the Australian men became detached from their companies and lost until they could connect up with other Australian soldiers, sometimes from their own company, sometimes not.

By 11am Harry and D Company had reached The Nek, a thin strip of ridge that connected to Baby 700. The area was being held by Captain Lalor and men of the 12th Battalion. Lalor was the grandson of Peter Lalor, the man who had led the revolt at Eureka. With him on that morning on the approaches to Baby 700, Lalor carried a magnificent sword, said to be the one used by his grandfather at that famous stockade. Swords had been prohibited to be carried during the landing, but Lalor had disregarded the order.

Across The Nek on the slopes of Baby 700, Turkish troops were gathering. Joining up with Lalor's group, the newly arrived men of D Company formed up and charged the Turkish troops, driving them back into a gully before advancing up Baby 700. After reaching the summit, D Company started to dig into that hardscrabble ground. The Turkish troops they had driven before them had retreated, but only to a previously unseen trench, and from here they poured heavy fire on the entrenching D Company. It was here that D Company's commander, Major Blair Swannell, was killed on that first morning, shot dead just as he had earlier predicted he would be to his mates aboard the *Minnewaska* in the predawn fog before the landing.

Against the fierce Turkish assault, the Australians had only their rifles (when they worked), bayonets and pistols. The naval guns offered no support, as those manning them were afraid of firing on their own troops in the complicated mess of invaders and invaded that swarmed the hills of the peninsula. A few artillery guns had been brought ashore at midday but were then ordered to be sent back out to the boats.[5] Other commanders had refused to allow their guns to be landed, such was the chaos on the beaches, and it wasn't until dusk that the first artillery guns came into action in support of the Australian troops.

The Australian firing line on Baby 700 could not hold, and over the course of the morning the Australian troops moved over the summit only to be thrown back by vicious counterattacks no fewer than five times. In the midst of the fighting there was Harry Freame, moving from position to position, scouting the ground and enemy positions, running messages between commanding officers. At one point he came across Lalor's discarded sword, retrieved it, then lost it himself as the fighting intensified in the afternoon.[6] Lalor would have no further use for it. He had been killed earlier, felled by a Turkish bullet as he stood to rally his battalion.

At one point Harry and a small group of men drove a contingent of Turkish troops from a trench. But having gained the trench they found they were then held in place by persistent enemy fire. The men hadn't heeded the words of Lieutenant General Birdwood, and who could blame them, but they were out of water, exhausted and near death. Without water they felt that they would soon perish or be forced to surrender. Harry called for volunteers to brave the bullets and shrapnel and go for water. None raised a hand or spoke a word, so over the side of the trench he went, collecting water bottles from those who would never thirst again, fallen soldiers whose twisted repose could never be mistaken for the sleeping, a last look, a last thought of home or their best girl held fast in a glassy eye like a butterfly trapped in amber. When Harry returned he brought not only precious water but food and pickaxes for the grateful men.

All day the fighting raged on Baby 700, with ground taken then lost, the attackers and counterattackers continually changing roles, the air perfumed with the smell of the wild thyme that had been lashed by the bullets and shrapnel bursts. And as the day stretched on, still the men had no idea where the firing line was, only supposing that it was somewhere ahead of them, always somewhere over the next ridge, and that they must get to it. And if they could not advance, then at all costs they tried to hold on to whatever patch of land they had come to stop on.

At around 4.30pm as D Company, reinforced now with New Zealand troops, fought to hold the right side of the Baby 700 slope, a massive Turkish counterattack was launched that peeled the Australians off the slope. Alfred Shout, who had been with Lalor when he was killed, had earlier left Harry and fourteen men at The Nek with orders to hold it no matter what. The small group came under intense fire and before long only nine men were left, and by the time Shout returned, retreating from Baby 700, only Harry and one other man held the position. The rest lay dead or dying about them. Shout ordered them both to follow him in retreat towards the beach.

After regrouping on the beach, Shout and Harry then set about rounding up men from various battalions, a combination of the stragglers and shirkers, the lost and the shell-shocked. Harry collected around two hundred men[7] and led them back up the slopes to reinforce the New Zealand troops who were holding Walker's Ridge, a key position leading back to Baby 700, which was by now firmly in Turkish hands.

Recording the efforts of Lance Corporal Harry Freame on that chaotic first day at Anzac Cove, official war correspondent Charles Bean wrote:

> With such fighters as Lieutenant A.J. Shout, Lieutenant G.A. Street and Lieutenant Jacobs, all of his own battalion, he and others held vital positions in that constantly moving and changing fight but none was so ubiquitous as he, now holding a key position on The Nek leading to Baby 700, now finding for his commander the scattered parts of his battalion.[8]

As night fell on the evening of 25 April, the fighting abated only somewhat; rifle fire and shrapnel bursts echoed through the night. At around midnight Lieutenant General Birdwood sent an urgent message to his commander-in-chief, Sir Ian Hamilton, urging an immediate evacuation of the peninsula. Hamilton, from the comfort of the HMS *Queen Elizabeth*, was having none of it, advising Birdwood that he had 'got through the difficult business and you have only to dig, dig, dig until you are safe'.[9]

The following morning, 26 April, the hills of the peninsula rang with the sounds of shovels, digging, digging, digging. Those not digging or engaged in holding a position were out scouring the ravines and hillsides for the wounded and missing, and it was while thus engaged that Harry came across a detachment of men under the command of Captain Harold Jacobs sheltering in a trench at Quinn's Post. The men had had no water to drink and were in a desperate state. Harry offered to go for water and without a second thought braved the enemy fire that came in from unseen snipers and dashed back down the valley from where he had just come. He soon returned with the promised water, allowing the position to be held.

Realising that Lieutenant-Colonel Leonard Dobbin, the company commander, would need information on Captain Jacobs's position and situation, Harry was again up and over the side of the trench, making his way back down the valley to where Lieutenant-Colonel Dobbin was located. As Harry approached Dobbin's trench, he was heard to yell out, 'All right!' Arriving he delivered his message to Dobbin. Mission accomplished, it was only then that Harry revealed that on the descent he'd been struck twice by snipers' bullets, once through the fingers of the left hand and once through the left arm.[10]

For the duration of the fighting at Gallipoli, Quinn's Post remained the Anzacs' most advanced position and the key to their defensive positions. It would never have been held if not for the bravery of Harry Freame.

Charles Bean later noted that very few men received decorations for the deeds performed at the Anzac Cove landings. But when the recommendations came out, the name Harry Freame was first among them. His citation read: 'Has displayed the utmost gallantry in taking water to the firing line, though twice hit by sniper fire.' Harry's commanding officer further reported:

> Since I have assumed command of the Brigade, Serjeant Freame has almost daily performed some action worthy of recognition in the shape of carrying out night reconnaissance, conveying messages through dangerous zones etc etc. He is a fine fearless soldier who I strongly recommend for recognition.[11]

The recommendation was heeded and Harry, for his work over those first days of Gallipoli, was awarded the Distinguished Conduct Medal. Writing both publicly and privately years after the war, Bean offered the view that Harry should have been awarded the Victoria Cross and that the only reason he wasn't awarded the VC was because, 'Australian Commanders hesitated to set up for that hallowed decoration any standard short of the impossible. I think that it is safe to say but for that Harry would have been awarded the highest decoration.'[12]

More than a hundred years have passed since that tragic week in the northern spring of 1915, and such was the carnage and chaos faced by the Australian, New Zealand, British, French, Canadian and Indian troops that despite the hundreds of thousands of words that have been written describing and detailing it, it is still difficult to know exactly what happened or when it happened, or who did what and how, in those first few days with any level of detail and certainty. The 1st Battalion's official war diary doesn't even report the events of 26, 27 and 28 April. It merely records that when the battalion was re-formed on the morning of 29 April, of the 972 men of 1st Battalion who had landed, 366, practically a third of the force, were either missing, killed or wounded.[13]

Possibly the best description of what occurred on the peninsula in the last week of April 1915 can be found in the diary entry of Lance Corporal Eric Harford Ward of Harry's D Company, 1st Battalion. Reflecting on that first week of fighting, on 1 May Ward wrote, '1st 4 days perfect Hell on earth'.[14]

Chapter 2

Born Between Worlds

On 27 February 1880, in the Japanese port city of Nagasaki, Sei Kitagawa and William Henry Freame welcomed their third child, Hidetsugu Kitagawa, into the world. Given the English name Wykeham Henry Freame, this was the boy who would grow into the legend Harry Freame.

Harry's father, William Henry, had arrived in Japan from Melbourne in 1867, and at the time of Harry's birth was working as a telegraph clerk for the Mitsubishi Mail Steamship Company. But he would not live long enough to see his third-born son become the Marvel of Gallipoli. On 7 December 1880 just eight months after Harry's birth, William Henry Freame died from an aneurism of the heart. He was just thirty-nine years old.

Harry and his two older siblings, brother Shunichi and sister Grace, were not only left fatherless but also stateless, thanks to the complicated life of William Henry before he arrived in Japan.

At the Church of Saint Paul in Swanston Street, Melbourne, on 20 June 1867 William Henry Freame had taken Ellen Jane Coker to be his lawfully wedded wife. If the family and friends of William Henry and Ellen Jane had wished them a long and happy marriage on their special day, they were to be disappointed, for the marriage was neither long nor happy. The nuptials had been hastened on by an unplanned pregnancy. The impending arrival of a newborn notwithstanding, William Henry had deserted his marital home by mid-October 1867, leaving his heavily pregnant wife to fend for herself.

In divorce papers filed with the Supreme Court in 1870, Ellen Jane stated that from the very first day of their marriage William Henry had stayed out late, frequenting bars and brothels and cavorting with prostitutes. It wasn't until the middle of December 1867 that Ellen Jane learnt that William Henry had not only abandoned his young family but the colony of Victoria entirely, swapping the charms of Melbourne for those of the Japanese port city of Yokohama.

William Henry Freame, whether by design or accident, landed in Japan at the dawn of the Meiji era, a period that would see Japan transform from a feudal society to a modern nation-state under the guidance and reforms of the young Emperor Meiji.

In 1854 Japan and the United States signed the Kanagawa Treaty, which ended a 220-year policy of self-imposed isolation for Japan. The treaty gave the United States access to Japanese ports and the right to install a US consul on Japanese territory. The Japanese were at first reluctant to enter into the treaty but soon changed their minds when US Navy Commodore Matthew C Perry showed up off the coast of Japan with four gunboats and threatened to proceed to Tokyo and burn it down.

Nursing a deep sense of humiliation at the forced nature of the signing of the Kanagawa Treaty and fearing that, with their ports now thrown open to the world, they would become victims of the process of Western colonisation that was already evident in mainland Asia, Japan's leaders set out on an ambitious program of reform to modernise the nation. They determined to develop, or import where needed, scientific, technological, philosophical, political, legal and aesthetic skills and ideas. The policy was designed and executed with one goal in mind: to bring Japan onto an equal footing with the world's other great powers.

In April 1868 Emperor Meiji released what became known as the Charter Oath. The oath consisted of five principles that would pave the way for Japan's modernisation. The fifth principle declared: 'Knowledge shall be sought throughout the world in order to promote the welfare of the empire.'[1]

The most fundamental knowledge needed by the Japanese, if they were to play on the world stage, was proficiency in the English language. This created a need for English teachers, and so in 1872 William Henry reinvented himself as a self-styled professor of English in Tokyo.

But all was not well in Meiji Japan. There were parts of Japanese society that resented a turning away from the old ways in favour of this pursuit of the modern. The sword-wielding class of samurais had seen their station in life brought down by the young Emperor Meiji and his pivot towards the West and modernisation. Their class privileges were revoked after all classes were declared equal, and they were later banned from wearing their samurai swords. While some samurai adapted and moved into business and politics, for others the emperor's reforms generated feelings of shame. They considered his desire for modern ways a disgraceful pandering to Western ideas and power. This resentment spilled over towards foreigners and bubbled ominously below the surface of life in Meiji-era Japan. As a consequence, William Henry and the rest of the estimated three to four thousand foreign teachers then resident in Japan were never safe.

In early 1871 two foreign teachers, Americans by the names of Dallas and Ring, were set about by two sword-wielding rōnins in a Tokyo street as they wandered the night searching for female company. Though badly cut, both men survived to teach again. Commenting on that period in Japan's history, academic Edward Beauchamp wrote, 'Anti-foreign feeling ran so high among the ronin that they often felt that it was an act of the highest patriotism to cut down a foreign "barbarian" in the street.'[2]

Writing of the early Meiji period and the constant and vicious attacks upon foreigners, diplomat and serious Japanophile Ernest Satow observed that 'Japan became to be known as a country where the foreigner carried his life in his hand, and the dread of incurring the fate of which so many examples had already occurred became general among the residents.'[3] WE Griffis, a teacher resident in Tokyo, wrote that, 'It is doubtful whether vice in Edo [the former name for Tokyo] was ever more rampant than in the third quarter of the nineteenth century ... life was held to be cheaper than dirt by the swash-bucklers, ronins and other strange characters and outlaws ... infesting Tokyo.'[4]

It may have been this latent threat of violence that led William Henry to abandon his search for pleasure and female companionship in the streets and bars of Tokyo and retreat to the relative safety and comfort of matrimony for a second time.

In early 1873 a petition was submitted to the Japanese Government requesting permission for Sei Kitagawa to marry William Henry Freame. The petitioner was Sei's father, Yasuaki Kitagawa, a man of the samurai class, a Confucian scholar, editor and government administrator. Born in 1857, Sei was just sixteen years old in 1873 and likely a student of William Henry's. Like other samurai families adapting to their much-changed position in society, the Kitagawas no doubt saw education, and particularly education in the English language, as important.

That William Henry married his sixteen-year-old student is completely in line with the class of foreign teacher that Japan's push for education attracted. Frederick Dickins, an English medical officer resident in Japan at the time, writing of the wave of foreign teachers flooding the country, claimed that 'the majority of the "Professors" in the schools of Tokyo were graduates of the drygoods counter, the forecastle, the camp and the shambles, or belonged to that vast array of unclassified humanity that floats like waifs in every seaport. Coming directly from the barroom, the brothel, the gambling saloon.'[5]

It is fair to say that William Henry fit this profile perfectly. One of his students, Miyake Setsurei, who went on to become a prominent journalist, thought very lowly of him, questioned his breeding and wrote that Freame 'had bad grammar and pronunciation'.[6]

Another of Freame's students, Sanae Takada, later recalled:

> In retrospect, the Western teachers at that school [Kyoritsu Gakko] were very poor, and my first teacher was a foreigner named Freame, a former British or American sailor. Therefore, his character was rather crude, and his teaching was rather violent. Although he was quite strict with his students, he was a strange teacher who smoked from a large pipe used by sailors even in the classroom. We students had to recite the conversation as a task, and if a student got stuck in the middle, he would hit the

student's hand with a broken edge of the slate so that the colour of the skin changed.[7]

Jiro Ando was another who suffered Freame's pedagogical abilities and recorded his impressions for posterity:

I knew this person [Freame] at Nagoya English School. He's British, but he's a British in Australia, and he should be called Australian. He was very rude. Once he got angry, and two or three times he made his way towards the student, slipped and fell, unable to get up. The students gathered and took care of him.[8]

Despite William Henry's dubious teaching qualities, permission for the marriage to take place was granted on 7 June 1873. It was a historic event, the first recorded marriage between a foreigner and a Japanese woman in the Meiji period.

But in the conservative samurai society of late-19th-century Japan, where notions of honour and courage and morality were taught to young Japanese through the Bushido code, William Henry's wayward lifestyle left an awkward and potentially dangerous legacy for Harry Freame. His father, a notorious cad, now dead, left him nothing but fair skin and the fate of a 'half-caste' in a society where foreigners were still viewed with deep suspicion, if not outright hostility.

Harry's mother, Sei, had been forced to give up her Japanese citizenship to marry William Henry. It was expected that in marrying a British subject, Sei would be granted British citizenship. But to do so William Henry needed to ratify his marriage before the British consul in Japan. This he never did. The British vice-consul at the time, Joseph Henry Longford, was aware of William Henry's previous, and still valid, marriage to Ellen Jane Coker, and therefore refused to ratify the bigamous marriage between Sei and William Henry. This situation left Sei Kitagawa and her three young children officially stateless, having lost their Japanese citizenship but not gained the British equivalent.

In 1882 Sei remarried, this time to Magohiko Koba, an active member of the Anglican Church. Koba was born into a samurai family in the Kumamoto prefecture in Kyushu in 1855. Though his father died when he was just six years old, he was raised as a samurai. He was trained to use a sword, and as a young man was drawn into nationalistic and anti-emperor politics. He joined an ultranationalist group called the Shinpūren. Koba was a member of the group's assassination squad and took part in the Shinpūren rebellion, which resulted in the assassination of several government officials in 1876. Around the same time Koba came under the influence of Anglican priests and his life changed radically. Under the tutelage of the priests, he started studying theology and English in the divinity school in Nagasaki.

After marrying Sei, Koba adopted all three of her children as his own and would later also father two more girls, Ayako and Yasu. However, neither Sei nor Harry and his siblings had Japanese citizenship yet. In 1885 Sei's brother, Shichiro, applied to have Sei and her young family registered as his dependents. Doing so enabled Sei and her three young children to regain their status as Japanese citizens.

Though Harry now had a stepfather in the form of Magohiko Koba to guide him, Koba's religion presented more problems for Harry. Christianity had been outlawed in Japan in 1587. Since that ruling both foreign and Japanese Anglicans had been openly persecuted, including the crucifixion, ten years later, of twenty-six Christians at Nagasaki. These Christians would be remembered as the Twenty-six Martyrs, beatified on 14 September 1627 by Pope Urban VIII, and canonised as saints on 8 June 1862 by Pope Pius IX.

The persecution of Christians took official form in the use of the fumi-e. Usually cast from bronze, fumi-e depicted images of Jesus Christ or the Virgin Mary. Government officials would order citizens to trample a fumi-e to prove that they were not Christians. This occurred at the beginning of each year. If a person refused to trample the fumi-e they were tortured 'by hanging them over a pit filled with excrement'[9] or in some cases executed by being boiled in hot springs. During this period over 2000 people died for refusing to renounce their Christian faith. When the ban on Christianity was finally lifted in 1873, there were just 20,000 Christians left in Japan, down from 500,000 before the persecution. The suspicion of Christians lingered and would only have contributed to Harry's feelings of being an outsider in the land of his birth.

Despite his Christian religion, Harry, as the son of a samurai family, was raised in the Bushido code, instructed by Magohiko Koba. By the mid-1880s the samurai class was adjusting to life under the Meiji emperor, but they still clung to the Bushido code.

Education in the code was built upon the three tenets of wisdom, benevolence and courage. Writing in 1899 when Harry was still a teenager, attempting to explain Bushido to a foreign audience, Inazō Nitobe wrote:

Bushido, then, is the code of moral principles which the knights were required or instructed to observe. It is not a written code; at best it consists of a few maxims handed down from mouth to mouth or coming from the pen of some well-known warrior or savant. More frequently it is a code unuttered and unwritten, possessing all the more the powerful sanction of veritable deed, and of a law written on the fleshly tablets of the heart. It was founded not on the creation of one brain, however able, or on the life of a single personage, however renowned. It was an organic growth of decades and centuries of military career.[10]

The Bushido code was constructed around seven principles: righteousness, loyalty, honour, respect, honesty, courage and consistency. Nitobe points out that the way of Bushido could be arduous for the children of samurai families:

Parents, with sternness sometimes verging on cruelty, set their children to tasks that called forth all the pluck that was in them. 'Bears hurl their cubs down the gorge,' they said. Samurai's sons were let down the steep valleys of hardship, and spurred to Sisyphus-like tasks. Occasional deprivation of food or exposure to cold was considered a highly efficacious test for inuring them to endurance. Children of tender age were sent among utter strangers with some message to deliver, were made to rise before the sun, and before breakfast attend to their reading exercises, walking to their teacher with bare feet in the cold of winter; they frequently – once or twice a month, as on the festival of a god of learning – came together in small groups and passed the night without sleep, in reading aloud by turns.[11]

Harry Freame learnt these lessons well, as we will later see. By the age of sixteen, though, the wider world called, and Harry left Japan and his family for England, to further his education. But Harry sought a different kind of education than the one to be obtained in an English classroom. As he later told Charles Bean, not long after arriving in England he 'took to wandering'.[12] The wandering led him to all corners of the globe, and it is here the first frissons of adventure, mystery, embellishment and a good dose of smoke and mirrors begin to appear in Harry's life.

Harry would later claim that he had served in the Mexican army under President Porfirio Díaz, rising to the rank of captain in the intelligence department. Some writers have argued that this could never have happened, that Harry couldn't have been in Mexico when he claimed to be.

The last Díaz presidency (there were three in total) started in 1884 and ended in 1911. We only have a reasonably accurate account of Freame's whereabouts from 1903 onwards. If he left Japan as a sixteen-year-old in 1896, as he told Bean he did, there is every possibility that sometime between 1896 and 1903 he served in the Mexican army under Porfirio Díaz.

There is further circumstantial evidence that supports Harry's claim. Among his possessions that he kept throughout his life was a small English–Spanish dictionary. But most compelling is the evidence of Harry's fighting ability. Among Harry's fighting comrades and officers on Gallipoli, he was noted for his marksmanship, able to 'blow the neck off six bottles, three shots with each hand, from a distance of 25ft'.[13]

To his marksmanship was married his skill as a battalion scout, with numerous reports and testimony from Gallipoli veterans attesting to his talents and fame as the finest scout on the peninsula.

The work of a scout was dangerous, more so than any other role in the infantry. During open combat the scout moved ahead of the main troop body, keeping a lookout for enemy troops or traps, reconnoitring the way ahead, locating strategic points. But once combat had moved to trench warfare, as it did at Gallipoli after the first week, the scout's work became even more crucial. And more perilous.

Describing the scout's work in trench warfare, Major Hesketh Hesketh-Prichard wrote in 1917, 'His theatre of action is No Man's Land, which comprises all the area between the two armies which are drawn up one against the other ... The work of the scout was, of course, to dominate the enemy in No Man's Land, and to this end he was continually patrolling it during the hours of darkness.'[14] Hesketh-Prichard described the scout as a soldier of special aptitudes, strengths and abilities that could not be trained: a man either had them or he didn't. Resourcefulness, a willingness to take risks, precise observational skills, an ability to see but not be seen, physical fitness and excellent condition, an ability to go long stints with little rest, accurate marksmanship and, above all else, intelligence. Their information had to be completely reliable as it would form the basis of decisions made at the very highest levels: whether to advance or retreat, and when and how to do so. Battalions of men lived or died on the quality of the scout's information.

Harry's skills with a revolver and his knowledge of scouting could only have been learnt in the heat of battle. His service in Gallipoli strongly points to a man with not only military training but hard-earned fighting experience, the kind one could be expected to pick up in the wars of Mexico at the turn of the 20th century.

Harry's first stint outside Japan lasted two years. A photograph of an eighteen-year-old Harry, looking like a young Benedict Cumberbatch, holding his stepsister Ayako, places him in Osaka in 1898. The next official record we get of Harry is on 7 January 1902, when he arrived by ship in Avonmouth in the United Kingdom and signed off from a sea voyage that took him to Genoa and through the Black Sea. Four months later in May 1902, Harry signed on for another sea voyage that would see him leave Hull bound for the River Plate in Argentina.

Working as a scullion, a ship's cook, and sometimes as a steward, Harry took to the seafaring life, finding in it an antidote to the strictures and rigours of a samurai upbringing. In the community of ocean-going men, a community of souls far more accepting of his mixed heritage than the still-conservative Japanese society, he found a place and an identity. Over the next ten years Harry made his life at sea, undertaking thirty-one voyages in all. Some were short trips of no more than a few weeks; others lasted for over a year.

Harry based himself in the United Kingdom, moving around the ports of the country looking for a berth on whatever ship would take him across the oceans. Liverpool, Newcastle and Glasgow all served as points of departure for Harry, but it was no coincidence that he spent most of his time at Middlesbrough. By the early 1900s Middlesbrough was home to a large population of Japanese, engaged mainly in shipbuilding and commercial trade, the result of both the Anglo–Japanese Treaty of Commerce and Navigation that had been signed in 1894 and the Japanese desire to go forth and bring back Western knowledge and expertise.

During one of his short onshore breaks at Middlesbrough, Harry met twenty-six-year-old Englishwoman Edith May Soppitt. Edith May came from a family with a strong connection to shipping. On 19 July 1906 the pair were married in Middlesbrough. A short honeymoon period was spent visiting Edith May's older half-brother, Frank Arthur, in Failsworth near Manchester. Here Harry met and formed a special lifelong bond with Frank's infant daughters. He would send them postcards and objects from all over the world that he picked up on his travels, always signing off as 'Windy Harry' or 'Breezy Harry'.

But Breezy Harry could not tarry long on family visits, and now with a young wife to support he signed onto another voyage, this time aboard the *Aislaby* on 1 September at South Shields.

When the *Aislaby* docked in Philadelphia on 24 October, Harry deserted the ship. It seems not to have been a happy ship, for as author Brian Tate points out, in addition to Harry a further fourteen of the crew abandoned the *Aislaby* during this voyage.[15] Harry would later tell how he worked for a while on an American farm before again crossing into Mexico and linking up with his old commander in the Mexican army, the German Colonel Zeigler. Zeigler convinced Harry to form up a band of mercenaries to fight alongside the German army in its African colonies. The adventure was a complete failure after nearly all the men succumbed to malaria, and Harry was forced to return to the seafaring life.

Writing in his insightful book *Australia's First Spies*, author and ex-intelligence officer John Fahey questions Freame's claims to have served in both Mexico and German East Africa. Fahey labels Freame a 'fantasist', arguing that 'the two gaps in Freame's seaman papers, 1906–07 and 1912–14, do not coincide with the Maji Maji Rebellion in German East Africa in 1905 or the presidency of President Díaz, which ended on 31 May 1911.'[16]

What makes it difficult to arrive at a hard truth on the question of Freame's whereabouts in those years is that both Freame and Fahey appear to have made errors. Fahey compounds an error from Freame when he argues that Freame couldn't have been involved in the Maji Maji Rebellion. Freame never claimed to have fought in this rebellion: he told Charles Bean that he had fought in the Herero–Nama Uprising – but he placed it in German East Africa, when it actually occurred in German West Africa, or modern-day Namibia. Whereas the Maji Maji Rebellion did occur in German East Africa. Was Freame obfuscating or confusing his geography almost two decades after the event? Without documentary evidence either way, it is difficult to tell.

There is no doubt that, over the years, Freame's backstory was embellished – sometimes by overeager journalists looking for an angle, sometimes by comrades repeating careless whispers and at other times by Freame himself. But where Fahey sees a fantasist, from what I know of Freame's parentage, his upbringing, of Japanese society in the latter part of the 19th century, I see a small boy of both Anglo and Japanese parentage losing his father before his first birthday, growing up in a society that looked down upon his mixed-race genetics, a boy who needed a story to explain his father's absence, to make of his absent father somebody to be looked up to, a boy who desperately wanted to belong, a boy who didn't seem to fit into the neat and rigid social structures of Japan in the late 1800s. And in that wanting to belong, to be accepted, he created stories to justify and explain his place in the world.

Poignantly the little boy who didn't belong would eventually find his place in no-man's-land, that stretch of ground between enemy trenches, where his courage and determination would make him beloved by the officers and men of the first AIF.

Harry signed on aboard his next ship in August 1907 and for the next five years continued to travel the world. His seaman's logbook shows that he rarely spent more than a few weeks at home before getting his next job. One can only imagine the strain this placed on the young couple's marriage.

There was not a part of the globe he did not venture to: Brazil, India, China, the United States, South Africa, Egypt, the West Indies and finally, for the first time on 9 December 1911, the land of his father, Australia. But he did not stay long in the great southern land, arriving back in England a few short months later on 11 February 1912.

After returning home Harry took the decision to give up the seafaring life and return to Australia. It is unclear from the records when he arrived for the second time, but by 1913 he was living and working in the New South Wales town of Glen Innes. His young wife, remained behind in England.

Also in Glen Innes in 1913 was a woman by the name of Josephine Clarke. Josephine had been born in nearby Tenterfield. Her sister, Bessie, had married saddle maker Joseph Higgins in 1900 and the young couple had moved to Glen Innes where Joseph was to run the local saddlery. In 1913 Bessie gave birth to their third son, Joe. It was at this time that Josephine Clarke travelled to see her sister and newborn nephew in Glen Innes. While there, she was introduced to a good-looking though very married young horse breaker called Harry Freame.[17]

Though we can only speculate on the seriousness of the relationship that formed between Harry and Josephine, we do know that in March of the following year Josephine gave birth to a baby boy. Though still a resident of Tenterfield, Josephine travelled to Brisbane to give birth. On the birth certificate in the space reserved for the father's name was written Walter Warner Collins. But Collins never existed. The motives are clear. Even assuming that Harry had hidden the fact that he was already married, for a young unmarried Catholic girl in 1913 to be in a relationship with, let alone fall pregnant to, a man of Japanese birth, and an Anglican to boot? It was enough to warrant any level of subterfuge. How much Harry was involved in this is unclear. It is possible that he did not even know that he had become a father.

Regardless, by 1914 events would overtake the young parents and Harry would be swept away to the war that would make his name.

Upon hearing the news that there was a war to fight and an adventure to be had on the other side of the world, like so many other young men in country Australia, Harry set off to Sydney to enlist. On 28 August at Kensington, Harry presented himself before the New Zealand–born carpenter Captain Alfred Shout.

Harry was just under 180 centimetres tall, lean and fit. He weighed around 150 pounds and had a tattoo of a snake on his right arm. Harry gave his age as twenty-nine years and three months and told the captain he was born in Kitscoty, a remote village in central Canada that had been founded three years earlier in 1911. Asked if he had any previous military experience, Harry simply wrote, 'Mexican army only'.

Men were needed, and Shout had before him a fine specimen of a man, eager and willing and – most importantly in the untested volunteer army that was being put together – one with fighting experience. No doubt caught up in the headiness of the early days of that Great War, Shout signed off Harry's attestation papers as being true and accurate. But they were far from it.

Standing before Alfred Shout, Harry must have been unsure if he would be accepted into the Australian Imperial Force. He was a Japanese national, and at the time the army was only accepting British nationals. This explains why Harry gave his birthplace as Kitscoty, Canada. It provided him with British citizenship, and he rightly assumed that nobody would ask for proof. Kitscoty also helped him explain his dark skin and Japanese accent, enabling him to pass as a man with Indigenous North American ancestry. Kitscoty also had the benefit of being just a dot on the map, even today as close to the middle of nowhere as geographically possible, meaning Harry was extremely unlikely to come across someone from there, or who had heard of the place, and who could therefore expose his falsehoods.

At the outbreak of the war Harry was over thirty-four years old. He must have been concerned that he would be considered too old for military service, so he simply shaved five years off his age by giving a false date of birth.

Whatever the reasons, the untruths on Harry's attestation forms worked and he was soon falling in with the other men at the training grounds at the Randwick Racecourse. On 18 October he boarded the SS *Afric* with the rest of the men of 1st Battalion. In a few short months he would be landing at Gallipoli, and the man born Hidetsugu Kitagawa would transform into Harry Freame. By the time Harry left the peninsula his name would be legend among the Anzac troops.

Chapter 3

The 'Mexican' Scout

Wykeham Henry Koba Freame landed on the beaches of Gallipoli a lance corporal in the first AIF, but by the end of those first three days of intense fighting he was promoted to sergeant. He had also been wounded again, this time receiving seven wounds to his left side from machine-gun fire.[1]

He had already been recommended for honours, which saw him receive the first Distinguished Conduct Medal of the Gallipoli campaign. His bravery over the first week of fighting would also earn him a mention in General Sir Ian Hamilton's dispatches. But his war, and his feats of courage and daring, were only just beginning.

Early on, possibly while training in Egypt, Freame was appointed as a battalion scout, and it was in this role that he performed his greatest feats.

Eric Edwin Longfield Lloyd was a second lieutenant with the 1st Battalion when he landed at Gallipoli. Though neither he nor Harry could have known it at the time, Longfield Lloyd would be an almost constant presence in Harry's life from here on – and ultimately mixed up in his tragic, mysterious death. Writing sometime after the war, Longfield Lloyd described Harry's work as a scout on the peninsula:

I saw him frequently in action, and as I had always set a high value on reconnaissance work, I early recognised in Mr. Freame one of the finest of scouts, tenacious, adhering always to the objective, and invariably bringing anything in which he was concerned to a satisfactory and definite conclusion. I often discussed reconnaissance problems with him and always welcomed his assistance in my particular sector. His scouting instincts were uncanny. His movements when so engaged usually defied detection and his endurance was as remarkable as his keenness. I recall an occasion when it fell to me to participate in an operation which would have had a very strong appeal to Mr. Freame. I would have liked him to have taken part too, but at the time he was having a much-needed rest and so he was not disturbed. He was afterwards thus greatly concerned to have thus missed one of the hazards upon which he seemed to absolutely thrive and it was typical of him that he welcomed the risky enterprise.[2]

Harry's endurance and keenness to be involved in every action was a defining trait of his work at Gallipoli. Colonel Frederick Kindon, second-in-command of 1st Battalion, recalled preparing to go on a patrol and finding Harry standing by his side. 'Hullo, Freame' he said. 'What are you doing here? You are not on this patrol.'

'I am on every patrol,' was Harry's reply.[3]

As April turned into May and May into June, Harry's reputation as a scout beyond compare continued to grow. He moved through no-man's-land like a snake or an eel, they said. He could move in a 25-foot circle around a colleague in 12 inches of grass and not be seen.

He modified his army-issue uniform to aid his reconnaissance work. Leather patches were sewn onto the knees and elbows where they contacted the ground as he slithered along towards the Turkish trenches.

He also abandoned the army-issue Lee–Enfield .303 rifle and bayonet, deeming it unfit for the work of a scout. Instead Harry sported two revolvers, one on each hip, a bowie knife in a boot pocket and a third Colt revolver secreted under his armpit. Harry reckoned that the job of the scout was to see and observe, and not to shoot unless you were engaged, in which case it would be at close quarters. Under those conditions a pistol was the weapon for the job.[4] And Harry knew how to use his six-shooters, a skill he had learnt and perfected serving in the Mexican army of Porfirio Díaz. Around his neck he wore a blue-and-white patterned bandana, a barrier against the dust and grime of his field work. On his head he wore his hat straight brimmed. Safe to say he cut a distinct and dashing figure among the other diggers.

At first his facial features, his dark skin and his 'peculiar intonation of speech'[5] caused suspicion among his colleagues. Some referred to him as the 'Mexican Scout' and said he had been born there. Others said that wasn't true: the dinkum oil – as rumours or any approximations to the truth were called – was that he was a French Canadian who had fought in the Mexican Revolution. Others didn't care. All that mattered was that he was a digger, he could shoot straight and his intelligence could be relied upon. His brothers in arms said they'd follow Harry anywhere, such was his prestige as a fighter.

Every night when the sun set beneath the ridges and darkness stalked the valleys, Harry Freame would sneak out into no-man's-land, exiting the Australian trenches through a hole that the sappers had accidentally made in a communication tunnel. Crawling across the ground with just the insides of his elbows and knees and the knuckles of his toes touching the earth allowed him to move quickly and silently across broken ground. (He taught this crawling technique to other Anzac scouts, and it is still employed today.) Harry would creep up to the edge of the Turkish trenches. He'd take note of trench designs, defensive emplacements and troop strengths in the trenches. Once done he would crawl back to the Australian trenches to report his findings.

One night he returned and reported on a card game between Turkish soldiers that he had followed unseen from the tops of the trenches.[6] But Harry grew tired of playing at what he called being a 'peeping Tom'.[7] He figured with his dark skin and Asian looks plus his ability to speak French, a language he had picked up on the sailing ships of his youth, which was also the language of the Turkish officer class, he would have a fair chance of passing unnoticed inside the Turkish trenches. If he could get away with it, he would only be repaying the Turks back in their own coin. In the early days of Gallipoli, Turkish spies had successfully infiltrated Australian trenches, passing themselves off as Indian officers and even giving orders to Australian soldiers, leading to Australian troops inadvertently firing on their own men.[8]

Harry figured it was worth the risk. He tried it twice successfully, moving about the Turkish trenches and eyeballing Turkish soldiers as he casually walked past them. But on the third night out, he was confronted by two Turkish soldiers, the points of their bayonets convincing Harry that the game was up, that surrender was the only option. The Turkish soldiers led Harry, their prize capture, back to their commanding officer.

Without waiting to be asked, Harry immediately handed over his two revolvers and bowie knife to the commanding officer. He then asked the man if he spoke French. The officer, whom Harry later described as a 'perfect gentleman'[9], was delighted and ordered up some coffee and offered Harry a cigarette. After a few minutes of cordiality amid one of the bloodiest confrontations in history, the commanding officer turned to Harry and said, 'Well, you've been captured in our lines in certain circumstances. You probably know the results.'

'Yes,' Harry replied.[10]

The officer called up an armed guard to escort Harry back to headquarters, where the best he could hope for was a quick death. Harry was under no illusions that his fate was to be shot as a spy. He expected no less. But Harry wasn't thinking about death. Harry was thinking of escape. The Turkish officer shook his hand, notably didn't wish him luck and told him he had a 5-mile march ahead of him. That was all Harry needed to hear.

As he set off with his escort of six armed Turkish soldiers, Harry was making his plan. He played the role of the perfect prisoner knowing that, with the heat of the day and the boredom of the 5-mile march, he could lull his captors into a false sense of security. He had two men at the front, one at each side and two bringing up the rear. Harry walked along, biding his time and, as predicted, his guards grew lazy. When Harry saw them swing their rifles onto their shoulders, he slipped his hand silently below his shirt and retrieved his still-hidden Colt revolver from under his armpit. After Harry had voluntarily handed in his two revolvers and bowie knife, his captors had not bothered to conduct a full-body search for weapons. Now with his Colt in hand, he shot the two men in front of him, turned on the soldier to his right, fired and missed, swung around and fired at the one on his left and missed him too, and then spun around and shot dead the two men coming up behind who knew not what had happened. The two soldiers whom Harry missed had dropped their rifles and scrambled off into the scrub leaving Harry by himself. He sought cover and awaited the coming of dark, and then, as he had done so many nights before, silently made his way back to the Australian lines.

By June 1915 the drudgery of trench warfare intermingled with the sudden interruptions of senseless deaths, and exploding shells and machine-gun fire were taking a toll on the morale of the Australians. Waking to a new day must have seemed just as great a miracle as getting to sleep at all.

There was always work to be done, another trench to be defended or taken. One Turkish trench, located opposite the Australian trenches at Steele's Post, was proving particularly troublesome, pouring machine-gun fire on the Australian troops day and night. Early in the war Australian soldiers had seen a couple of German officers occupying this trench, and from then on it had been known as German Officers' Trench.

The trench held one, possibly two, machine-gun emplacements. The field of fire offered by the position covered two key Anzac positions, Courtney's Post and Quinn's Post. On 3 June the men at Steele's Post received an order to destroy the machine guns in German Officers' Trench. The operation was to be used as a distraction, occupying the attention of Turkish troops and preventing them from reinforcing an area at Cape Helles where the Allied commanders were preparing a much larger attack. The raid was set for 11pm on the night of 4 June. Everybody knew that Harry Freame was the man for the job.

A party of eight men was selected by Lieutenant Geoffrey Street, but it was Harry Freame, the man who knew no-man's-land better than any other, who would decide the route to be taken to arrive at German Officers' Trench. The success of the mission depended on Freame's scouting skills. Following Harry out from the relative safety of Steele's Post, the men were placing their lives in the hands of Harry and his keen sense of direction. Between the Australian trenches and German Officers' Trench there was an old Turkish trench, which the Australian officers believed was unoccupied. The plan was for Harry to first lead the men into this trench and then set out by himself to find an approach to an area below where the machine gun was situated, before returning to the party and leading two engineers up to the edge of German Officers' Trench. The engineers would take over from there, planting the explosives that would blow up the machine gun and silence its deadly voice.

Harry and Street exited the Australian trenches and moved into the night, their men following close behind. At the supposedly unoccupied trench, Harry and Street threw their legs over the wall and prepared to drop down to the floor. But in the dark, they barely made out a group of Turkish soldiers at the bottom of the trench staring back up at them, taken utterly by surprise at the two Australian soldiers dropping in from above. Quickly Harry and Street backtracked as the Turkish soldiers fired indiscriminately but harmlessly into the night. Harry advised Street to get the men back to their trenches while he himself dropped down into a scrape in the ground, both revolvers blazing as the Turkish troops started to come up and over the side of the trench. In addition to the revolvers, Harry had on him four bombs, and these he now threw at the Turks as Street and the rest of the raiding party retreated behind him. All four bombs failed to detonate, but by now his men had reached safety and, seeing that he was alone, Harry himself retreated. All the men had made it back to safety with no casualties, but the operation was a complete failure. For his part, Geoffrey Street, who after the war would serve as Australian defence minister, never forgot the night that Harry Freame risked his life to save those of Street and his small party of raiders.[11]

A few hours later at around 1am on the morning of 5 June, news reached Steele's Post that Quinn's Post was being swept by machine-gun fire coming from the gun that Street and Harry's party had failed to take out. A decision was taken to send out another raiding party to finish the gun off. This party consisted of two groups, each of fifty men. The first party was led by Lieutenant Longfield Lloyd and was tasked with destroying the machine gun. Lieutenant Henry Wells was to lead the second group of men with instructions to make for the snipers' trench that had caused the problems for Street and Harry and put any Turks they found to the bayonet.

The engineers who had accompanied Harry's first raiding party had by now returned to their trenches, so Longfield Lloyd decided that he would make the raid without engineers and their explosives, deeming that too much time would be lost while he waited for the engineers to be found and recalled to the post. At 2.55am Longfield Lloyd and his men went over the top of the trenches again, making for where they knew the machine gun to be. Coming to the Turkish trenches they were hit by a wall of gunfire. Some of Longfield Lloyd's men returned fire into the Turkish trenches; others kicked at the sandbags that lined the top of the trenches, sending them crashing down on the Turkish defenders. Longfield Lloyd and another soldier, Lance Corporal Charles

The 'Mexican' Scout

Davis, located the machine gun. Longfield Lloyd emptied his revolver into the trench while Davis poured three rifle shots into the lock of the machine gun through the loophole. The job done, the men retreated back to the safety of their own trenches. All up the raid cost the lives of five men and wounded twenty-seven. For their night's work Lieutenant Longfield Lloyd received the Military Cross and Lance Corporal Davis the Distinguished Conduct Medal.[12]

Watching this second raid unfold, Sergeant Harry Freame noted that there was not one but two machine guns firing from German Officers' Trench. Over the course of 5 and 6 June, there was some doubt as to whether Longfield Lloyd and Lance Corporal Davis had been successful in taking out the first machine gun, despite their best efforts. Coupled with Freame's observation that there was a second machine gun in the trench, this led to Harry being ordered out into no-man's-land again on the night of 6 June. This time his job was to draw fire from the machine guns so that observers in the Australian trenches could ascertain exactly how many were operating and what their precise location was. A dangerous job, but one that Harry didn't flinch at undertaking.

Harry needed two additional men for the job. Offers to accompany him, to become one of his 'deathless band of men'[13] as the newspapers later referred to them, were always forthcoming. Now with a job at hand, Harry sought out two men who had previously expressed a desire to accompany him on one of his night raids. Finding them, Harry asked the first if he wanted to come along with him on a job.

'What's the job?' the man asked.

Harry explained what was needed.

'Not good enough for me,' the man answered.

'I only asked you because you offered to come along,' Harry said.

'Not good enough,' the digger repeated, unmoved.

Harry turned to the next man.

'What have you got on, Harry?' the man asked him.

Again, Harry explained how he had been ordered out into no-man's-land to draw the fire of the machine guns in German Officers' Trench.

'I hope you get back alright,' the man told him as he walked away.

Freame was unimpressed. 'Look, I'm not going to call you men cowards,' he said. 'Life's too short in these days for us to quarrel. I don't think you are cowards but if you don't mean what you say, don't say it.'[14]

It speaks volumes about Harry's self-belief, and also his standing among the Anzac soldiery, that as a dark-skinned man in 1915 in a basically all-white army he felt confident enough to openly imply the cowardice of these two men.

After these two diggers refused to go with him, Harry went looking for others who wouldn't shirk the dangerous work. He eventually found two volunteers to join him on his mission. One was a young bloke of around twenty-four called Walter Morris, a newly arrived reinforcement for the 1st Battalion. The other man went by the name of Edward Elart, twenty-five years old and an original with the 1st Battalion. A few weeks prior to being approached by Freame, Elart had been in the firing line when the soldiers directly to the left and right of him were killed by Turkish bullets. The near miss caused him to reflect on his life. In a quiet moment he sat down to write a letter to Brigadier-General Harold 'Hooky' Walker:

Sir, It is my desire to present myself as a defaulter before you. I am a deserter from the Royal Australian Navy. I am known

The 'Mexican' Scout

here as Edward Elart but my real name is Harry Hart. My rating was Stoker HMAS 'Australia' when I cut the painter at the time when war was least expected. When war broke out I left my job in Portland and went to Sydney with the object of surrendering myself. But when I reached there I thought of the long term of punishment to be gone through, and the reception a man would get on the ship, so I took advantage of the other outlet for my services to my country, and came as a soldier. It was my intention to remain silent and be 'Edward Elart' always. The reason why I do not remain so is the experience of that memorable Sunday and also the attack by the enemy a few mornings ago, when my mates were shot on both sides of me, and when I was also slightly wounded make me realise that the honour of death may now be any man's and I wish to go out with a clean bill. It is for my sister's sake. I know that the penalty for my crime is a severe one and to say the least of it I could lose everything. I have weighed it over in my mind for a few days. But I have also heard that a free pardon has been granted to offenders of my calibre. Perhaps the authorities in their clemency may pardon me and count this as part of my five years' service in the Navy (about 8 more years) when we go home again. I am writing this statement so as not to take up your valuable time in talking. My next of kin is Mrs G Turner, 40 Bronte St, East Perth. If she could one morning get a note saying that I could use my name again, it would be the finest present in the world I could make her. Trusting that I may have the matter put before the authorities so soon as a favourable opportunity presents itself.

I am your obedient servant
103 Edward Elart
14 Platoon 'D' Coy 1st Battalion[15]

Since landing at Gallipoli Elart had distinguished himself in the eyes of his commanding officers. Major Kindon noted his excellent work and his tendency to be the first to volunteer for even the most dangerous expeditions. So it was no surprise when Elart jumped at the chance to accompany Harry and Private Morris on their mission into no-man's-land on 6 June. Prior to the sortie Harry spent time teaching Elart and Morris his technique for slithering undetected across the ground. As darkness fell, the three men slipped out from the trenches via Freame's usual exit point.

Freame carried two revolvers plus five bombs, and Elart and Morris carried their rifles and two bombs each. Following Harry's lead, they slipped silently past the snipers' trench, which had again been reoccupied by Turkish troops after Longfield Lloyd's raid. The three men made their way towards German Officers' Trench and the place where Freame had seen the machine gun firing from the previous night. Attempting to provoke the firing of the machine gun so that it would give its position away, Harry lobbed two bombs into the trench. The result was a smattering of rifle fire in return. Harry crawled further along the front of the trench and lobbed a few more bombs inside. Again this was met with only a few rifle shots. Surmising that the trench was either lightly held or that the machine guns were indeed out of action, Harry led Elart and Morris back towards the snipers' trench. Here they lobbed their remaining bombs into the trench, causing its occupants to fire wildly into the night.

Their work almost done, the three men started to head back. In one last effort to provoke fire from German Officers' Trench, Harry raised himself up in open ground and unloaded both of his revolvers in the direction of the trench. Again only a handful of Turkish rifles answered his challenge. Contented, he turned the two boys for home. The three men crawled back in single file, Elart in the lead, followed by Morris, with Harry coming up behind Morris, guiding him through no-man's-land by way of touch: a touch on the left leg to send him left, a touch on the right leg to send him right.

There is some confusion as to what happened next, but as the men approached the Australian lines, Elart may have become entangled in a wire connected to some jam tins that had been set up as an early-warning signal against raiding Turkish soldiers. Other accounts say that when Elart uttered the password that would tell the Australian soldier on sentry duty that the party had arrived, the sentry, a newly arrived and nervous reinforcement, mistook the password, which was 'Freame', for a Turkish word.

In either case the nervy sentry loosed a round in the direction of the noise. The bullet struck young Elart through the eye, exited his neck, passed though the face of Morris directly behind him and lodged in Morris's shoulder. Harry, unmarked, was quick to react and dragged both men hurriedly into the safety of the Australian trenches. Morris would survive this incident with the loss of an eye, but Elart succumbed to his wounds eleven days later aboard the hospital ship the HMHS *Sicilia*. Whatever shame Elart had felt at his desertion, his actions at Gallipoli won him the admiration of his fellow soldiers, and not long after his death the pardon he had asked for was officially granted with the full backing of his commanding officers.

The death of Elart and the wounding of Morris by one of their own affected the men of 1st Battalion, even despite the amount of death and suffering they had witnessed already by June 1915. Maybe it was the senselessness of it, or the desperate poignancy of doing so much to survive the Turkish bullets only to be cut down by fire from your own side. The event is recorded in several diaries of 1st Battalion members, in the official battalion diary and in Bean's official history. Private John Gammage of 1st Battalion was certain about who was to blame for the death of Elart and the wounding of Morris. Writing in his diary at the time, Gammage recorded, '2 of our men shot by our own blooming fools, our officers to blame, one of which should be shot for manslaughter he is not fit to be in charge of Cadets in Australia'.[16] Who the officer was remains unclear.

The day after the shooting of Elart and Morris, official war correspondent Charles Bean visited the Australian troops at Steele's Post. There he met Sergeant Harry Freame for the first time. The two spent some time speaking and Bean faithfully recorded the conversation in his war diary, dedicating almost four pages to the remarkable Anzac scout. A major criticism of Bean's war reporting is the amount of time and attention he gave to the officer class at the expense of the rank-and-file soldier, but he certainly gave Harry considerable time and space in his narrative.

Harry told Bean the 'pitiable story'[17] of the previous night's doomed scouting expedition with Elart and Morris. Interestingly when Bean came to write up the official history of the war, he included the story of Elart and Morris as told to him by Harry but omitted the preceding incident in which two Australian soldiers had refused to accompany Harry and were indirectly labelled as cowards by him. It was typical of Bean to keep in mind that he was not only recording the events of a war but also birthing the identity of a nation, an identity that he was keen to mould and smooth out wherever possible.

Harry shared with Bean his approach to scouting, his choice of weapons and his technique for moving across no-man's-land, which enabled him to go about unseen. Bean complemented his diary entry with little sketches depicting Harry's instructions of how to perform his version of the leopard crawl, and how to not stand upright when crossing a ridge but to go over it like a snake, bending your body to the contours of the ridge to avoid giving the enemy snipers a profile to shoot at. Bean was clearly taken with Harry's story, and this is when he recorded how Harry had served in German East Africa and Mexico before the war. Harry told Bean that when not engaged as a soldier of fortune, he had been a rancher on an American farm and had also worked for Standard Oil, during which time he had had the opportunity to visit Turkey. How much of this was true and how much of it was Harry trying to disguise his Japanese past is still unclear today, but Bean had no doubts about Harry Freame. His actions, from the first day of the landing until that day in June 1915, had proven that Harry Freame was a soldier beyond compare.

But if Harry was trying to hide his Japanese nationality from Bean, he was only partly successful. Bean recorded that Harry was born in Canada but was 'clearly of Chinese or Japanese blood'.[18] Bean's fascination with Harry is made even more curious by the fact that Bean, at that time in 1915, was a public and lively supporter of the White Australia policy. Writing in 1907 Bean had declared that 'for the good of either Australia or England, a Western and an Oriental race cannot live together in

Australia' and that 'the probability of an Oriental invasion, peaceful or warlike, is enormous, and justifies urgent measures.'[19] The threat of an Asian, and specifically a Japanese, invasion had occupied Bean's mind for some time, and he had followed with interest the Japanese victory over the Russians in the 1905 Russo–Japanese War.

'No one can deny the danger of an Oriental overflow who knows the facts,' Bean wrote. He continued:

> In truth, no one does. There are some three million odd whites in Australia inhabiting three million square miles. To the north, at its very gates, up to within a day's sail, are eight hundred million Orientals. The island of Java alone, three days' steaming from tropical Australia, holds thirty millions. The Eastern question, famine, plague, overcrowding, a vast coastline to hold – three men to hold it against every eight hundred – that is the quality of the danger. The weakest point that I can see in the Australian case is here, in the moral problem. Have we, so few, a right to keep out those hordes and save Australia for ourselves? But, then, is it for ourselves, or for the forty million white men to come after, and for the perpetuation of our race and the ideals we believe in, and, above all, for our children? Are they to look to us for a healthy home – or for that mixed horror?[20]

Later in life Bean was to change his views on the White Australia policy and Australia's Asian neighbours. In arguments in favour of Asian migration, he would cite the example of Harry Freame, a loyal man dedicated to Australia.

Bean finished his diary entry of 7 June 1915 with one last observation of Harry. 'It is his ambition to go home to his people in Canada as a commissioned officer.'[21] After obscuring so much of himself from Bean, Harry's admission of this ambition is an amazingly frank moment. It was an ambition he would pursue relentlessly over the next year of the war.

Chapter 4

In Search of a Commission

On 11 June 1915 Harry and the rest of 1st Battalion were sent to Braund's Hill for 'rest', though it was a commodity hard to come by on the Gallipoli Peninsula. But it was from here on 14 June that Harry found time to write to his wife, Edith May. This is the only surviving letter written by Harry during his time in the Dardanelles:

My Dear May,

Just a few lines to you hoping to find you all well at home as I myself doing fine and well. I hope you are getting all my P.Cs and letters in due course which I am sending to you at every possible opportunity. Of course, it isn't much but best I could. I suppose you have seen in the papers that I have won the D.C.M as you P.S'ed in your last letter of May 25th 'play the game well and you will be rewarded.' I am doing my best. We cannot write any other news anyhow. You will get all the particulars and full account of our doing on the newspapers. Bye [sic] the way you may send us some light reading book if you can. Nothing too heavy as we want some amusement or something to take our mind away for

a few minutes even as all we get is fight fight bullets and shells. As well blood.
Love to you all, heap to yourself
From your loving Harry[1]

Again in this letter we see Harry's plan to use his wartime experiences to gain the rank of commissioned officer. He is playing the game as best he can. A position as a commissioned officer would set Harry up in life; it would allow him to take Edith May to Australia after the war, to settle down and start a family, and to enjoy a way of life that his seafaring days had never afforded him. This clear ambition may go some way to explaining Harry's extraordinary acts of courage and daring, his willingness to be front and centre whenever danger was present, to do what other men of the Australian Army would not or could not do. His plan of course was dependent on two things: gaining the commission and surviving the war. And neither was guaranteed no matter how good a soldier Harry Freame was.

On 29 June 1st Battalion did receive the rest they had been promised. Most of the battalion were taken off the peninsula and sent to the nearby Greek island of Imbros. But even on board the ship they were not completely safe, with the battalion diary recording, 'when on the water we had one man hit by a stray bullet and another bullet embedded itself in the butt of R.S.M. Melville's rifle'.[2]

For the men of 1st Battalion, after two months of heavy fighting, of bomb and shell, it must have felt like there was no escaping the reach of that brutal war. The men arrived at Imbros at 2.30am on 30 June. By now the battalion strength was just nineteen officers and 536 men of other ranks. At Imbros they recovered as best they could, but by 8 July they were back on the peninsula, in the trenches, among the rats and the blood and the dead and the dying.

In July Harry was wounded again: this time a bullet wound to his right thigh. He was operated on and the bullet was removed. Towards the end of the month, after weeks of waiting for a Turkish counteroffensive that never eventuated, dinkum oil started to filter through the trenches that an Australian offensive was brewing. On 1 August Harry was shot yet again, taking a bullet through the joint of his left big toe.

It wasn't until 5 August that Harry Freame had the rumours confirmed by Colonel Cyril Brudenell White, who stopped by the trenches to speak with Harry and wish him luck for the coming attack. Harry later wrote of the excitement that he and the other soldiers felt at getting the news:

> We were all quite ready and happy in the thought of some active reaction from the monotonous trench warfare. Even I myself was pleased in anticipation of giving an official call to the Turkish trenches instead of repeating my old practice of crawling to these on my belly like a 'peeping Tom'.[3]

The attack that White whispered news of into the ear of Harry Freame would come to be known as Lone Pine, a battle characterised by losses that no cross could mark and terror that no prayer could disperse. The 1st Battalion diaries describe it as:

> one of the most gallant Australian adventures in the history of the ill-fated Gallipoli campaign ... [that] involved days and nights of

slaughter; of fierce hand-to-hand encounters; of men struggling through dark tunnels towards the enemy; of inspired heroism as Turkish counterattack after counterattack was flung back as violently as it was launched; of screaming shells and blinding flashes; of nerve racking nights and red dawns shot with blood.[4]

The attack on Lone Pine was to be led by the 2nd, 3rd and 4th battalions, with Harry's 1st Battalion held in reserve. In the early afternoon heat the men sat around the trenches preparing white calico patches and bands to be applied to the backs and arms of their uniforms. The calico would help their own men avoid firing upon them, but as they fixed the patches to their uniforms they also knew that that it would help identify the expected, inevitable casualties of the battle to come.

At around 4pm the Allied bombardment of the Turkish trenches began. Harry and the rest of the members of the 1st Battalion were sheltered in Browne's Dip, and now the men of the 2nd, 3rd and 4th battalions started to make their way past them through the trenches, heading for the jumping-off point from where they would launch their assault on the Turkish positions. Writing in *Australia in Arms*, reporter Phillip Schuler recalled watching the men of those battalions moving through the trenches in complete silence, lest they be heard by the Turkish forces who were no more than 100 yards away. 'At various points their comrades from other battalions, who watched the line of heroes who were "for it," dashed out to shake some comrade by the hand. There was a warmth about these handgrips that no words can describe.'[5]

The Allied bombardment was answered in kind by the Turkish guns, their shells 'falling like hailstones'[6] into the valley where the Australian troops were gathered. Diarist Private Eric Vial recorded that the Turkish shells fell on a 'graveyard close by and huge pits were made by these. Then in many cases the bodies of our comrades, buried weeks before, were being unearthed and blown into the air'.[7] It was only a fraction of the horror that was to come.

At 5.30pm the bombardments stopped and the officers' whistles blew their call to death and glory, whichever found you first, sending scores of young men from the 2nd, 3rd and 4th battalions up over the tops of their trenches, hurtling across no-man's-land towards the Turkish positions.

Coming upon the enemy trenches, the Australian troops were surprised to find that they were topped with wooden beams. The artillery bombardment had failed; the defences were intact, unscathed. The beams needed to be pried up before the trenches could be entered into, a task made all the more difficult by the unceasing fire of the Turkish artillery. Some Australians stayed on to open breaches in the beams while others charged on, heading straight for the uncovered communication trenches that were laid out behind the first line of Turkish trenches. The Anzacs who remained at the first line of trenches eventually removed enough of the heavy wooden beams to allow the Australians to drop down feet first into the dark galleries of the Turkish trenches and start the dangerous, dirty work of clearing them of enemy soldiers.

The work was done with bayonets and bullets and bombs (homemade, fashioned from old jam tins) and hand-to-hand combat. By 8pm, two and a half hours after the attack had begun, the final company from 1st Battalion occupied the Lone Pine trenches. The Australians had taken the first, second and third lines of the Turkish trenches. Now the job was to hold these new positions in the face of wave after wave of ferocious Turkish counterattacks.

The trenches filled with dead men from both sides, making movement through them almost impossible. Captain David Fallon recalled, 'A thousand corpses were in the trench system after the occupation and to make room for the fighting men these were stacked in piles at intervals between the traverses.'[8] Private Vial recorded that 'Stacks of dead and wounded were lying about and in some cases four feet high.'[9] Private Gammage recorded his horror at the 'moans of our own poor fellows and also Turks as we tramped on their wounded bodies'[10] as the Australians pushed further into the enemy trenches. Captain Jacobs of 1st Battalion later recalled that after the initial fighting had finished:

> [the] trench [was] so full of our dead that the only respect that we could show them was not to tread on their faces, the floor of the trench was just one carpet of them, this in addition to the ones we piled into Turkish dugouts.[11]

One man absent from the horror of those trenches was Sergeant Harry Freame. At 6.30pm on the evening of 6 August, as he stood waiting with the rest of D Company to be thrown into battle, Harry was tapped on the shoulder and called away on 'special duty'.[12] He reported to headquarters and was asked how long it would take him to dig a communication trench from the Australian trenches to the newly captured Turkish trenches and how many men he would need. The communication trench would allow men and officers to move safely from the Australian trenches to the now occupied Turkish trenches without being exposed to the withering fire of the enfilading Turkish artillery, which was still sweeping the open ground between the trenches.

Harry set off to reconnoitre the terrain, reporting back that he would need sixty men and could have the job done before daybreak the next day. Harry then rounded up sixty-two men, all recently arrived recruits whose bodies had not yet been depleted by the excesses of war. Immediately they set to work. The trench was to be 6 feet deep and take a zigzag form. The men worked through the night and 'with entrenching tools and shovels they dug in as bullets and shells swept the open area between Lone Pine'[13] and the Australian trenches. And all through the night there was Harry Freame, running back and forth, dodging shell and shrapnel, marking out and pegging the course of the trench, cheering on and encouraging the men. By morning the communication trench was completed, the first to the newly held positions of Lone Pine.

Over the next three days the men fought to hold on to the hard-won trenches. The Turkish counterattacks didn't cease, waves of enemy soldiers coming down the maze of trenches both day and night. The Australians would not be safe until every Turkish soldier had been cleared from the area. On the morning of 9 August, Captain Cecil Duncan Sasse and Harry's constant companion Captain Alfred Shout set about clearing the Turkish communication trenches of enemy soldiers with bombs and revolvers.

Charles Bean wrote of Shout going about the work with a sense of gaiety, and Schuler, recalling Shout's actions that day, wrote: 'Reckless of his life, he hurled the missiles as if they had been so many cricket balls.'[14] Sasse and Shout worked their way along the trenches, clearing a section then establishing a small barricade of sandbags before moving on. So pleased were they with their morning's work that they decided on a repeat performance in the afternoon. After lighting three bombs, Shout threw the first two but the last exploded before it had left his hand, severely injuring him. Bean wrote that as he was taken out of the firing line, Shout was 'still cheerful, he sat up and drank a pannikin of tea, vowing that he would soon recover'.[15]

Shout's optimism was misplaced and he later died aboard a medical ship. For his work that day he received the Victoria Cross. His citation read:

> with a small party, Captain Shout charged down trenches strongly occupied by the enemy, and personally threw four bombs among them, killing eight and routing the remainder. In the afternoon of the same day, from the position gained in the morning, he captured a further length of trench under similar conditions and continued personally to bomb the enemy at close range under very heavy fire until he was severely wounded, losing his right hand and left eye, this most gallant officer has since succumbed to his injuries.[16]

In total, seven Anzacs received the Victoria Cross during the battle of Lone Pine.

With the Australians settling into the newly captured trenches, Harry was again back at work as company scout, collecting intelligence on the enemy's new positions at Lone Pine. On 15 August, nine days after the initial attack, Harry was determined to pinpoint the direction from which enemy machine-gun fire was peppering the Australian positions. He raised himself above the Australian trenches and, finding what he was looking for, he passed word back down about the location of the machine gun. But as he climbed back into the safety of his trench, he was struck by a 75-millimetre Turkish shell. The bullet smashed his right arm, fracturing the humerus and leaving the bone protruding from the skin. Harry fell backwards into the trench, landing awkwardly on his shoulder and fracturing his collarbone.

The shell ended Harry's time at Gallipoli, but he was determined that it would not end his war. He knew that there was still a game to be played.

Before the Great War, New End Hospital in Hampstead, London, had served as accommodation for the unemployed, the destitute and unmarried mothers and their children. But with the outbreak of hostilities in 1914, the building was converted into a hospital to treat the wounded and shell-shocked soldiers returning from the various fronts across Europe.

Harry was evacuated from the peninsula aboard the hospital ship *Andania*. His first stop was Mudros Harbour on Lemnos, an important staging post for the Allied operations in the Dardanelles Strait. But after two weeks there his wound was deemed serious enough to require evacuation to London. He was admitted to the New End Hospital on 31 August 1915.

From his rooms at New End, Harry may have been able to catch a glimpse of the dome of St Paul's Cathedral – but he had little time for views. There was a war to be fought and a plan to be executed. Harry was determined to make it back to the front, this time as a commissioned officer. For a while he toyed with the idea of taking on a job as an observer in France with the balloon section of the imperial army. He was eventually dissuaded from this idea by Brigadier-General Harold Walker.

On 16 January Freame received a letter from Brigadier-General

Walker. Although he was an Englishman, Walker had taken command of the 1st Australian Division at Gallipoli – after the death of the Australian General Bridges in the early weeks of the fighting. Walker arrived at Gallipoli with rich military experience, having fought campaigns in the Sudan, Egypt and India. He was an officer who liked to lead from the front, a man at home in the thick of the action. Of Walker's time at Gallipoli, Charles Bean wrote that he was:

> constantly visiting corners into which he would not allow anyone else to go. He knows every point of the defence line, as possibly no other man in the Division knows it, and knows men, and is known by them, in a way which is seldom possible for any high officer.[17]

Unusually for the British officers leading Australian troops at Gallipoli, Walker was respected, and 'every man seem[ed] to count him his friend'.[18] When Harry wrote to him, Walker was also in England recovering after being badly wounded in October, having taken two rounds from a Turkish machine gun, one through the hip and one through the arm. Brigadier-General Walker wrote:

> Dear Sergt Freame,
> I have discussed your promotion question with Col. Buckley our representative at 72 Victoria Street – he says it is impossible to make recommendation for commission while you are at home. Commission from the ranks are only given to men on the spot. You will have to rejoin before you can put in an application for

a commission. Let me know when you have a board and are fit for service. Until you are so passed you cannot rejoin your regt. I hope that you are able to. I shall always remember your splendid service and when the time comes I will do what I can to honour your wishes.

Yours sincerely,

H.B Walker[19]

Harry copied Walker's letter out word for word and sent it off to Edith May. The excitement and pride in being able to bring good news to his wife is clear. Signing off the letter, Harry writes:

So you see, he remember me. But I will take any steps unless I am pass for active service and then I might as well claim commission, what.[20]

Walker's response must have buoyed Harry in his convalescence, but it also set down a challenge. To achieve his dream of gaining an officer's commission, Harry would have to get back into the field, and the field seemed a long way away from London in that cold January of 1916.

Though he had Brigadier-General Walker's endorsement, Harry was determined to strengthen his case for a commission, and during the next month more letters of recommendation in response to Harry's own arrived at his bedside. The first to arrive on 3 February was from Lieutenant-Colonel Alfred Joshua Bennett. Bennett had seen action in the Sudan during Australia's first overseas military engagement in 1885 and later served in the South African War. When war broke out in 1914, he enlisted and was named second-in-command of the 3rd Battalion. In the early days of Gallipoli, he was promoted to lead the 4th Battalion and then later led the 1st Battalion during the Lone Pine operations. Bennett was known for his enforcement of discipline, earning the nickname 'Defaulter's Waterloo' due to his treatment of stragglers, shirkers and malingerers. Like many of the Anzac soldiers in the second half of 1915, Bennett had come down with typhoid and had been evacuated from the peninsula. He was happy to provide a recommendation for Harry:

> No. 764 Sergt. Freame H. served with 1st Bn 1st Aust. AIF from formation of Bn to 16 August when he was wounded at Lone Pine. He was frequently employed as a scout and won the D.C.M. and was promoted by General Walker for excellent services. Sergt. Freame is now rejoining after passing a medical board which at first had declared him unfit for further service and I can confidently recommend him for further promotion.
> A.J Bennett Lieut. Col. 1st Bn.[21]

It seems from Bennett's letter that Harry may have given him a false impression of where he was at in his recovery by this stage, as he had still not been passed fit for active service, the wound he had suffered at Lone Pine taking more time than expected to heal, such was the severity of the damage done.

Two days later a letter from Major Cecil Duncan Sasse arrived at Harry's bedside. Sasse, Alfred Shout's bomb-throwing partner during the heroics of Lone Pine, wrote:

No. 764 Sergt. Freame H. was in my company in the 1st Bn A.I.F from the formation of the Battalion till he was wounded at Lone Pine on August 16th.

During his service on the Peninsula Sergt. Freame was awarded the DCM and was specially promoted [by] General Walker G.B commanding the 1st Australian Division, for his excellent services.

During the whole of the fighting, Sergt. Freame was under my command and proved himself to be the most reliable & capable man I had. He is a splendid fighter, excellent disciplinarian and always had the confidence of the men under him, and I confidently recommend him for a commission which he thoroughly deserves.

C.D Sasse Major, D.S.O 1st Battalion A.I.F.[22]

The next letter to arrive was from Captain Jacobs, the man who Harry had taken water to on that first day on the peninsula, high up at Quinn's Post, saving Jacobs and his men from thirst and enemy fire. What shines through in Jacobs's letter is the warmth and camaraderie between Jacobs as an officer and Harry the rank-and-file soldier. It seems that whatever differences existed on Gallipoli between officers and soldiers, differences that have been well documented over the years, they were not evident in the relationships Harry enjoyed with his commanding officers. Harry was accepted as an equal among them, a place he won by his bravery, courage and discipline.

Jacobs wrote:

In Search of a Commission

My Dear Freame,

I received your letter this morning & was indeed pleased to get it. I cannot really tell you when the next draft is going out as no one down here has any knowledge of it. I was surprised to see by your letter that there is talk of me commanding the next draft as I have not been told anything of it, indeed I have not yet been passed as fit for active service though I expect the result of my last test to be through in a couple of days.

I saw Genl Walker several times when I was in London & he tells me he was trying to get you a commission. I put a good word or two in for you. He was awfully wild when he heard the story of the D.S.O I didn't get from the little job up at Quinn's in the early days, he tells me he knew nothing about it & says I should have told him about it when he was out in the Peninsula, as it is, he says he will look into the matter for me, so if you see him you can tell him the facts of the case.

You asked me about your camera some time back well I lost your address so could not answer you so will tell you its history now. Well, after you left Lieut. McGregor came to me and asked me for it, he said you asked him to get it off me & mind it for you so I gave it to him, when I left the regiment on 30th September he still had it. Hoping to see you down here at an early date.

I am yours sincerely,

H. Jacobs[23]

On 16 February Brigadier-General Walker wrote again to Harry and this time included a letter of recommendation to Cyril Brudenell White:

Dear Sgt Freame,

Yours of 10th has followed me round hence the delay in replying. I enclose you a note for General White, tho' as I have passed my own Board I shall, I hope, be out as soon as you are. I am afraid I'm not in a position or have any right before the Medical Authorities any instructions as regards passing you out but said better ask them before you out as soon as you can – in any case in Egypt. I'm sure they can find you a job that need not necessitate carrying a rifle. Let me know what they decide.

Yours Sincerely

H B Walker[24]

The note that Walker enclosed for White read:

My Dear White,

The bearer of this is Sergt. Freame who you know as well as I do. He's had some difficulty about getting PASSED for service on account of his arm and he will not be able to carry a rifle. He's too valuable a fellow to lose however – He wants a commission – personally I think he has earned one but Gen. Godley may not like to give one to a Mexican – Still you will be short of officers and the 1st Battalion thought no end of him. I daresay I shall be out as soon as he is. Yours very sincerely, H.B Walker.[25]

A staff officer, White had planned the Anzac landing at Gallipoli with General Bridges and had also been the architect of the evacuation of Gallipoli, the most successful operation of the whole campaign. It was

White who had stopped by the trenches in Browne's Dip prior to the attack on Lone Pine to confer with Harry. By February 1916 his control of the Australian divisions administration was almost total. Winning his support would almost guarantee that Harry's ambition would be fulfilled. That Hooky Walker was under the impression that Harry was Mexican points to either Harry's ability to obscure his true origins or the nature of rumour among the troops on the peninsula. What is most interesting, though, is that Walker is unconcerned by Harry's background: whether Mexican or not, Walker felt he deserved a commission based on his splendid service. Walker's suspicion that racial prejudices – in this case Godley's, but not uncommon among the British officers of the time – would play a part in deciding Harry's fate were not unfounded.

Walker's letter was all the encouragement Harry needed to get himself passed fit and back to his beloved 1st Battalion. An officer's commission was all but assured if he could get himself to Egypt, where the troops were awaiting deployment to Europe after having been pulled out of the Dardanelles. Nothing was going to stop Breezy Harry from claiming it.

On 2 February the medical board declared Harry fit for 'any duty abroad not necessitating the carrying of a rifle'.[26] Once discharged in March 1916 Harry made his own way from London down to the Montevideo Camp at Weymouth on the British coast. The camp served as a base for Australian and New Zealand soldiers who had been wounded at Gallipoli, sent to England to convalesce but ultimately deemed unfit for service. From Weymouth the wounded men would be repatriated to Australia or New Zealand. Over the course of the war almost 120,000 Australian and New Zealand soldiers passed through the camp.

After arriving at Weymouth, Harry told his story to the officers in charge and explained how he needed to find passage on a ship back to Egypt, where his battalion was re-forming. But the officers didn't believe him, put off by his strange appearance and stranger accent.[27] Anzacs didn't look or talk like Harry Freame, not in their experience. There was nobody about the camp to vouch for Harry, none from 1st Battalion who had witnessed his heroics on the peninsula. To the officers in charge Harry was just a brown-skinned man with an accent and a tall tale to tell.

Unperturbed, Harry knocked around the camp for a few days and by chance struck up a conversation with an Englishwoman who told him that her husband was about to set sail for Salonika in Greece with the Border Regiment at 3am the next morning aboard the troopship *Huntspill*, a German ship that had been captured by the British at Alexandria at the outbreak of the war. Salonika wasn't Egypt, but to Harry it was at least a step in the right direction, and at 3am he presented himself aboard the *Huntspill* dressed in the uniform of the Border Regiment. A few days' sailing out from Weymouth, Harry discarded this disguise and, dressed in his Australian hat and uniform, presented himself to the *Huntspill*'s commanding officer and confessed his story. He was immediately placed under arrest. Of his time aboard the *Huntspill* with the British soldiers of the Border Regiment, Harry only had this to say: 'they didn't speak good English like me.'[28] However, he was well treated and when the *Huntspill* arrived at Salonika, Harry was sent on to Egypt, disembarking at Alexandria on 6 April 1916.

But Harry arrived too late. Brigadier-General Walker, having made a full recovery from the wounds he suffered at Gallipoli, had resumed command of the Australian 1st Division on 14 March and a few days later left Egypt for France. Though Harry was bitterly disappointed to find that he had missed Walker by a matter of weeks, he was still not beaten.

At the time Harry arrived in Egypt, the Australian 53rd Battalion was being formed up with both Gallipoli veterans and new recruits recently arrived from Australia. The 53rd was to be deployed on the front lines of France, and Harry assumed that a man of his fighting experience would be highly valued. He assumed wrongly.

He presented himself and was initially made company quartermaster sergeant, but when he saw a young, inexperienced, recently arrived recruit made a regimental sergeant, Harry questioned the decision and protested loudly. His protest was not well received, and for the second time in a matter of weeks, the hero of Gallipoli found himself under arrest. Fortunately Lieutenant John Storey of the Army Medical Corps, a Gallipoli veteran, witnessed the arrest and recognised Harry from his days on the peninsula. Storey quickly admitted Harry to hospital, which meant he avoided imminent incarceration.[29]

Over the months of May and June, Harry was in and out of hospital receiving treatment for his arm, first in Tell El Kebir and then Heliopolis. On 24 June, against his wishes, Harry was finally invalided out of Egypt, his medical report noting a 'deformed right arm'[30] a result of the gunshot wound suffered at Lone Pine.

Harry left the Suez on 24 June 1916 aboard the *Port Sydney*, bound for Australia, where he disembarked on 22 July. On arrival Harry made his way to Kensington, where his adventure had started on 28 August almost two years before. There he again pressed his case to be sent back to France, back to his men, back to his battalion, back to his war. But his pleas were ignored and on 22 November 1916 Harry Freame was discharged from the AIF, deemed unfit for service. Harry's war was over.

Writing on the crucial role of scouts in World War I, Hesketh-Prichard had this to say:

> the ideal scout ... should be looked up to. Their immense value should be realized, and due credit and honour given to them for their skill. The scouts of a battalion should be the pick of that battalion, and the fact that a man has attained the rank of scout should be signalized by his receiving extra pay and extra consideration.
>
> As long as war lasts it will be necessary to find out what is in the enemy's mind, and this is so important, that those who prove themselves capable of discovering and of giving warning of what is about to occur, should be objects of admiration and respect to all their comrades.[31]

Harry got none of this. The war had left him maimed, forgotten and discarded. In all he was wounded eighteen times at Gallipoli, including the shattered right arm that put him out for good. The war had wrecked his body, but it was the Australian high command and their refusal to make him an officer, to give him his due, that inflicted the most pain upon this gallant soldier.

In private notes written after the war, official historian Charles Bean (himself a captain) wrote that Freame's ambition for a commission:

> was never fulfilled. It was known to General Walker, but Walker was away, badly wounded, at the time of the evacuation of Anzac, and I feel that though not unsure of Freame, whose character

and achievements he well knew, he was not sure how Australians would accept him as their officer. In this, I am sure he was for once completely astray – they would have leapt to Freame's skill and daring and the nobility of his leadership.[32]

Bean does Brigadier-General Walker a disservice here. Walker was in favour of giving Harry his deserved commission. It was Godley who Walker believed would have reservations about Freame's ancestry, though he had mistaken Freame for a Mexican. Maybe Bean was putting his own prejudices into the mouth of Walker, unjust as they were. The letters of recommendation from Cecil Sasse and Harry's other commanding officers show clearly that Harry had the confidence of the men around him and none held any concerns about a promotion for Harry.

But in the early days of the AIF, a man's courage under fire, discipline and having the confidence of the men around you meant little when it came to commissions. The story of Lieutenant Geoffrey Street, Harry's raiding companion on German Officers' Trench, shows this better than most.

When war broke out in 1914, Street, a law student at Sydney University, signed up with the Australian Naval and Military Expeditionary Force, which was sailing off to fight in New Guinea. But before leaving Street had second thoughts and, taking advice from his father that the real war would be fought in Europe, he decided to sign on with the New South Wales Infantry Brigade. This brigade was formed by a Sydney lawyer and the 1st Battalion commander was led by another solicitor, Lieutenant-Colonel Dobbin. As Cameron Hazlehurst writes in *Ten Journeys to Cameron's Farm*, 'Legal connections and militia experience made law graduates, and even students, prime candidates for commissions. Thus, after four days as a private in the Australian Imperial Force, 20-year-old Geoffrey Street ... was commissioned 2nd Lieutenant in Dobbin's battalion.'³³

Harry didn't have any connections. He was never a lawyer. He never attended Sydney University. He was a horse breaker, a sailor, a cook, a fighting man. And he had dark skin and a strong accent. But he had a lot more experience than four days as a private.

In May 1913 the Royal Military College, Duntroon, had changed its entry requirements for those seeking to become officers in the Australian Army. When Afghan-born British subject Abdul Wade attempted to enrol his Australian-born son into Duntroon, the attorney-general, in collaboration with General Bridges, intervened to change the admission requirements of enrolling cadets to stop that happening. From May 1913 those wishing to complete the officers' course needed to be 'substantially of European descent'.³⁴ The use of 'substantially' was intentional, to allow for any potential officer with Asian, or Mexican, descent to be excluded. The new wording was designed to be arbitrarily applied after the previous wording, 'of pure European descent', had proved too hard to enforce as it required the tracing back of lineages over generations.

Harry had played the game. Played it better than anybody else on the peninsula. He had proved himself over and over again, night after night on the deathly grounds of no-man's-land. The war needed Harry, and men like Harry – the Maori and Indian and Indigenous, and the Black African soldiers of the French forces. But while they could play the game, men like Harry, men with darker skin and different intonations of speech, could never win. The game was rigged.

Chapter 5

A Hero's Return

When Harry stepped ashore at Woolloomooloo Bay in late July 1916, he, along with the other returning soldiers, received a hero's welcome. The Liverpool Depot Band struck up a version of 'Home, Sweet Home' and Red Cross members handed each returning soldier a sprig of wattle and a packet of cigarettes before waiting cars whisked them off to the general hospital. Newspaper reports told of the splendid physique of the men returning, naively noting that they seemed to show little effect of the fighting they had gone through. One ship's officer was heard to comment that it was a pity that such good material had to be returned as unfit for service.[1]

But of all the returning soldiers that day, none captured the attention of the waiting newspapermen as much as Sergeant Harry Freame, DCM. One soldier tipped off a reporter that Freame was a 'household word' among the Australian soldiers on Gallipoli, such was his fame. But even without that information, as early as September 1915, almost twelve months prior, the Australian public had become familiar with Freame's name through a report in the Australian papers.

In that article Freame was described as the smartest scout in the army, a man who ventured out nightly to inspect the Turkish trenches, but tellingly, 'has very little to say'.[2] The reporters who awaited Freame in Sydney likewise found him reluctant to speak. When a journalist from *The Sun* asked Harry how he had come to win the Distinguished Conduct Medal, Harry simply replied, 'Just for carrying water.'

'How much water?' the reporter pressed.

'Oh, two bottles,' Harry said.[3]

Another reporter described Harry as 'close as an oyster' when trying to get information from him about the exploits that earned him his war medal. After much probing Harry finally described winning the DCM as 'merely a bit of luck'.[4]

The Australian public hungered for news of their soldiers, longed to hear that their men had stood up to the enemy, had gone bravely into battle, had done the country proud. And though he was reluctant to speak, Harry Freame's feats of bravery were soon splashed across the pages of Australian newspapers.

On 29 July the most extensive interview with Freame appeared in *The Daily Telegraph* under the title 'From Mexico to Gallipoli'. In it Freame, described as 'tall, dark and lithe',[5] told his interviewer:

> I have been through several revolutions in Mexico as I went back a few times after wars broke out and before I came to Australia I had a Captain's commission in the Mexican Army. I joined the Australian forces at Glen Innes and left with the 1st Battalion and took part in the first landing. The landing was bad enough, but our real troubles were only beginning. A few days after, I was with a party of 28 men in a trench when we found ourselves cut off. We

were being shelled, sniped at and peppered with machine guns but there we had to stay and do our best. Our food and water ran out, and we found ourselves right up against it. We were also short of tools with which to make ourselves a little more secure. We had to have water and tucker but how to get it was the problem. My job had been scouting and after we had a talk a call was made for volunteers to try and get water. I had been wounded five times but I was able to knock about so I volunteered to go out and make a try. The Turks kept pegging away at us, but I got out and back safely and also brought a few picks and shovels. We were relieved that night. There were many incidents of the same kind. Water was always the trouble in those days. That night we got word of another lot who were in a bad way. They were the men under Captain Jacobs, of New South Wales. They had been cut off for three days without water. I got a message into them at daylight, and as I was coming away I got winged by a sniper. That made six wounds all told, but they were not much and I managed to keep going. That night I got water into this lot of men. It was here that the heaviest fighting took place. For my part in these incidents I got the D.C.M.[6]

Freame described how he ended up being evacuated to England:

I stuck to Gallipoli and saw a good deal of fighting here and there. You could not miss that. At Lone Pine however I took the count. We had a bad time there. We were again stuck in a trench and we were trying to get a bit of our own back by bombing. I wanted to have a look to see how we were doing and stood up on the parapet to have a look and just as I did so I stopped a seventy-five projectile with my right shoulder. I had to leave then. Yes, I had about four months of as fine fighting as anybody could wish for. I was sent to England and there I met General Walker, who had recommended me for a commission. He told me if the board would pass me he would try to get me a commission. The board however turned me down as permanently unfit. You can't pass the medical board with a smashed shoulder and useless arm. General Walker had given me a letter to General White, who was in Egypt so I was determined to get out there again if I could. There was only one way to do it so I stowed away on a transport and landed in Egypt all right and again commenced training. I did not last long though. The doctors spotted me and I was sent back. That's about all I think. I'd like to go again, but I suppose I won't get the chance.[7]

Freame's interview is a candid account of his time on Gallipoli and his dealings with Brigadier-General Walker. Freame kept the letters he referenced among his most treasured possessions. But he was not so candid about himself. In all the interviews he gave after returning to Australia, he is reported as being born in Canada. No mention was made, either by Freame or reporters, of his Japanese ancestry. And with good reason. The Australian public was hungry for news of the heroic acts of their soldiers, stories they could build a national identity around, feats of war they could be proud of, that would place them among the brave nations of the Allied forces. But they were not yet ready to learn that their bravest soldier, the finest scout at Gallipoli, the first Australian soldier to win the Distinguished Conduct Medal, was a Japanese national called Hidetsugu Kitagawa.

For while Australia's soldiers were still battling German troops in Europe, at home all attention was on the emergence of a potential new enemy: Japan.

Part II
Bread and Jam and a Cup of Water

Chapter 6

Japan and Australia

Contact between Australia and Japan was limited throughout the better part of the 1800s. The opening up of Japan to trade opportunities in the 1850s attracted little interest in Australia, and it wasn't until 1861 that the two countries had their first trade contact. Until then Australian minds had been occupied with money-making ventures closer to home as the goldrush era swept Australia.

Men such as William Henry Freame were a rarity. The goldrush served to distract attention away from Japan by focusing Australian minds on Chinese migration, which many Australians disparagingly referred to as the 'Yellow Peril'. The rushes attracted thousands of Chinese immigrants, and this influx had the unintended consequence of causing Australians to consider the tenuous hold they had over the vast tracts of land they had spent the better part of a century stealing from its Indigenous inhabitants. How to stop Chinese migration became an intense focus of the colonial parliaments throughout the second half of the 19th century, and one that saw the introduction of an immigration restriction Act in Western Australia in 1897, followed closely by one in New South Wales in 1898.

It wasn't until the early 1890s that Japan came into focus as a possible threat to the white population in Australia.

Forced into the realm of Western civilisations at gunpoint by the warships of Commodore Perry, Japan had done exceedingly well in replicating the technological, scientific, educational and, most importantly, military advances of the Western powers. In conjunction with their rise came a feeling of public dissatisfaction inside Japan that the Western powers had failed to recognise their great leap forward and still treated Japanese citizens unfairly. This unjust treatment manifested in the number of unequal treaties that Japan had been forced to enter into with various countries, treaties designed to keep Japan subjugated, if not colonised.

In 1894 this changed. For in that year Britain signed the first Anglo–Japanese Treaty of Commerce and Navigation. This put an end to the string of unequal treaties that had come before it and recognised Japan as a rising power, to be treated as an equal by the existing powers of Europe and the United States.

In 1894 Australia was still very much an outpost of the British Empire, and here the treaty's signing was met with alarm. The terms of the treaty granted Japanese citizens reciprocal rights of travel and residence. However, Britain – no doubt anticipating the unease the treaty terms would cause in the Australian colony – allowed the British territories and dominions a period of two years to decide whether they would adhere to it.

A year after the signing of the treaty and well within the two-year decision period, Japan went to war with and defeated China in the First Sino–Japanese War. This victory served to warn Australia of the rise of

Japan as a serious military power.

In May 1901 Australia's federal parliament sat for the first time. The Immigration Restriction Bill 1901 was the first major piece of government business, having as it did the full support of all the major political parties and players. To the Japanese consul at the time, Eitaki Hisakichi, this would have come as no surprise.

From as early as 1899, Eitaki had advised his government that 'after the Federation of the Australian colonies, this issue (restriction of coloured immigrants) is very likely to resurface, and the Japanese government should be well prepared to handle the situation'.[1] Now, in May 1901, Eitaki wrote to Prime Minister Edmund Barton, stating:

> My Government recognises distinctly the right of the Government of Australia to limit in any way it thinks fit the number of those persons who may be allowed to land and settle in Australia, and also to draw distinction between persons who may or may not be admitted. As Japan is under no necessity to find an outlet for her population, my Government would readily consent to any arrangement by which all that Australia seeks, so far as the Japanese are concerned, would be at once conceded.[2]

The problem the Japanese had with Australia's Immigration Restriction Bill was not that it excluded Japanese migrants. The problem was that in excluding Japanese citizens it lumped them in with other nationalities that the Japanese had spent the last fifty years separating themselves from. As Eitaki wrote:

> The Japanese belong to an Empire whose standard of civilization is so much higher than that of Kanakas, Negroes, Pacific Islanders, Indians, or other Eastern peoples, that to refer to them in the same terms cannot but be regarded in the light of a reproach, which is hardly warranted by the fact of the shade of the national complexion.[3]

The Japanese sympathised with the prerogative of a nation to exclude a certain class of migrant; they had for many years enforced their own immigration restriction Act based purely on race.

The Immigration Restriction Bill was one of the most highly debated pieces of legislation to ever pass the Australian parliament. A strange fact given that there was virtually no opposition to the Bill itself. Central to the debate was the key question of what language would be used in the dictation test. Edmund Barton proposed using English, but his parliamentary colleagues rejected this idea. They argued that Japan was quickly modernising, and the uptake of the English language meant that soon anybody from Japan would be able to pass a dictation test conducted in English.

Alfred Deakin, chief architect of the Bill, tried to support Barton. He told the parliament that:

> When it becomes necessary for us to exclude people like the Japanese it is reasonable that we should exclude them in the most considerate manner possible, and without conveying any idea that we have confused them with the many uneducated races of Asia and untutored savages who visit our shores. To lump all these

peoples together as Asiatics and undesirables would naturally be offensive to a high-spirited people like the Japanese, and surely without any request from the British Government or without any representations from the Japanese people mere considerations of courtesy, such as should exist between one civilized people and another, should lead us to make this distinction. Considerations of simple politeness, such as honorable members extend to each other in this House, should at least govern the actions of civilized nations in their dealings with one another.[4]

Deakin was immediately challenged from the floor. 'Does the Attorney-General advocate Japanese immigration?'[5] asked Senator Conroy.

'No,' Deakin replied. 'I say that the Japanese require to be absolutely excluded ... I contend that the Japanese require to be excluded because of their high abilities. I quite agree with the honorable member for Moreton that the Japanese are the most dangerous because they most nearly approach us, and would, therefore, be our most formidable competitors.'[6]

The Australian senators knew of the offence that the *Immigration Restriction Act* would cause the Japanese, but they cared very little for the sensitivities. These men had a bigger goal in mind, the preservation of a white Australia.

This attitude was summed up by Senator William 'Billy' Hughes when he told the parliament, 'We want a white Australia, and are we to be denied it because we shall offend the Japanese?'[7]

Unbeknown to the Australian Government, while they were debating how best to keep the Japanese out of Australia, the British were in the middle of negotiating a military alliance with Japan. The Anglo–Japanese

Alliance was a crucial piece of strategic diplomacy that would allow Britain to withdraw its naval fleet from the Pacific and bolster its fleet in European waters in readiness for any confrontation with Germany, the likelihood of which was increasing.

On 23 December the *Immigration Restriction Act 1901* gained royal assent and became Australian law, effectively excluding permanent Japanese settlement in Australia for the next half a century. Just over a month later on 31 January 1902 the Anglo–Japanese Alliance was announced. This alliance would be the catalyst for Japanese workers migrating to the United Kingdom, in particular to the shipyards of Middlesbrough – and among them was one Harry Freame.

When the veil of secrecy was lifted from the successful negotiations, Australia welcomed the signing of the Anglo–Japanese Alliance. This might seem a surprising response given the hostile words that had been aimed at Japan and its citizens over the preceding six months during the debates around the Immigration Restriction Bill. But Australian politicians and the public alike saw the alliance as a logical way of balancing Russian power in the Pacific. It was Russia that presented the greatest military threat to Australia at the time.

For their part, the Japanese saw the alliance as affirmation of their newly acquired great power status, confirmation that their program of modernisation was bearing fruit. The program may have started out on the backs of English teachers such as Harry Freame's father, men dragged from the bar rooms and brothels of Yokohama, but now the Japanese were sitting at the same table as the great Western powers, inferior to nobody and no nation.

By December 1903 international observers felt that Russia and Japan were headed for war. The issue was control over the territories of Korea and Manchuria (modern-day northeastern China), the expansionist dreams of Russia and Japan rubbing up against each other with neither willing to back down. The military build-up was noted in Australia, and one politician in particular, Dr John Mildred Creed, began to wonder what it would mean for Australia if Japan were to defeat Russia.

In December 1903 Creed wrote to Deakin advising that the Australian Government change its approach to the question of Japanese migration. Creed argued that if Japan were to win the war, 'her standing among the nations will be so vastly increased that she is not likely to tamely submit to what she considers a national humiliation and what would now be a graceful concession will then possibly have to be yielded to superior force'.[8] Deakin heeded Creed's advice and set in motion a process that resulted in the Japan–Australia Passport Agreement of 1904. This agreement allowed Japanese merchants, students and tourists to enter Australia without restriction but crucially still denied them the right to settle permanently in Australia. But it still didn't resolve the Japanese question in Australian minds.

Japan's eventual victory in the Russo–Japanese War had shifted Australia's thinking on Japan. Where previously Japan was considered an immigration threat, it was now perceived as a military threat. Addressing the Australian parliament in 1905, Senator William Knox of Kooyong warned his colleagues that there was no sense in belittling a country that had clear military superiority:

> It is idle to suppose that the Japanese who are so rapidly pushing their way to the first rank among the nations of the world, will

allow themselves for many years longer to be kept out of Australia by a hypocritical measure, such as we now have in force ... The honorable and learned member for West Sydney [Billy Hughes] spoke about the people of Japan knocking at our door, and demanding admission. If it were not for the alliance between Great Britain and Japan, we might regard the nearness of Japan to Australia as a very great danger, deserving the most serious consideration. But are we under the circumstances, justified in assuming a confident attitude? Is it to be imagined that the 4,000,000 people who are scattered over this great continent could effectively resist the Japanese if they chose to attack us, and we were unsupported by Great Britain? The supposition is so absurd that the statesmen of Japan who read the speeches of some honorable members will regard them as ludicrous. We can maintain our present position only with the help of Great Britain, and Japan, in the years to come, will not allow us to continue to hold an enormous unoccupied territory if her own country becomes overcrowded. The time will come when, treaty or no treaty, the Japanese will demand from us the same consideration that we extend to other civilized races. They have shown readiness to adapt themselves to the conditions of Western civilization, and conducted themselves with the utmost humanity during the terrible war in which they were engaged with Russia. It is ludicrous for honorable members to attempt to belittle a people who, by sheer force of their virtues, have attained an exalted position among the nations. How could we effectively resist the Japanese if they thought fit to attack us?[9]

Knox had hit upon the very problem that was to keep Australia's policymakers awake at night for the next two decades. That Australia had been able to bring in and enforce a racially discriminatory immigration policy while being situated on the doorstep of Asia was only made possible by the presence of the British Navy in the Pacific. But with the signing of the Anglo–Japanese Alliance, the British had withdrawn their fleet to European waters. In doing so, the British entrusted the defence and security of the Pacific to the Japanese fleet. For security Australians were now relying on a people they had not only banned from their country but whom they feared may invade. To Australian politicians following the Japanese victory over Russia, it must have been quite alarming to think that Britain had left the fox to guard the chickens, and they were the chickens.

Over the next few years, under Alfred Deakin, Australia took steps to shore up its maritime defences. Then in 1909 the first Intelligence School of Instruction was formed. The school was set up to equip intelligence officers and staff with the skills they would need to meet what was perceived as the growing Japanese threat. One of the first graduating officers was a man called Edmund Piesse.

Born in Hobart, Piesse graduated from the University of Tasmania in 1900 with a degree in science. He then went on to study law, graduating in 1905. He joined the intelligence service in 1909 and after completing the intelligence course was deployed to conduct a geographical survey of Tasmania. Over the next decade and a half, he would become the leading Australian thinker on Japan and its relationship with Australia.

With the fear of Japanese invasion leading to the creation of an intelligence agency, it was only a matter of time before that intelligence network would begin to find signs that supported that fear. Though evidence of Japanese espionage activities in northern Australia was collected, Australia's intelligence officials were at a loss as to what to do with it. In a minute paper of late May 1909, the chief of the general staff wrote:

> If Japanese spies are being employed in Japan a secret service is not required to know that they are employed for the benefit of Japan and not of Australia and that the information would be used in the case of hostilities. If the statements are believed we ought to attempt to prevent them acquiring information though how this can be done I do not see. Careful study of the Estimates, Government Gazette and the Press will afford any trained officer all the military information he requires and it is the general policy to make the resources of the country known as widely as possible.[10]

It reads as a rather fatalistic piece of advice from the organisation charged with the nation's security.

On 9 December 1911 the British ship the TSS *Gothic* docked in Sydney after completing its long journey from London. The passenger list recorded those aboard the ship, including one Freame, HK, ship's scullion, born in Japan. Travelling under the name Henry Koba Freame, this was the first time Harry set foot in the adopted homeland of his father, William Henry Freame. Harry did not stay long, with his seaman's journal placing him back in London a few months later, in February 1912. He only spent a very short while in Australia, but whatever he saw and did must have convinced him that his future lay here. Whatever prejudices that were held against the Japanese people, they had no effect on Harry's plans. In February 1912 Harry abandoned the seaman's life.

By 1913 Harry was back in Australia, working as a horse breaker at Glen Innes. There is no evidence to suggest that Harry held British nationality. His birth had never been registered with British authorities in Japan. All evidence suggests that when Harry entered Australia for the second time he did so technically as a Japanese national.

Harry could have entered on a Japanese passport, which would have allowed him to stay in Australia as a non-permanent resident and renew annually his right to stay for a period of five years while exempt from the dictation test. The dictation test would have held no fears for Harry anyway; he could speak seven languages to varying levels, picked up on his long voyages around the world. The other possibility is that Harry simply absconded from whichever ship had brought him to Australia and slipped into the anonymity of the Australian outback.

Chapter 7

A Mis-start at Montavella

Harry set sail from Albany, Western Australia, on 1 November 1914 bound for Egypt aboard the *Afric* with the rest of the 1st Battalion diggers. If he had ventured on deck, he would have seen the Imperial Japanese Navy battleship *Ibuki* cruising alongside, keeping a protective eye over the Australian fleet as it headed off to the Great War. The *Ibuki* provided an escort for the Australian ships all the way to the Middle East and formed part of the Japanese commitment to the Allied powers' cause in World War I. This wartime support was a product of the Anglo–Japanese Alliance, which had been reaffirmed and extended in 1911, the year Harry first arrived in Australia. The treaty did not oblige Japan to fight alongside the British, but at the outbreak of World War I, the Japanese offered to support Britain, asking in return for the possession of the German territories in the Pacific that lay north of the equator. The German territories that lay south of the equator were to go to Australia.

Over the next four years of the war, Japan asserted its military might throughout the Pacific, even cruising by to visit Australian ports. Rather than reassuring Australians, these visits by the Japanese navy only stoked the fears of Japanese invasion that had never abated. Australia did not see Japan's effort to support the Allied cause in the Great War as a positive, as strengthening the bonds between the British Empire and Japan. Australians saw the war as their worst nightmare playing out before them. Britain, as they had long feared, was bogged down in a struggle for survival in Europe and could not spare any resources to come to the rescue of its far-off dominion in Australia. Additionally, Australia's best fighting men were also on the other side of the world. Australians felt further from the protective lap of the motherland than ever before. In an undefended Pacific, Australia was now at the mercy of Japan. Recognising this, Japan tried to press its advantage.

In February 1916, a few months before Harry Freame returned to Australia for a third time, the Japanese Government passed a resolution aimed at ending anti-Japanese actions in Australia. The man behind the resolution, Konishi Kanau, complained that 'Australia humiliated Japan by treating its citizens like Chinese and Indians and demanded that all barriers to Japanese immigration and trade in Australia and South Pacific islands be removed.'[1]

The Australian Government, first under Prime Minister Andrew Fisher and then under Prime Minister Billy Hughes from October 1915, had fobbed off Japanese diplomatic pressure, claiming they were much too busy with the war to start discussing commercial treaties. Their concern, of course, was the same old fear: that Japan's insistence on Australia's adherence to the treaty was merely a back door into Australia, a way to find an outlet for their surplus population. And now with the Japanese occupying the former German territories just north of the equator, the Japanese were closer than ever to Australia's coastline.

But the Japanese were not so easily denied. In early 1916 when Britain requested further naval assistance from its Japanese ally, Japan replied that they would need some signs of friendship from the British before they would provide it. The Japanese made it clear that convincing Australia to sign up to the Anglo–Japanese Treaty would do nicely as an indication of Britain's commitment to remaining an ally.

However, for Australian politicians this manoeuvre only confirmed their suspicions that sooner or later today's ally would become tomorrow's invader. Prime Minister Hughes wrote from London to his minister for defence, George Pearce:

> My dear Pearce, I hardly know how to begin to tell you the story of what is going on in England ... all our fears – or conjectures – that Japan was and is most keenly interested in Australia are amply borne out by facts. Grey told me that the Japanese Ambassador had been pressing him before my arrival about the Commercial Treaty ... Grey believes Japan will stand behind Britain – he admits however that there is a large and growing party in Japan who look askance at the alliance and with favour on Germany. It is to me quite clear that in the event of temporary reverse to the Allies, the Japanese government might not be able – even if they so desired – to keep Japan behind Britain ... The position is aggravated ... by the fact that Britain has approached Japan with a view to obtaining naval assistance – say in the Mediterranean – and that the Japanese Government, while ready enough to grant this, ask for some evidence of Britain's friendliness towards her in order possibly to justify her action or placate the opposition ... I

told Grey that Australia would fight to the last ditch rather than allow Japanese to enter Australia.²

A month after Harry Freame landed in Australia, Prime Minister Billy Hughes also returned home, after an extended trip to Europe to deal not only with the war but with the ever more insistent Japanese diplomatic advances. Hughes's mind was on the upcoming referendum on conscription. Japan and the spectre of Japanese invasion played a big part in the referendum. The 'Yes' side, those in favour of introducing conscription, argued that conscription was necessary because – in the words of Prime Minister Hughes – 'Japan would challenge the White Australia policy after the war, [and] ... Australia would then need the help of the rest of the Empire, and that if she wished to be sure of getting it she must now throw her full strength into the war in Europe.'³

For those advocating a 'No' vote, the spectre of Japanese invasion was equally important. It was madness, they claimed, to conscript and send away as many men of fighting age as possible. A land empty of defenders would only encourage the Japanese to attack. Best to have as many men at home as possible.

Some in the parliament took offense that Japan, a valued ally, was being used in such a way. Senator William Maloney tried to reason with his colleagues, telling them:

> I know that some of our cities would have been blown to pieces if it had not been for the protection of the Japanese Fleet. The *Australia* is a splendid ship, but even she could not guard our coastline from Brisbane in the north to Perth in the west, and

the remaining units of the Fleet would not have remained afloat for three hours before that powerful German fleet which sank a British Fleet off the coast of America, and was in turn sunk by a British Fleet of stronger tonnage. We must thank the Japanese. We know that they protected our transports which were conveying our soldiers across the sea ... I can point to treaties which England has broken, notably the treaty re Copenhagen, but I cannot place my fingers on a single treaty which Japan has broken, and much as I love our White Australia – I would give my life to-morrow in order to keep the flag of a White Australia flying – my lips must speak the truth of what I know our Allies have done for us ... I say it is idiotic to blame Japan; it is not fair to Japan, to an ally that has saved our cities from destruction and our soldiers from losing their lives in the perilous journey to Egypt.[4]

But Maloney was in the minority and throughout the war, despite their assistance to the Allied war effort – and despite the fact that there was at least one Japanese soldier fighting among the Anzacs at Gallipoli – suspicion of Japan continued to grow in Australia.

To the Japanese, still very much an ally that Australia relied upon for its maritime security, this must have all seemed quite surreal and not a little ungrateful.

If Harry Freame thought when he stepped off the boat in Sydney in July 1916 that he was stepping onto the soil of a Japanese ally, one where he would be welcomed as wholeheartedly as he was in Gallipoli, he would have quickly realised his Japanese ancestry was still something to be hidden, just as it was when he first signed up to the war. And sure enough, in 1916 we see Harry once again reverting to the old story of being born in Canada, claiming himself as a French Canadian to explain away his accent.

The politics of the day placed Harry in an uncomfortable position, and maybe he reflected on the similarities to his own childhood and upbringing. Growing up in Japan, he had witnessed a government insisting that the country embrace Western ways – the ways of his father (minus the drinking and whoring) – and yet on the street he saw these same Western ways pilloried by the public and he heard stories of samurais cutting down foreign men: men like his father. And now in Australia he saw a government allied to the country of his birth, the country of his mother, and at the same time he saw the deep fear and distrust the Australian public had of people who looked and sounded like him. But if Harry felt any confusion or divided loyalties, he kept them strictly to himself.

After being discharged from the army on 20 November 1916, Harry travelled to Montavella, one of the first soldier settlements established for the returning diggers, located a short distance from the NSW town of Bathurst. In 1916 the Federal Government had purchased Montavella, a 200-acre working orchard, with apple, pear and cherry trees ranging from three to four years old, from a Mr Wolstenholme. Wolstenholme had come to prominence a few years earlier after inventing a mechanism that allowed farmers to combat frost on orchards by way of a thermometer connected to a bell that would alert them when the temperature fell to freezing. Thus alerted, the farmer would rise from his bed and light kerosene tins around the base of the trees, raising the ambient temperature. Newspapers of the day described the invention as 'ingenious', though unsurprisingly it seems it never caught on.

A survey of soldiers taken in 1916 reported that around 25 per cent of Australian soldiers dreamed of farming after the war. Tellingly the same survey found that, of those 25 per cent, only 50 per cent possessed any experience of farm work.[5] The soldier settlement programs aimed to overcome this, and there was great excitement around the prospects of Montavella as a suitable fruit-growing area, based mainly on the claims of those who sold the land to the government. The presence of Harry Freame only added to the sense of expectation connected to one of the first soldier settlement programs. One newspaper reported:

> An instance of successful settlement may be quoted – the Montavella orchard, at Bathurst, where our old friend Sergt. Harry Freame, D.C.M., the Marvel of Gallipoli, is one among a lucky dozen. The Montavella orchard was planted out some years ago by a very clever orchardist named Wolstenholme who was formerly expert to the Bathurst Government Experimental Farm.[6]

For the first year of the program, Harry and seven other returned soldiers worked the orchard in return for a wage. For the men who had bled for their country on the battlefields of Europe, the Montavella soldier settlement, like other soldier settlements across Australia, was a chance to heal the scars of the war in the open air of rural Australia, and a means for them to become self-sufficient, to live and support their families off the back of their own toil.

Under the scheme the government provided the men with a working orchard and capital, the cost of which would be paid back over a thirty-year period. The government described the objective of the program as 'To

A Mis-start at Montavella

give the settler an advantageous start in life and so to provide him with the basic requirements of his occupation as to enable him to make the farm productive of income at the earliest possible season, and to ensure that the expansion of the farm shall depend solely upon the intelligently applied industry of the farmer.'[7]

Despite the inexperience among the men at Montavella, by July 1917, six months after arriving, things were going well. Five thousand cases of fruit had been sold, all of high quality with very little incidence of disease or pests reported. Until that point Harry and the other soldiers had merely been working the property for a wage, but in July a ballot was taken and orchard blocks allocated to the soldiers. Harry drew Block 4, and the government also appointed him as foreman of the Montavella Soldiers' Settlement, making him responsible for coordinating the produce of the other men for sale and liaising with the government authorities responsible for the administration of the settlement.

The role suited Harry well. There is a surviving picture of him from this time. In it he holds a box of fruit, most likely cherries, beautifully arranged in a geometric pattern. As was his way, he stares proudly into the camera with his face shining below a stiff-brimmed hat.

In March 1918 the Montavella Soldiers' Settlement received a distinguished visitor, Governor-General Sir Ronald Munro Ferguson. If Sir Ronald was expecting to bathe in the glow of some good publicity connected with the state looking after its returned soldiers, he was in for a rude shock. Led by Harry, the soldiers took the opportunity of the governor-general's visit to air grievances that had been building over the previous year, particularly about housing. Most of the men at Montavella had been unable to afford the cost of constructing suitable housing and were living in wooden shacks. Others were still camping in tents.

Sir Ronald explained that there was nothing he could personally do for them and beat a hasty retreat. However, a few journalists had accompanied Sir Ronald, and soon there were enough news items about the dissatisfaction of Australia's returned soldiers at Montavella that members of the NSW Parliament started to ask questions. Following an invitation from Harry Freame, the member for Bathurst, Valentine Johnston, visited the settlement to find out for himself exactly what was going on.

A delegation of men met with Johnston and explained that they had voiced their complaints publicly after growing exasperated by the lack of response from the secretary for lands William Ashford, and the director of soldier settlements, John Bryant. Under the terms of the soldier settlement scheme, Harry and the other men received a line of credit of £500 with which to go about building their new life. However, as the men made clear to Johnston, the credit line was proving difficult to access. Permission to pay for necessary farm equipment or labour was not given by the department, leaving fruit to rot on trees or seeds to go unplanted. Where the soldier settlers had bought equipment on credit from local businesses, the money had not come through from the department to pay off the debt. One soldier described how he was embarrassed to show his face in town on account of his unsettled debts. What further concerned the soldier settlers was the absolute lack of clarity around the sale of their fruit.

Under their agreements with the government, all fruit was marketed through the department's agent, but the soldiers were kept in the dark as to how much their fruit was sold for. Nor were they told the state of their accounts despite numerous promises from the department to provide the accounting.

What upset the soldier settlers most was the uncertainty around the land itself. A year into the program, the men still did not know 'exactly on what terms they were holding the land and for what or whose benefit they were "working from sunrise to sunset". They knew that they were not exactly tenants; they were not proprietors; they were not lessees, or sharefarmers.'[8]

One returned soldier told Johnston that the situation at Montavella was so bad that 'If I were physically fit I would a thousand times sooner battle with the Huns in Flanders than battle with the diseases and disadvantages confronting the returned men at Montavella.'[9]

After hearing the men out, Johnston told them, 'I have listened with amazement to what you have told me, and have come to the conclusion that the amount of mismanagement or want of business capacity on the part of the Government is simply amazing.'[10] Johnston left Montavella promising to get a better deal for Harry and the other soldier settlers of Montavella.

Government mismanagement of the scheme was bad enough, but Harry and the rest of the men had other problems to deal with at Montavella. It soon became apparent that the area was no good for orchards. The trees were soon infested with pests such as woolly aphids, codling moths and black spot. Reports soon surfaced that the original owner of the property, Wolstenholme, had never been able to make it function as an orchard. He had sold the property to the government for far more than it was worth. It became obvious that the government had overpaid, meaning that the repayments being made by the soldiers were higher than they needed to be.

Adding to the settlers' problems, the individual blocks were proving to be too small. No matter how hard a man worked to improve his block, no single block was large enough to grow enough fruit to sell to allow him and his family to pay off what was owed to the government, let alone to get ahead. The men felt like they were slowly choking in the open country air.

When the then NSW minister for agriculture, William Ashford, visited Montavella in the early days of the scheme, he told the old soldiers that he looked upon them 'with a certain amount of sympathy, as being returned men, they were not quite right in their heads'.[11] In this unsympathetic appraisal, the minister had touched upon another absurdity of the soldier settler program.

Harry and the other men of Montavella were expected to work the land and to make it profitable, with the first of those profits to be returned to the government coffers. But no thought was given to how a man such as Harry, who had been discharged from the army because he couldn't hold a rifle, was meant to wield an axe or a hoe, to chop wood, to cut down trees, to plant trees, to till the soil. And Harry was one of the luckier ones.

The sad history of the World War I soldier settler schemes is littered with the stories of returned soldiers sent out to farms suffering from the wounds, physical or otherwise, of war. Men missing an arm or a leg. Men who couldn't walk a hundred metres without gasping for breath, their lungs destroyed from exposure to German gas warfare in the trenches of France. Men missing eyes and ears and hands and feet. Men still carrying bullets in their bodies or with bodies ravaged by the diseases that swept through the trenches of Europe, which they had spent months or years in.

Then there were the men who carried their scars on the inside, those who couldn't sleep, or who woke up every night dreaming they were dying, that they were burying another mate, or being buried beneath a shell blast deep in the French mud.

Some of the wives of these men found themselves in rural Australia with a man they no longer recognised, a man who was at turns silent and moody, dark and violent, a man who had died once on the battlefields of Europe and now stood dying again before their eyes.

In their examination of the soldier settlement experience in Australia, historians Bruce Scates and Melanie Oppenheimer highlight that the wellbeing of the soldier was never front of mind for the policymakers. They write:

> Making the injured man productive was the clear aim of repatriation policies: even badly disabled men should be weaned off 'unmanly' reliance on State assistance or private charity and work towards a goal of '100% efficiency'. Repatriation officials encouraged former soldiers to adopt 'a civilian state of mind', 'pick up the threads' of their former lives and return to their natural role of breadwinners and providers.[12]

After the press reported the outcome of Johnston's visit to Montavella, not all voices were supportive of Harry and the other soldiers. One local paper reported:

> Of the original nine settlers; five left after working for six to nine months, and their places have not been filled. The deserters all duly drew their weekly allowance, however, and it is said by persons with good opportunity for observation, that some of the

men that have left did not overtax their strength at any work to which they set their hands, although they were diligent in the pursuit of pleasure night after night in the not-far-distant city.[13]

Another report argued that 'It is not necessary to believe that there are no grumblers among the returned soldiers, or that there are not among them men that are never satisfied, and that will suck the government dry if they are allowed.'[14] The report did concede that the soldiers deserved some sympathy for their plight, but it was a concession dripping with condescension: 'Nevertheless, the soldier settlers at Montavella, if their story is not a tissue of falsehoods from beginning to end, would appear to have real grievances; And their most serious hardship, and the one that will win them sympathy from every manly independent farmer, is that they are nurse-maided by government officials.'[15]

A cartoon captioned 'The Baby-Farm at Montavella' ran below the article. In it a soldier sits in a highchair depicted as a crying baby, surrounded by bureaucrats dressed as nursemaids. For Harry and the returned men of Montavella who had served their country, it must have been a particular humiliation.

On 20 July 1918 Harry gave up his soldier's block at Montavella. Still unable to fully straighten his right arm, which was now significantly shorter than his left, and unable to raise the arm above the height of his shoulder, the manual labour required proved beyond his physical capabilities. But even so, Harry's record shows that during his time at Montavella, he never lost a day of work through illness or injury. Over the next few months the rest of the soldier settlers also began to abandon Montavella, unable to make it work, unable to overcome the challenges of being sent out to farm unprofitable land with neither the training nor physical condition to succeed. By the end of 1918 not one of the original settlers remained at Montavella and the Repatriation Committee ordered an investigation into what had gone wrong.

Unsurprisingly perhaps, attempts to find out what had happened at Montavella were blocked by William Ashford, the secretary for lands. He prevented any members of the Repatriation Committee accessing Montavella. The committee eventually thwarted Ashford's efforts and launched an enquiry that found that 'the conditions at Montavella were not good enough for returned soldiers. The fact that not one of the original settlers was there now was sufficient evidence that there was something radically wrong ... One thing was obvious; that Montavella had been over-rated and should be re-valued.'[16] The overvaluation of the land had a cruel impact on the men sent to work it. As the committee concluded, 'the men were being robbed, owing to the big interest they had to pay on the over-estimated valuation of the estate'.[17]

Another newspaper sent an investigative reporter to ascertain what had gone wrong and who was to blame. The ensuing report largely confirmed the legitimacy of the complaints of Harry and the other men. But by then Harry, the Marvel of Gallipoli, had already left the settlement. His leadership and good service defending the rights of the men of Montavella did not go unrewarded, with newspapers reporting that after he left, the remaining settlers took up a collection of funds and purchased a 'comfortable chair'[18] for Harry and sent it on to him. Given the dire financial situation all the settlers were in, this shows the high regard in which Harry was held.

Chapter 8

'Repugnant Restrictions' and Corruption at Kentucky

In 1873, the year that William Henry Freame married Sei Kitagawa, an illustration appeared in a Japanese book depicting the moment that Isaac Newton was prompted to begin his thinking on gravity. But in the Japanese illustration, Newton isn't contemplating a falling apple. Instead Newton watches a Japanese plum fall from a tree. The illustrators surmised that the Japanese public would not recognise or even know what an apple was. And they were probably right, as prior to the beginning of the Meiji period the apple was unknown in Japan.

Agriculture played a prominent part in the Meiji modernisation push. As early as the 1870s, the Japanese were importing large amounts of seeds, plants and animals in an effort to replicate the agricultural practices and products employed in the West. The first shipment of apples arrived in Japan via China in the 1860s but did not immediately find favour with the Japanese people, the fruit arriving damaged and past its best. However, that changed in 1875, when a large shipment of apples arrived directly from the United States. The hitherto unknown fruit created such wonder that it set off an enormous sustained effort among the Japanese to cultivate their own apples.

That samurai families led this agricultural charge is no surprise, considering that traditionally they had the means, in terms of both capital and landholdings, to position themselves for agricultural success. Additionally, in samurai culture fruit and the gifting of fruit had always played a large role in celebrating important dates and moments.

When Harry Freame walked off the Montavella Soldiers' Settlement in 1918, he accepted a position as postmaster and storekeeper at the Kentucky Soldiers' Settlement located about 40 kilometres from the town of Armidale in northern New South Wales. While the Montavella settlement had been a failure, in the orchard life Harry had found something that appealed to him, something strong enough to draw him back to the orchard and give it another go. Maybe life among the apple and pear and cherry trees had spoken to the samurai spirit that resided deep in Harry Freame.

At first Harry owned no land in the Kentucky settlement, but soon after arriving he was granted a block of 12 acres, the smallest block in the settlement. His right arm never fully healed, never regained its previous strength, and in cold weather it ached and swelled. He could only engage in light manual labour and for other jobs such as heavy lifting or ploughing Harry would pay fellow settlers to do the work for him.

At some point in 1919 Edith May made the long voyage from England and joined Harry at Kentucky. It is remarkable to think that since they married in 1906 the Freames had not spent more than a few months together at any one time. Now, in Australia, Harry had found the place where he could finally settle down, where his breezy life could find some stability among the apple and pear trees of Kentucky – and Edith May's arrival cemented this.

Interest in Harry Freame, sailor, soldier and now orchardist, never seemed to wane, and in December 1919 a reporter travelled to Kentucky to interview Harry. 'His skin is dark,' the story ran, 'but no born white man, even an Australian, ever possessed a whiter, larger or more generous heart. He and his English wife are very comfortably situated in a nice home on Kentucky, and the visitor there is received by them most hospitably.'[1] It would be an offensive compliment today, and possibly it was to Harry even back then, but you get the picture. Harry Freame was loved.

The reporter noted that Harry was a 'French Canadian by birth' and that Harry had a large selection of 'fine pictures of Gallipoli' hanging on his wall. Harry shared with the reporter his experiences at Gallipoli, claiming to have advanced further inland than any other soldier there. 'I was the first man of the A.I.F. to cross Anafarta Ridge,' he told the reporter. Then he added, dryly, 'It was as a prisoner of war though.' Freame repeated the story of his daring escape from his Turkish guard, the reporter no doubt enthralled by Freame's laconic retelling. 'How did you manage it [the escape]?' the reporter asked. 'Oh, I killed the three of them,' Harry replied.

The storytelling, and even the habit of keeping pictures of the Gallipoli landscapes, show a fascinating side of Harry Freame, one that continued throughout his life. Many veterans of the Great War never spoke of it to friends or family, let alone strangers, instead burying their memories and experiences. But Harry had no such disposition. The walls of his house hung with reminders of his time on the peninsula. Throughout his whole life he kept reminders of the war: a bullet with the word 'Dardanelles' carved on it and letters from his commanders and comrades. He would happily discuss the war with reporters and was known for giving lively talks recounting his experience during the war. He gravitated to the soldier settlements, where he was surrounded by other veterans, men who had shared his experiences. Gallipoli was the most important thing that ever happened to Harry Freame, and he was reluctant to let go of the memories, the camaraderie and the love he felt for the men of the AIF and they felt for him in turn.

Soon an opportunity for Harry to return to the company of military men would present itself – and in an unexpected way.

Unlike most military men of the day, at the outbreak of the Great War, Edmund Piesse, one of the first officers through the Intelligence School of Instruction of 1909, did not rush off to the battlefronts of Europe. He was firm in his belief that he was 'bound only to the defense of Australia'.[2] Piesse stayed in Australia, moving to Melbourne to work in the intelligence section of the Directorate of Military Operations. The work of collecting and analysing intelligence appealed to the scholarly Piesse. By 1916 he held the rank of major and the title of Director of Military Intelligence. In this role Piesse directed operations to monitor enemy aliens in Australia. The work sometimes extended to keeping an eye on the citizens of supposed allies, particularly the Japanese. The Japanese question had long fascinated Piesse. Shortly after completing the intelligence course in 1909, he wrote to his fiancée and told her that he was 'recommending new and more relevant mathematical questions for the school examination, such as the distance of Tokio from Port Darwin'.[3]

Unlike other policy thinkers of the day, Piesse did not base his thinking on racial prejudices or hearsay. He wanted his opinions and policy advice to be anchored in the bedrock of fact. From 1916 onwards Piesse dedicated a large amount of time to the Japanese question, gathering information from the NSW trade commissioner based in Kobe, the British ambassador in Tokyo, newspapers and Australian Government files. His scholarly mind was frustrated at the unreliable nature of the information obtained, and he began to learn Japanese so that he could consult Japanese sources and read Japanese newspapers for himself without relying on the translations and interpretations of third parties.

Piesse doubted the quality and reliability of information to be obtained through British diplomatic channels, writing that 'it is not sufficient for us to rely on what we get from British representatives. There seems to be a blight over British policy in the Far East – some British representatives are not in sympathy with our interests.'[4]

After reviewing all available material, Piesse concluded that 'our policy of defense against Japan is inadequately supported by evidence'.[5]

For Piesse the solution was clear. Australia must build its own Commonwealth intelligence service and 'employ someone who knows the main trends of international policies and who has knowledge of Eastern languages'.[6] In a paper to the Australian defence minister, George Pearce, Piesse argued that if Australia could obtain more complete information about Japan, the government could tailor its defence spending accordingly. For Pearce and the Australian Government, which was still paying for the war in Europe, the economics of the argument proved appealing. Piesse wanted to build a Commonwealth office that could gather reliable information on Australia's international concerns – for example, Japan's attitude to the White Australia policy – and provide reliable advice to government. His work would eventually lead to the creation of Australia's first foreign office.

As a consequence of Piesse's research, his views on the threat represented by Japan softened. In his thinking he was much influenced by a man called James Murdoch.

Born in Scotland, Murdoch came to Australia in 1881 and taught first at Maryborough Boys Grammar School and then at Brisbane Grammar School. By 1887 Murdoch had left the teaching profession and was working as a journalist for *The Boomerang*, a Brisbane-based newspaper founded by William Lane. Two years later Murdoch left Australia and settled in Japan. He did not stay there long, leaving in 1893 and travelling to Paraguay, where he expected to take charge of the schools under William Lane's ambitious utopian project founded in the jungles of Paraguay.

Following the defeat of the Shearers' Strike in the early 1890s, Lane, a prominent trade unionist and writer, came up with the idea to start a utopian colony in South America, a place where his ideals could be lived fully. He acquired 463,000 acres at no cost and, by 1893, 220 colonists had arrived at what was then known as New Australia. However, by the time Murdoch arrived, utopia had dissolved into a community of disease, disaffection and disaster. He stayed only long enough to contract a mysterious illness and returned to London to recover. Murdoch had travelled to Paraguay with his twelve-year-old son but strangely decided to leave him in South America, where he would live for the rest of his life.

After a few months in London, Murdoch returned to Japan, again going into the teaching profession. In November 1899 he married Japanese woman Takeko Okada. Murdoch remained in Japan until 1917, when he was recruited by Edmund Piesse as an Australian intelligence asset. That same year the Australian Government paid for Murdoch to travel to Australia and set him up with a professorship in Oriental Studies at the University of Sydney.

Murdoch based his views on the Japanese on his long experience living in Japan. He convinced Piesse that Japan's opposition to the White Australia policy was based solely on the offence such a policy gave to the Japanese by placing them on an equal footing with groups of people whom the Japanese considered themselves superior to.

Murdoch's role was not purely academic. Under the terms of his contract, he was to dedicate two days a week to teaching the Japanese language at the Duntroon Royal Military College. There was also a provision in his contract that he would be allowed to travel back to Japan once a year at the expense of the Australian Government. On this annual trip Murdoch was expected to gather intelligence and report back on the current Japanese thinking on questions of policy deemed important to Australia. During these trips Murdoch corresponded with Piesse using a crude code to evade Japanese scrutiny. As he wrote to Piesse, 'the Japanese were watching all correspondence very carefully'.[7]

In Sydney Murdoch recruited a team of Japanese teachers. Some he brought in from Japan but, as he wrote to Piesse in April of 1919, one was a returned soldier, whom he had installed at Fort Street High School in Sydney. The soldier was none other than Harry Freame, the Marvel of Gallipoli.

How Harry came to the attention of James Murdoch may be explained by the identity of one of the Fort Street High School pupils, Eric Longfield Lloyd, formerly of the 1st Battalion, AIF. Like Harry, Longfield Lloyd had led raids against German Officers' Trench machine-gun positions and participated in the Lone Pine attacks. He had been evacuated from Gallipoli not long after Harry himself had been taken off the peninsula. Suffering from typhoid, the disease that had swept through the Australian trenches in the last few months of the Gallipoli campaign, Longfield Lloyd returned to Australia in January of 1916, where he took up a position with the intelligence section of the general staff. Harry and Longfield Lloyd stayed in contact once both men were back in Australia; indeed, they became lifelong friends. If James Murdoch was looking for trusted Japanese speakers, then it is likely that Longfield Lloyd provided the name of his old 1st Battalion comrade, Harry Freame. And if it was Longfield Lloyd who provided Harry's name to Murdoch, then he must have been one of the few officers of the AIF with whom Harry felt enough trust to disclose his true Japanese identity.

The job must have posed a dilemma for Harry. In one sense, it placed him back among the officers of the Australian military and intelligence establishments, the officers he had once dreamed of joining in the commissioned ranks. The work also offered a much-needed income. However, to accept it would mean exposing his Japanese ancestry, which he had hidden and obfuscated for so long, at a time when anti-Japanese feelings and paranoia were reaching a crescendo, despite Japan's formal status as an ally. Harry must have felt like he was once again in no-man's-land, neither ally nor enemy. The fact that he accepted the job, with the risks that it posed, demonstrates the confidence Harry had in his ability to blend in where needed, to reveal only enough about himself to get by, to go about unseen but still get the job done.

Around the same time that Murdoch recruited Harry Freame to teach Japanese to Australia's intelligence officers, Piesse closed in on his objective of being named director of the service he had advocated for, the

Pacific Branch of the Prime Minister's Department, effectively Australia's first foreign office. Confirmation came through of Piesse's position at the end of May 1919. Ever the scholar in search of facts, Piesse immediately made plans to tour the countries and colonies of the Far East, including five weeks in Japan. He planned to gather information and judge for himself the threat to Australia presented by Japanese policy.

He set out on this trip in September 1919 and didn't return until March 1920. During his time away Piesse consulted with and interviewed all manner of experts and diplomatic staff of friendly nations based in Japan, and even managed to secure a meeting with Japan's vice-minister of foreign affairs, Masanao Hanihara. From this extensive research trip, Piesse concluded that Japan posed no threat to the territorial integrity of Australia. He argued that any Japanese military build-up or expansion south could be explained by Japan's desire to deter a military threat from the growing power in the Pacific, the United States. Piesse found that while Japan was front of mind for Australia's military planners, in Japan Australia barely seemed to register: it was considered of little to no importance when set against the growing might of the United States.[8]

Piesse submitted his conclusions to the Australian Government – conclusions that flew in the face of the opinions held by the Australian and British military establishment and even the personal views of Prime Minister Billy Hughes. These men, their views anchored in race prejudice and with little knowledge of the nation or its people, still believed Japan to be the biggest threat to Australia's desire to maintain a white Australia, and nothing Piesse could say, no matter how many facts he could bring to the table, was going to change their thinking.

Prime Minister Hughes's opposition to Piesse's findings was

predictable. In January 1919, at the conclusion of World War I, the 'great powers' – Japan among them, as one of the five victor powers – convened in Paris for the Peace Conference. There representatives of the victorious nations drafted the peace treaties and produced a draft Covenant of the League of Nations.

Proud of their role in the war and seeing an opportunity to finally be recognised on the international stage as a player whose citizens were equal to those of the European nations, Japan took a modest proposal to its victorious allies. The Japanese representatives asked that a clause be inserted in the Covenant of the League of Nations affirming the principle of racial equality. For the Japanese, the successful adoption of this clause represented the culmination of the long process started under the Meiji emperor in 1868 to achieve equality in all things with the West.

There was also a certain level of political pragmatism behind the Japanese Government's proposal; it was as much to do with domestic politics as international affairs. At the time of the Paris Peace Conference, Japanese public opinion ran against Japan joining the proposed League of Nations. The Japanese still resented what they saw as an unfair resolution to the Russo–Japanese War, when the United States did not enforce the payment of indemnities by the defeated Russians. Now, in 1919, many Japanese people saw the League of Nations as another measure by which the West would attempt to keep Japan from its place among the world powers by confirming member nations' rights to exclude Japanese citizens based on their skin colour, despite all that Japan had contributed to the Allied war victory.

Newspapers in Japan argued that there could be no world peace unless the racial discrimination perpetuated by Australia, the United States and

Canada was addressed. One newspaper wrote that if American president Woodrow Wilson 'who had been advocating justice and humanity' did not support abolishing this racial discrimination, 'he would be the world's biggest hypocrite'.[9]

On 13 February 1919 Japan presented its proposal, which had been developed in close consultation with the American delegation, to the conference. The clause stated:

> The equality of nations being a basic principle of the League of Nations, the High Contracting Parties agree to accord, as soon as possible, to all alien nationals of States members of the League equal and just treatment in every respect, making no distinction, either in law or in fact, on account of their race or nationality.[10]

Japan's proposal seemed fair to the attending delegates. There was only one hurdle: Australia.

Prime Minister Billy Hughes led the Australian delegation at the Paris Peace Conference. He viewed Japan's racial equality clause as nothing more than an attempt by the Japanese to open the door for unlimited migration from Japan to Australia. To Hughes the clause represented a direct threat to the White Australia policy. He was determined to oppose its insertion at all costs.

The Japanese delegation did not abandon their efforts and ramped up pressure on Hughes, seeing his as the crucial opposing voice – which indeed it was. Over the next few months, the Japanese delegates discussed with Hughes how they might water down the language of the proposal to make it more amenable to Australian sensibilities and provide a guarantee that racial equality did not equate to an immigration free-for-all. But Hughes was not for listening, telling one New York newspaper at the time:

> Australia cannot agree to the incorporation of the principle of equality of races in the League of Nations Covenant. Australia will not agree to the adoption of the principle of equality of races in any other form by the Peace Conference if it conflicts with our interests. We cannot deviate an inch from our expressed position in regard to the Japanese question.[11]

The message was clear: racial equality was not in Australia's interests. Hughes never deviated from this and the racial equality clause was never included. But to say that Hughes's views were that of Australia as a whole would be a misrepresentation. While some people in Australia supported Hughes's stance, others – Edmund Piesse among them – had a more nuanced and sympathetic view of what Japan wanted.

An editorial in the Hobart *Mercury* argued that what Japan was asking for at the conference was 'the removal of all the irritating and rather degrading disabilities now too commonly imposed on coloured immigrants'. The editorial was sympathetic to this position, arguing, 'unquestionably the great services lately rendered to the Allies by India and Japan in particular entitle the inhabitants of those countries to relief from restrictions which are repugnant not only to their material interests but to their self respect'.[12]

We can only speculate what Harry Freame made of this debate. He had experienced 'repugnant restrictions' firsthand – the restrictions that prevented him from obtaining an officer's commission in the AIF. If Harry were to take time out of his day to question the inequality of races, his mind may have gone back to a night in June 1915 when he called out two Australian soldiers for cowardice. He may have gone back further to the morning of 26 April when, along with Alfred Shout, he rounded up 200 stragglers and shirkers and drove them up the Turkish hills and back into the front line. But maybe as a returned soldier, and importantly not a returned officer, Harry did not have time to ponder such things.

~

With his wife Edith May installed in his little home in Kentucky and his orchard coming along nicely, Harry split his time – taking the train back and forth – between Kentucky and Fort Street High School in Sydney, where he taught the Japanese language to Australia's intelligence officers. But did Harry only teach the intelligence officers or was he himself engaged in intelligence operations for Edmund Piesse's department? This remains an open question.

James Murdoch recruited and oversaw the Japanese teaching staff. In addition to Harry Freame, Murdoch had employed four other Japanese nationals as teachers. There is no doubt that Murdoch himself was providing intelligence on Japan to Piesse, obtained during his frequent travels to Japan.[13] There is also evidence that at least one of the other Japanese teachers was similarly employed. In his book *Australia's First Spies*, author John Fahey asserts that one of the Japanese teachers, Manzi Koide, was likely deployed as an Australian intelligence agent inside Japan.[14] If so, it is quite possible that the other Japanese teachers were not just training the intelligence officers but actively engaged in intelligence collection and analysis themselves.

Given Edmund Piesse's penchant for facts and information, it is unlikely that he would not have made use of Harry's intelligence background and Japanese language skills. If Harry was only being used as a teacher, it would seem a waste of an invaluable resource: a military man, loyal to Australia, with a cultural and linguistic understanding of the Japanese.

But whether he was engaged in intelligence activities or not, Harry had other enemies to battle much closer to home.

In February 1920 the director of soldier settlement for New South Wales, John Bryant, escorted a party of journalists around the Kentucky Soldier Settlement. After the fiasco of the Montavella Soldiers' Settlement, Bryant and his minister, William Ashford, were keen to parade before the world the successes that were forthcoming in Kentucky.

The settlement was founded in 1918 and Harry Freame was one of the first men to arrive. The area was divided up into forty-four orchard blocks, and by 1920 around 23,000 apple and pear trees had been planted. It would take four or five years before the trees would begin to produce fruit in commercially viable quantities, so in the meantime the soldier settlers grew cash crops of potatoes, corn and onions to supplement the meagre government stipend they received.

The visiting journalists were impressed by the settlers' achievements. Gangs of men, mostly returned soldiers, had cleared large areas of farmland ready for the planting of more fruit trees or cash crops. The blocks were neatly fenced and the fruit trees all netted, protecting them from parrots and other pests. The onion and potato crops in particular looked promising.

As usual the journalists were drawn to Harry Freame. A reporter from *The Sydney Morning Herald* told this anecdote about his day touring the settlement:

'One of the boys won the first D.C.M. handed out to the Australians,' said the manager. 'He was one of Walker's Scouts on Gallipoli, and the excitement of crawling about in no-man's-land doesn't seem to have unfitted him for this quiet life.' Just then the object of the conversation, dressed in khaki shirt, riding breeches, and leggings, strode forward and was introduced to the party. 'Settler Freame, late of the First Battalion,' said the manager, turning to the party, and thereupon they were invited to inspect his quarters. This settler's home was a revelation to those of the party who naturally expected to see primitive conditions in a home built only a few months ago. A cool verandah overlooks the valley, the interior is tastefully furnished, and on the walls hang a fine collection of water colours of Gallipoli. There is a large bedroom, living-room, pantry, and back verandah; at the back a stable and poultry run, and a few yards on either side the growing crops stretch to the boundary fences.[15]

The journalists continued their tour of the settlement and Bryant proudly told them of the work his department had completed in looking after the men who had served their country so gallantly. Bryant was not shy of boasting of his own frugalness, telling the journalists that the cost for the construction of the sixty dwellings at the settlement had come in under budget by £1000. He also pointed out that the following month, construction would start on coolstores. Once finished these would allow the settlers to keep their fruit in the best possible shape for the market, guaranteeing high prices for the settlers.

A few months later Ashford would be out of the ministry, Bryant would be exiled in London and all of Australia would know about the Kentucky coolstores and the under-budget cottage construction.

In early January 1920 the NSW secretary for lands, William Ashford, travelled from Sydney down to Melbourne. While in Melbourne he met with WJ May, an expert in the construction of coolstores. Ashford's plan, supported and encouraged by Bryant, was to equip the solider settlers of Kentucky with cool storage capacity for their fruit crops. After meeting with Ashford and a further meeting with Bryant in Sydney, May visited Kentucky to inspect the proposed site of the coolstores. He then submitted to Ashford and Bryant a proposal for the construction of the coolstores with a capacity to hold 20,000 cases of fruit at a cost of £13,000. Ashford and Bryant accepted May's proposal.

As the vice-president of the Returned Soldiers League in Kentucky, Harry Freame held a prominent position in the Kentucky soldier settler community, just as he had at Montavella. When General Birdwood visited Kentucky in April 1920, Freame led the guard of honour for the man known to the diggers as the 'Soul of Anzac'.

Though a British general, Birdwood had the faith and trust of the Australian soldiers. He also appeared to appreciate, if not entirely share, the diggers' irreverent sense of humour, often directed at commanding officers. Captain David Fallon tells the following anecdote in his book *The Big Fight*:

A certain sentry didn't salute General Birdwood, who at that time wore no emu feather in his hat, an omission the Australians resented.

'What do you mean, sir,' demanded General Birdwood, 'by not saluting me? Do you know who I am?'

'No, who are you?'

'I am Birdwood.'

'Then,' said the sentry, without any loss of his own dignity, 'why don't you wear a feather in your cap as a bird would?'

The general stared hard at the man for an instant, tried to frown, but laughed instead, and there was no court martial.'[16]

Before inspecting the Kentucky settlement, sans emu feather, and seeing firsthand how the men he had met on the peninsula were adapting to civilian life, Birdwood stopped in at Harry Freame's house to reminisce about the Anzac days – a general stopping by to chat with a sergeant. Even in peacetime, this demonstrates the remarkable esteem in which Harry was held.

So when Harry Freame spoke, the men of the Kentucky settlement listened, and when Harry found out about the coolstores being proposed by Ashford and Bryant, he was concerned. He no doubt recalled his unpleasant dealings with both Ashford and Bryant at Montavella; maybe that was enough to alert his suspicions. From the outset he opposed the construction of the coolstores and recommended that the other settlers at Kentucky do the same. The cost seemed too high and, more importantly, at that point in time there was still no fruit even being grown at Kentucky. The coolstores wouldn't be needed for at least another three years. In the meantime the cost of construction, with interest, would have to be paid off by the settlers, in the form of an increase in the repayments they were already making to the government. Something smelled wrong to Harry Freame.

A few months after the journalists' visit to Kentucky, in May 1920, reports started to emerge of strange dealings in the soldier settlements of New South Wales, and the names at the centre of every accusation were William Ashford and John Bryant. By that time Ashford was no longer secretary for lands, his party having been defeated at the April election. Bryant, fearing what was coming, had escaped to London, having taken up a plum position with the Agent-General's Office just before the election.

The allegations against the two were serious enough for the Public Service Board to launch an inquiry into the management of the NSW soldier settlements. That inquiry, held throughout June, quickly turned up enough information against the men to warrant a royal commission.

Led by Justice Street, the royal commission was held in September and took no time in getting to the bottom of a cynical, disingenuous plan by Bryant and Ashford to enrich themselves off the backs of Australia's returned soldiers. One of the first men called to testify was Harry Freame.

Freame told the commission, 'I have been everything from a cowboy to a sea cook; I have been all over the world and have seen cold stores.'[17] And based on what he had seen, Harry was against the stores for Kentucky as being too costly and unnecessary. Before leaving the witness box, Harry was asked by Justice Street if he had won the DCM at Gallipoli. *The Armidale Express* recorded Harry's response: 'Freame, who became nervous with this change in questioning said, "yes" a reply which elicited from Mr. Justice Street his congratulations on such an achievement. "You well earned the distinction," remarked his honour.'[18]

This exchange provides a fascinating insight into Harry's character. A humble man, modest, unwilling and uncomfortable to claim the status of war hero.

Other witnesses at the royal commission told of how, under orders from Bryant, all construction of houses and cottages on the soldier settlements was to come in at 10 per cent under the proposed costs, with the promise that the government would still pay the full amount. The 10 per cent difference would then be split between the builder and Bryant. From his cut Bryant would then kick up to the minister. The scheme was being run at various soldier settlements around New South Wales, including Kentucky.

Unique to Kentucky, though, were the coolstores. The initial Public Service Board inquiry had already halted their construction. Now the royal commission found that their construction was never justified, nor had Ashford or Bryant ever put out a tender for the works, instead handing the contract directly to the Victorian firm of May.

The royal commission found that Minister Ashford had acted corruptly and that Bryant had conspired to defraud the government. The findings did little to appease Harry Freame and the other soldier settlers of Kentucky. Their lives continued just as before, trying to eke out a living on the land to support themselves and their families.

If Harry questioned the commitment of his adopted country to repay his service with a fair go and a leg up, he never voiced it. Instead, he went back to work.

Chapter 9

Slim Pickings

A few months after his appearance at the royal commission, Harry Freame was mentioned in an article in *The Armidale Chronicle*:

> Mr. W.H. Freame, DCM, has all his crops in and things being equal, he expects a bountiful harvest this year. Mr. Freame believes in all the latest improvements and all the latest labour-saving devices. His block is a model of what a block should be. He is to be heartily congratulated on the wonderful strides he has made since he took over.[1]

Indeed, in that summer of 1920 things looked good for Harry Freame. He was still teaching Japanese to the next generation of Australian intelligence officers at Fort Street High School, his soldier's block was cleared and his orchard was thriving, though still not yet bearing fruit. The cash crops he had planted were expected to do well. And he had his wife Edith May by his side for the first time in many years. The frustrations and disappointments about an ungrateful soldier settlement bureaucracy seemed finally to be behind him.

If you were in Sydney in late 1920 and happened to pick up a copy of *Everyones*, which described itself as a midweek journal for the 'tram, train, boat and home', you would have found on page 15 a section titled 'Who's Who in Sydney'. And there you could read about George Robertson, one of the founders of the publishing firm Angus & Robertson. You could read about how Robertson brought Henry Lawson's poems to the world and how he was putting his whole heart into the next book he would publish, *Birds of Australia*. Then, if your eyes skipped a little lower, you would read the following:

> Freame, W.H: Born Canada. Cowboy, sea-cook, and digger. On Gallipoli took three Turkish trenches single handed. Won the first DCM awarded Australian soldier.[2]

The piece appeared not long after Freame's testimony to the royal commission. And at the commission he had given his birthplace as Canada, most likely deeming it prudent to keep his Japanese ancestry under wraps given the climate of persecution and fear that was being whipped up by Prime Minister Billy Hughes.

It is remarkable that at this time, when Japan, and the Japanese, were public enemy number one in Australia, Harry succeeded in hiding his ancestry so completely, despite looking and speaking like a Japanese national. And of course he also had to hide the work he was doing for Piesse's intelligence department. It shows Harry's remarkable ability to live two lives simultaneously. It also shows that despite the fear of the Japanese, the average Australian had very little contact with or knowledge of either Japan or the Japanese.

Slim Pickings

Harry was spending less and less time in Sydney. On 30 October 1921 James Murdoch died suddenly at his home in Sydney, and with Edmund Piesse already on the outer with his political masters, the government's Japanese language program came to a halt. Harry took the decision to move permanently back to the country, for as he told a reporter he preferred soldiering rather than playing at soldier. And Harry would soon have compelling reasons to spend more time at home.

A letter written in the early months of 1921, from Edith May to her English family back home, provides an insight into early life at the Kentucky settlement, its challenges and small sparks of joy and entertainment. Some of those challenges were those of any small rural community, then or now: Edith May reports to her family that she has withdrawn from the Red Cross committee due to the inability of its members to agree on anything. She also makes mention of the persistent battles with the soldier settlement authorities who, despite the public embarrassment they had experienced over the revelations of corruption heard at the royal commission in 1920, were still making life difficult for the settlers.

Edith May writes:

> We are having several little changes here in Kentucky lately. The young fellow who took over the Store & Post Office from Henry, has given it up to open a Store here on his own. He naturally desired to take the Post Office with him, but the Department were up against him for that, & they have taken further steps, and retained it at the Government Store. He was evicted from his position as Postmaster at a minute's notice last Friday night

at 12pm, by an official from Sydney with no reason at all. On the Sat. morning all the settlers protested against this action & passed a motion to that effect sending it down to Sydney for further actions to be taken. I don't know whether it will do any good or not. The Settlement Manager received a very quick notice of transfer to another settlement further north.[3]

The Australian diggers were known for their antipathy towards officers and authorities, and after surviving the Turkish and German shrapnel on the battlefronts of Europe, they should not have had to battle bureaucratic harassment and bungling back home. The settlements, supposedly designed to help them rebuild their lives with dignity, often proved to be just one more source of stress to men already at their limit. Unfortunately for Harry, relations between the soldier settlers and the authorities would worsen before they improved.

What comes through clearly in Edith May's correspondence is a deep longing for the Mother Country. She dedicates most of the eight-page letter to enquiring after family and reminiscing about, and lamenting the absence of, the small things, little comforts and familiarities. In the soldier settlement of Kentucky, Edith May must have felt a million miles away from life in England:

To tell you the truth Lizzie, that is one of the things I miss most out here ... we only have service once a month & that is held in the little Iron Hall, which is scorching hot in summer & stone cold in winter. Since Mr. Comie has left we have not had even those regular, but there is another minister who has been given the Call

& who we have heard & we hope he may accept & then perhaps we may be able to get into a regular way again.[4]

And through Edith May we learn just how hard Harry and his wife were doing it, trying to wrench a living from the Kentucky soil, to make enough money to feed themselves and pay back the money owed to the government:

> We have got the Diggers here harvesting our Potato crop, but sorry to say so far we have not benefited any by the marketing of them. Henry got the returns from a ton sold yesterday, & he benefits to the amount of 4/- so you see farming is like everything else it varies. Last year was a good year, & of course we were able to buy lots of things that were required and pay the Dept. their dues, after which we were able to keep ourselves from the last of the crop until now, without drawing any further sustenance (which makes all the less for us to have to pay back to the Dept.) Of course we hope prices & sales may improve as time goes on, & then we have the turnips nearly ready for harvesting, & hope we may do well with those. I am pleased we are not like a lot of the Settlers in so much debt, as we have paid for all things as we got them, & Henry has more implements etc than anyone else. So you see if we are losing a bit, we have got value in another way.[5]

It was a cruel irony that the department itself was obstructing the settlers' ability to make money when the money was to be used to pay the department. But bureaucratic strictures were not the worst of the problems at Kentucky. Soon, despite early promises to the contrary, the Kentucky climate would reveal just how unsuitable it was for the growing of fruit.

As Edith May sat down at her writing desk in the little soldier settlement of Kentucky and poured out her thoughts and hopes and concerns to her loved ones across the sea, what she did not write was that she was carrying her and Harry's first child.

On 5 December 1921, Henry Wykeham Freame, to be known as Young Harry, was born at the Uralla hospital. Tragically, whatever pleasure the new parents felt about his birth was short-lived. Already missing home and now with the responsibility of caring for a baby with no family support in the scorching heat of an Australian summer, Edith May fell into depression.

When Edith May had arrived in Australia in 1919, Harry had promised her mother that he would take her home to England for a visit within five years. But with the orchard not yet yielding fruit and the money from the cash crop being used to pay back the government debt, invest in improvements and machinery for the property, and – with the little leftover – to buy food for his family, Harry had been unable to keep that promise. Now, in a perilous state of mind, Edith May insisted that she return to England.

Unable to afford the expense, Harry offered a compromise solution. Somehow he would find the money to hire domestic help for Edith May. He kept this promise and in early 1922 Josephine Clarke – Harry's one-time lover – arrived at Kentucky and took up the position of housemaid in the Freame household.

At the time Josephine had been living in Paddington, Sydney. She arrived at the settlement of Kentucky not as Josephine Clarke but as Josephine Collins, a widow who had been married to Walter Warner Collins, a fictitious surveyor from Brisbane and father of her only son. Since Harry had left Glen Innes for the shores of Gallipoli back in 1914, Josephine had never married and had raised their son, Chappie, by herself. When she left Paddington to take up the position of housemaid with the Freames, Josephine left Chappie, now eight, in Sydney in the care of family friends.

It is unlikely that Edith May knew of the previous relationship between Harry and Josephine, so she probably felt some relief at the arrival of Josephine Collins – an extra set of hands. But if so, this relief was fleeting. Not long after Josephine's arrival, Edith May, Master H Freame aged just six months and Josephine Collins all set sail for London aboard the *Benalla* passenger ship, which docked in London in July 1922. Harry senior was not aboard. He had stayed in Kentucky to take care of the farm.

With his wife and newborn baby over the seas in England, life only became tougher for Harry Freame. While the orchard plantings still looked promising, fruit-yielding years were still a way off, and the cash crops that the government had hoped would tide the soldiers over had proved a failure. The continued meddling of bureaucratic staff only added to the pain of the settlers. Newspaper reports claimed that some soldiers and their families at Kentucky were starving, and ventured that rather than supporting the reintegration into civilian life of those who had given everything in the Great War, the soldier settlement scheme was a scam to enrich the bureaucrats charged with administering it. There were irregularities with the running of the government store at Kentucky, price gouging was occurring on basic goods and when settlers requested information on the current value of their land and equipment, they were fobbed off by department officials in Sydney.

The money that was being siphoned out of the soldier settlement program by corrupt and heartless government officials meant that there was less money left for the soldiers themselves. A further blow came when, claiming financial hardship, the Department of Lands reduced the sustenance subsidy provided to settlers and their families. With crops failing and government subsidies reduced, settlers started to abandon their blocks again. Unable to make ends meet, incapable of sustaining themselves and their families and no longer willing to wage the daily battle against the harsh realities of the Australian bush, these men and women chose to take their chances back in the cities.

Not long after Edith May left Australia, at an extraordinary meeting of returned soldiers, a committee of men chose Harry along with one other settler to make the trip down to Sydney and present the settlers' grievances, once again, to the minister. Clearly the ex-soldiers still held Harry Freame in high regard. For Harry the situation at Kentucky must have felt like Montavella all over again.

In Sydney Harry met with the NSW minister for lands and agriculture, Frank Chaffey. Chaffey had served with the Light Horse Brigade and came from a farming background himself. He listened to Freame's complaints on behalf of the settlers with a sympathetic ear. So it was a shock when, shortly after returning to Kentucky, Harry received a notice from the government demanding immediate payment of all outstanding debt on his property. Never mind that other settlers owed more and were further in arrears.

Slim Pickings

For Harry the connection between complaining about the conditions on the settlement and the calling in of the debt was obvious. If you spoke up, there would be recriminations. But he had faced sterner tests than the faceless bureaucracy of the lands department and he wasn't about to take a backwards step. He fired off a letter to Lieutenant-Colonel Michael Bruxner, a member of the NSW Parliament. Before the war Bruxner, who was schooled in Armidale, had worked at farming in the Tenterfield area. When war broke out he joined the 6th Light Horse Regiment and was wounded at Gallipoli. It is likely that Harry had a personal friendship with Bruxner, and his appeal to his friend was heeded. Bruxner questioned the Department of Lands as to why Harry was being persecuted for his debt. The department, taken off guard by Freame calling in an influential friend, responded to Bruxner that the debt notice had been sent in error and withdrew it immediately.

Harry would have been pleased to know that there were people who still remembered his deeds in the war and were willing to go in to bat for him. But it didn't solve all his problems. Other settlers were so upset about the treatment Harry had received that they leaked news of his circumstances to a local paper. Soon a journalist arrived at Kentucky, looking to investigate Harry's situation. Harry himself was reticent; he merely confirmed or denied what others had said. But after speaking to the other settlers, the paper reported on the sobering circumstances of the Marvel of Gallipoli.

The reporter found Freame's orchard in good condition and noted that Harry had ploughed 18 acres of land ready to plant his cash crops. Harry's farm included a small menagerie of animals, a few cows and pigs and chickens. But after Edith May left for England (the report mentions her 'suffering from a serious illness'[6]), Harry's government ration had been cut, reduced to that of a single man, even though everybody knew that Harry was married with a small child. And though Harry had ploughed and readied his land for planting, he had no money for seeds. He fed his animals before he fed himself, and Harry admitted to the reporter that:

> he had not had enough to eat for some weeks past; that he had been living on dry bread; that the struggle to make ends meet was getting the better of him. He had been working hard in order to keep his mind off the subject of Departmental blundering and to retain his sanity.[7]

The article continued: 'there are times when this war hero would give almost anything he had for a good square feed.'[8] Harry Freame, Australian war hero, was starving to death.

~

Harry may have been reluctant to raise too much of a fuss in the media for reasons of self-interest, for in the final months of 1922, in the lead-up to a federal election, Japanese ownership of NSW land became a major political issue.

On 11 August 1922, writing on letterhead from the Sydney Press Club, George Part, a watchful official from the federal taxation department, found it necessary to bring to Prime Minister Hughes's attention some disturbing and alarming behaviour he had recently witnessed. 'Dear Sir,' Part wrote:

I beg to draw your attention to an incident that happened at La Perouse, last Sunday the 6th instant. On going towards the ferry for Kurnell, I noticed four Japanese each carrying a camera ($30 would not buy any of the cameras). As I have done a little amateur photography myself I could plainly see that these Japs were not taking photos from a Photographer's point of view, as they would have us believe, but were taking very carefully the whole of the entrance and the bay.

In the best Walter Mitty tradition, Part continues:

They were correcting one another in their alignments and each photo they took the four cameras were used in the same alignment. They were joking and laughing making out they were novices at the game as each was correcting the other, but believe me, they were experts at it. Three hours later they were over the Kurnell side of the Bay doing the same thing. This, Sir, meant only one thing, they were taking a panoramic view undoubtedly for military or naval purposes; this is why they were so careful to get their correct alignment.[9]

Reinforcing Part's conclusion of nefarious activity was the fact that 'These Japs appeared to be highly educated and were immaculately dressed'. Lest his reports not be taken seriously by Hughes, Part stressed that he was not an alarmist, only that he believed that 'prevention is better than cure'.[10]

Hughes thanked Part for his report and immediately forwarded it to Captain Eric Longfield Lloyd of Military Intelligence for further investigation. Encouraged by Hughes's positive receipt of his amateur counterintelligence efforts, Part went back to work and a few months later wrote again to the prime minister. This time Part's sleuthing skills would blow up spectacularly in Hughes's face.

Part's correspondence of 23 October 1922 read: 'Dear Sir, Following on from my letter of the 11th August re Japs with cameras, I have just come across the following list of land purchased this year by a Jap Kinjira Onishe.'[11]

Part had gone to the effort of digging into the NSW property registry and had discovered that Japanese nationals owned 86 acres of land in New South Wales. This represented a tiny fraction of the 197,968,000 acres that make up the state of New South Wales, but to Part and Hughes it was alarming. Part had also discovered an until then unknown loophole in the White Australia policy. While 'coloured' migrants could not enter Australia, if by some means they did enter there was absolutely nothing to prevent them from purchasing land. They held the same rights to purchase land as any other British subject.

Newspapers splashed the story across their pages. 'WHITE AUSTRALIA MENACED. STRATEGIC LAND SOLD TO JAPS. DEALS THAT MAY LEAD TO AUSTRALIA'S DOWNFALL' screamed the headlines of the Brisbane *Daily Mail*. 'JAP PENETRATION. SENSATIONAL STORY EXPLODED' ran another headline. One can only wonder what Harry would have made of these sensationalist, racist headlines after he came in from a long day's work.

The newspaper stories detailed how a 'sinister Japanese syndicate'[12] had been buying up strategic points of land along the NSW coastline. Hughes came out and, in a bold-faced lie, denied there had been any land

The young samurai Hidetsugu Kitagawa pictured with his stepsister Ayako in Osaka, 9 May 1898. Hidetsugu would grow up to become Harry Freame, the bravest scout at Gallipoli.

Harry Freame in 1904, aged 24. This photo was taken at Newport in Wales, not long after his completion of a three-month voyage to India.

Harry and Edith May Freame in 1906, taken a few weeks after their wedding. The honeymoon was short and Harry was soon sailing again.

Harry Freame, ship's cook, about to embark again. He sent this postcard to his wife, Edith May, signing off as 'Breezy Harry', a testament to his wandering ways.

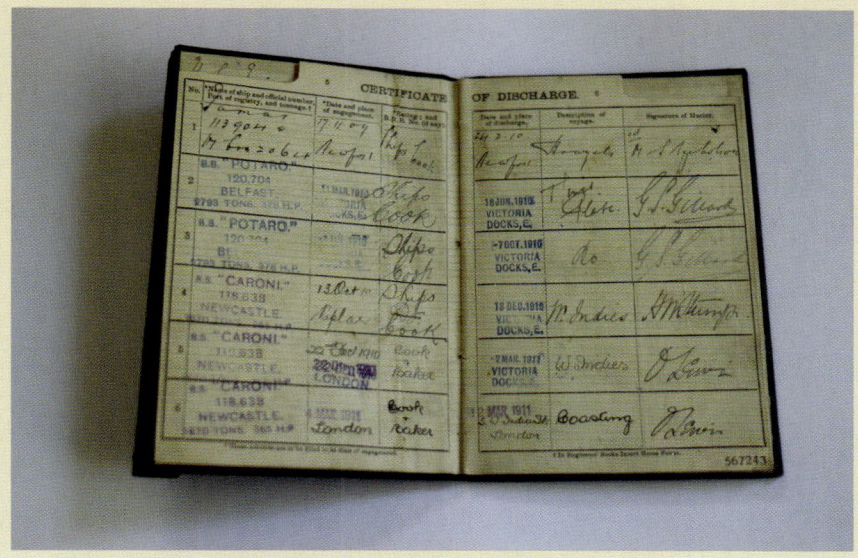

Harry Freame's Seaman's Record, issued by the British Board of Trade. Between 1902 and 1912, Freame made over 30 voyages, travelling to all parts of the globe, working as a ship's cook and baker.

Harry Freame in Egypt in early 1915. As scout for D Company, 1st Battalion, in the Australian Imperial Force (AIF), he landed at Gallipoli on the morning of 25 April 1915.

Harry Freame at Gallipoli on 8 June 1915. Freame is looking out over Turkish positions through a loophole cut into the Australian trenches in Wire Gully. It was from this hole that he would venture out each night to map the enemy positions and launch raids on the Turkish trenches. This photo was taken by Australian war correspondent Charles Bean, who interviewed Freame on 7 and 8 June 1915.
(Australian War Memorial G01029A)

For his work on the morning of the Anzac landing, Freame was decorated with the first Distinguished Conduct Medal (left) awarded to an Australian soldier. Charles Bean always maintained that it would have been a Victoria Cross if not for the colour of Freame's skin. His other medals from left to right are the 1914–15 Star, the British War Medal and the Victory Medal.

Freame (fifth from the right) following discharge from New End Hospital in London after being wounded in the Lone Pine attacks. Shortly after this photo was taken, he stowed away on a ship to Egypt, desperate to re-enlist in his battalion and get back to the war.

After being discharged from the AIF on medical grounds, Freame (left) was one of the first men to be given a block of land at the Montavella Soldier Settlement. Despite a promising start, the settlement was to be plagued by government corruption. (State Archives and Records Library of New South Wales)

After abandoning Montavella, Freame made his way north to the Kentucky Soldier Settlement in northern New South Wales. On his lapel he proudly wears the Silver War Badge that was issued to members of the armed forces of the British Empire who were wounded in battle and subsequently discharged.

Freame's house at the Kentucky Soldier Settlement. Edith May joined her husband, Harry, in Australia in 1919, and they set about building a life together. Journalists who visited noted that the walls inside were adorned with paintings of Anzac Cove. Note the Japanese design over the front gate.

General Birdwood (white coat) was known as the 'Soul of Anzac'. Here he is seen emerging from the house of Freame after visiting the Kentucky Soldier Settlement in 1921. Freame is pictured front right, partially obscured.

In December 1921, Harry and Edith welcomed their first child to the world, Henry Wykeham Freame, known as Young Harry. Here, the family is pictured with Reverend George Comie and housemaid Josephine Clarke. Unbeknown to Edith, Freame had fathered a child to Josephine in 1913.

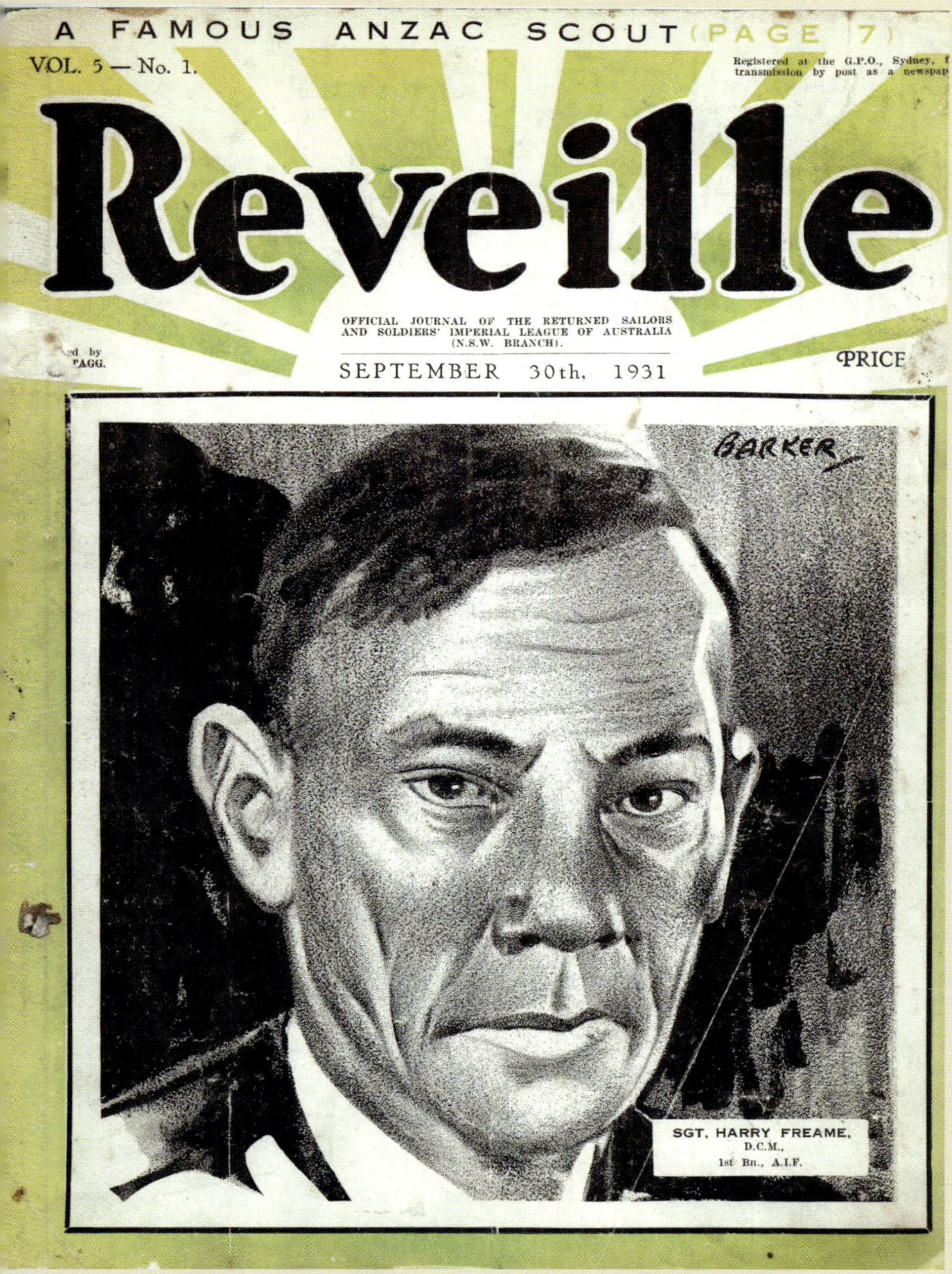
A FAMOUS ANZAC SCOUT (PAGE 7)
VOL. 5 — No. 1.
Registered at the G.P.O., Sydney, f
transmission by post as a newspap
Reveille
OFFICIAL JOURNAL OF THE RETURNED SAILORS AND SOLDIERS' IMPERIAL LEAGUE OF AUSTRALIA (N.S.W. BRANCH).
SEPTEMBER 30th, 1931
PRICE
BARKER
SGT. HARRY FREAME, D.C.M., 1st Bn., A.I.F.

In 1931, Freame made the cover of *Reveille*, a magazine for returned diggers. Seven pages were dedicated to the amazing feats of courage performed by him during the Gallipoli campaign.

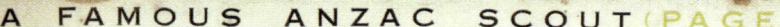

In 1927, Freame fathered a second child with Josephine Clarke. Josephine Grace, known as Gracie, was adopted by Harry and Edith May but grew up not knowing the identity of her biological mother. Here, Freame and Gracie are pictured in Sydney in the late 1930s.

Freame walking along the Sydney streets with his old first battalion comrade Eric Longfield Lloyd on Anzac Day 1939, no doubt discussing the coming war. Longfield Lloyd was the head of the Commonwealth Security Service, a forerunner of ASIO.

Freame's last march, Anzac Day 1940. Five months later he would embark on the mission that would cost him his life.

When Australia appointed Sir John Latham as the minister to Japan, Military Intelligence recruited Freame to act as Latham's interpreter in Tokyo. Issued with his diplomatic passport, Freame sailed for Japan in October of 1940.

Though his business card said 'Attache', Freame's real job was to spy on the Japanese, gathering information on Japanese intentions towards Australia in the lead-up to their entry into World War II. Unbelievably, his work as an intelligence agent was leaked by the press before he left Australia.

While in Tokyo, Freame reconnected with his Japanese family and recruited his niece Kazuko (pictured) to help him in his house.

Freame pictured on the streets of Tokyo some time before the attack that would cut short his life. After his death, the Australian Government denied that he had ever served as an intelligence officer.

Young Harry: gifted sportsman, courageous soldier. After graduating top of his class from the Royal Military College, Duntroon, Young Harry deployed to fight the Japanese in Borneo. Harry was killed on 8 May 1945, after a Japanese soldier threw a grenade under the bed where he was recovering from a dental operation.

An ornate Japanese box that contains a lifetime of letters, memories and memorabilia of Ha[rry] Freame – lovingly preserved first by his daughter Gracie and now by her friend Susan McG[...] who kindly provided access to this trove.

purchases. Coming as it did on the eve of a federal election, Hughes put the story down to election propaganda designed to tarnish his reputation as a defender of White Australia. In a bid to bolster his White Australia credentials, he asked the Australian public: was it not he who had prohibited foreigners from owning mining licences?

The following day newspapers reported the facts of the purchases and details of the letters shared between George Part and the prime minister's office. Hughes was then forced to admit that, yes, there had been land purchases, but they had been done with the approval of the NSW Government, and no blame for allowing the penetration of Japanese nationals along the NSW coastline could be laid at the feet of the Federal Government. Hughes promised that any land contracts owned by Japanese nationals would be cancelled where possible.

The Sydney-based *Sun* newspaper tracked down Kinjira Onishe. Rather than finding the head of a sinister Japanese syndicate intent on infiltrating Australian navy bases, the *Sun*'s reporter found Onishe to be a well-respected businessman, an Australian resident for some thirty years who had bought the land in question from a real estate agent. Onishe had been trying to sell the land for the past decade but had been unable to find a buyer. One block of land at Woy Woy he had simply given away after failing in all attempts to sell it.

In any event Hughes survived the election, but a few months later in February 1923, he was forced to resign his position as party leader and prime minister.

Edmund Piesse might have thought that a change of prime minister would resurrect his career, but he was sorely mistaken. There was no place in the new government for a man seen to be soft on the Japanese threat.

Piesse's pragmatic approach to Japanese relations was seen as pro-Japanese and his cards were marked.

Rather than continue on the outer, his advice going unread and unheeded, in August 1923 Piesse resigned from his role as director of the Pacific Branch. With Piesse's resignation, Australia lost one of its clearest and sharpest thinkers on not just Japan but Australia's foreign policy and position in the Pacific.

Though reluctant to share his privations with the press, in a letter to Edith May's family written in January 1923, his situation still unimproved, Harry opened up about the struggles he faced, not just with the unyielding environment but also with the mental anguish brought on by his separation from wife and son:

Dear Sis Lizzie,
Yours of the date 22–12–22 to hand this morning & I thank you all for good wishes etc.

Say! I am sorry to say that I noticed in your letter that you have lost your dashing & cheeky style. I hope that I have not done anything to offend you. or do you feel that way. But it was such a formal letter from you. Well, to tell you this truth all the things are 6&7 at Mt. Salisbury But I am trying to do my best & look cheerful. I was not feeling too good as yet. But much better than I was. I have laid up for 5 weeks & under the Doctor and he ordered me to go away for a few week's change. But what a chance have I got to go away just at this time as all the crops either need looking after or else wanted put in, beside one dose need money to go away. May does not know that I have been ill.

Bye the way what do you think of the people at 'Parkhurst' do you believe me that they have left me along for 16 weeks without any news of May or my baby and again they missed this English mail which brought yours & I may say that yours was only the one I got from home & I am begging them to let me know how May is by just a few lines.

I have being very unfortunate in my farming this last two years in fact I was loosing at any thing & everything that I undertook. But since Baby came I have to work twice harder to keep things going now I am up at 4:30am & working until about 6:30pm that is the hour of sunset. But am please to say my luck has too turn for the good I think as my crops are looking a promising lot. I hope so for all concern it is a hard work to work the Orchard as well farm myself. But then when Orchard are bearing will bring in a good income. while I was down in Sydney with May last April I was offered the professorship of the Oriental Studies at naval College but I have made & spend my energe for this home so I stayed here.

I must inform you this trip of May is home well it was from beginning she never consulted me nor asking my consent. she just wrote & borrowed money to go home. I have had to consent at finish when I saw that she meant it ~ Begged her to wait another year, as it may be a better year for me to meet all the expenses. But she would not, just fancy I had to meet all the hospital expenses, getting a lady to live with us & help May with baby, Besides keep all our stock on £69–10–0 per year!! on top of that I have had to pay for all seeds, living, clothing etc. Oh well, better days are coming I hope.

Only this neglect that I haven't had pleasure of watching my little man growing from or to say changing out of babyhood to a little boyhood. just to fancy me getting up at 4:30am feeding horses, milking cow, then start to light fire for my breakfast. Dinner time many a time I was too tired to worry about fire so just wash down bread & jam with a cup of water. I tell you if there was 24 hours of daylight I could make more of it is not much fun in one man farm when you can not get any home comfort.

I am sorry when I came to read this letter why!! ~ I am just as bad as you.

I am longing to see you all. I must try & work a bit harder to save up the fare!

Give my love to my two little sweethearts, Flossie & Lily & Jamie.

Why your letter give me hours of pleasure!

Yours

Henry

My arm is till giving me some what for. They wanted to operate last May when I went to see Doctor at Military Hospital. Write again soon.[13]

The letter contains all the hope and heartbreak of the soldier settlement scheme. A man trying to make it work, trying to keep his family together, still battling the scars, seen and unseen, of war and always the hope of something better to come.

Edith May's health must have played on Harry's mind. So too the thought he would never see Young Harry again. It is instructive that Harry does not write to Edith May but to her family. Nor does he complain about Edith May not writing to him but rather that her family has not provided news of her. This must indicate the gravity of the illness she suffered.

But there is also resolve in his letter. Maybe Harry had in his ears the words of General Hamilton at the end of that first fateful day on Gallipoli. Maybe he felt he had got through the difficult business and only had to dig, dig, dig until he was safe. How else to explain his cheerful resolve, his admonishing himself for complaining, his promise to work a bit harder on nothing more than bread and jam and a cup of water, to keep hoping for better times ahead. At least at Gallipoli hope was rewarded with immediacy: the hope to survive the day was answered by the blushing of the dawn; the hope to be spared a bullet was answered with the rasp of your next breath. But at Kentucky, hope just dragged on, from one day to the next, never denied, never granted, stretching from dawn to dusk, from one frost to the next, from summer to winter.

~

After spending just over a year in England, on 28 August 1923 Edith May, Young Harry and Josephine Collins boarded the passenger ship *Esperance Bay* in London and set sail for Australia, arriving at the end of October 1923. Their homecoming must have been bittersweet for Harry. Though reunited again with his wife and his little boy, it also meant there were three more mouths to feed. Conditions at Kentucky had not improved in Edith May's absence. Newspapers described the New England winter of 1923 as one of the worst in the history of the area. At Kentucky the crops had failed, and while the orchards were still expected to yield up to 60,000 cases of fruit in the coming years, for 1923 they produced only 2000 cases in total.

Edith May's health only added to Harry's concerns. Despite her year away, her mental state remained precarious. A letter from her mother to a family member not long after Edith May's departure for Australia gives an indication of the condition that she was in: 'she would sit day in and day out, night after night and have no conversation and I was always with her.'[14] Her mother adds, though, that she felt Edith May's health had improved by the time she left for Australia. But whatever improvement Edith May might have experienced soon dissipated. In February 1924, only months after returning to the hardscrabble life of Kentucky, she received news that her beloved mother had passed away. Once again for Edith May, the distance between New England and Old England must have echoed and ached in her soul.

It is around this time that Edith May disappeared from life at Kentucky. Author Brian Tate argues that it is likely that she was admitted to a mental-health institution.[15] Given the stigma around mental health in those years, Edith May's previous struggles and her complete disappearance from the records of Kentucky life in the following years, this does seem a likely eventuality. Whatever the case, it would be seven years until Edith May appeared again in Kentucky.

Left to raise Young Harry with the assistance of Josephine Collins, Freame was not idle, demonstrating an appetite for hard work and an unshakeable faith in the prosperous future of the Kentucky settlement. Throughout 1924 Harry spent time organising the other fruitgrowers on the settlement into a working union, taking away the power of the

Department of Lands-backed Kentucky Cooperative Society (KCS), which until then had controlled the marketing and sales of the growers' meagre output. That arrangement had lacked clarity and Harry was determined to forge a new path.

At a meeting of assembled settlers Freame told the men of his scheme to launch the Kentucky Fruit Growers' Union:

The scheme I wish to place before you I feel sure will be acceptable to you, as it will be clearly seen that you have nothing to lose and all to gain. As you all know, I was a member of the K.C.S. but was not satisfied with it and resigned. A movement of this kind, in my opinion, is premature, and judging by the views expressed by many who are present they were not satisfied to join the K.C.S. and have a board of directors controlling their destinies. You have the business ability amongst you that can do it far better for yourselves. I will quote one instance that has been strongly remarked upon – and that is of the men who are on the 6-year-old blocks, only three have joined the K.C.S. Well, I take it you are not prepared to join the K.C.S., or you would not be present. What I propose to do is to form a Kentucky Fruit Growers Union that will be governed by a round table conference. Each member will be a director, the only officers being a Secretary and Treasurer, the Chairman to be elected at each meeting. If you join this, we can buy all your requirements, in bulk. That will show a great saving. Then there is the question of selling in bulk – Each grower could pack his own fruit, which will be labelled with the K.F.G. label, which will show the quality, count and grower's number, and the buyer will thus be able to trace any fault the case might contain, and suitable action could then be taken by the Union to see that the grower does not repeat this again. We would thus be able to place on the market a fruit guarantee by the Union. Then there is the question of distribution of fruit at assured prices satisfactory to all. If there are any growers who perhaps do not know how to grade and pack their fruit, they can bring it along to my large packing shed and be taught how to do it. I intend to get grading machines and other modern machinery that will be at their disposal. I would like to impress upon you that it is necessary for every grower to know how to pack his fruit. Later on you will have to employ packers, and you must then know if these men are doing their jobs correctly. Don't leave the superintending of your business to others – set to work and learn how to do it yourselves, and then the mistakes, if any, will be your own fault.[16]

Harry's fellow settlers, tired of working with the yoke of bureaucracy around their necks, welcomed Harry's words. Here was the chance for these proud soldiers to come together, free from government interference, and determine their own fates. And if they failed, well, it would be their own fault. At least that was better than waiting for a faceless bureaucrat in Sydney to determine what price your fruit sold at, where it was sold and what your future looked like. Unsurprisingly, most of the men signed up to Harry's Kentucky Fruit Growers' Union.

Harry's promise to bring in grading machines and modern machinery is indicative of his great love of modernity and the progress machines represented. Harry's embrace of the modern is a clear result of his upbringing in early Meiji Japan, where the push for modernisation created a national thirst for the new, for technology and for machines. No matter how far he roamed from home, Harry always remained a son of Japan.

The local papers took great delight in reporting Harry's acquisitions of the latest technologies and gadgets. In 1924 Harry introduced wireless radio to his household, the first settler to do so. A journalist from the local paper, *The Uralla Times*, travelled to Kentucky to report on the development:

> Mr. Freame sent out a list of invitations to his numerous friends. I was fortunate enough to be included ... the audience had the pleasure of hearing a very clear and distinct voice from somewhere in Sydney giving the market and weather reports. Thence a programme of instrumental and vocal items was given, following the 8 o'clock chimes of the G.P.O. clock. It was indeed a revelation to those of the audience who had never listened in before, and their interest and attention spoke volumes.[17]

Freame was not just another settler at Kentucky. When Governor Sir Walter Davidson visited the small settlement to lay the foundation stone at the Kentucky community hall, he took the opportunity to address the gathered settlers, imploring them to keep the faith despite the recent troubles and setbacks. He told the men and women that, whatever the trouble, they would get through it as long their heart was in the job. He then told an anecdote of how the year before he had encountered

General Birdwood and Birdwood had told him of how he had met Harry Freame during his own tour of Kentucky. Birdwood confirmed to Sir Walter that Freame was one of the foremost scouts at Gallipoli, the first man to win the DCM and that they 'had a great common bond in the comradeship of the fighting line, which would be regarded dearly as the years passed by'.[18]

The anecdote shows two things. First, Freame's ability to mix and mingle with the British aristocracy and, second, his ability to make an impression on those he met. When Freame spoke, the men and women of Kentucky listened. He held important positions in the institutions of the settlement, including the Freemasons Lodge and Returned Soldiers League. His opinion held sway in matters of business and dealings with the government. He set himself up as an agent for various companies, selling modern equipment and machines to the other settlers on behalf of Sydney-based companies. And he worked tirelessly in support of the social affairs of the community.

Fancy-dress balls were a regular occurrence on the social calendar, and year after year Freame's name appears as a winner of some category or other, including most original dress – 'Mr. H Freame as a turnip'[19] – and Harry Freame as Granny Smith, no doubt a nod to his apple trees. One article referred to him as the 'Kentucky Sausage King'.[20] And if there was a picnic that needed organising, a tennis court that needed building or a hall that needed decorating, Harry was the man to get it done. Such was his prowess it was always done well, and his reputation only grew. 'The hall decorations were carried out by Mr. H. Freame,' reported *The Uralla Times* after one event, 'and presented a fantastical riot of colours, softly illuminated with Oriental lighting effects. I understand before the war Mr. Freame was engaged as a high class ballroom decorator.'[21] If the claim is true, Freame must have cut quite the figure around Glen Innes, a horse breaker by day and a decorator of ballrooms by night.

Throughout the second half of the 1920s, Harry travelled to agricultural shows, in the local region but also as far away as Sydney and Brisbane, and everywhere he went his displays of fruit caught people's attention. 'An exhibit which attracted the eye at Tamworth Show was Mr. H.W. Freame's collection of apples and pears from his Mount Salisbury orchard, Kentucky,' ran one article. It continued:

> In the form of a pyramid, the fruit provide a beautiful color scheme, the red of the Jonathans showing out in sharp contrast to the brilliant green of the Granny Smiths, and the yellow of the five crowns. On one side pears in several varieties make a fine blend of green, browns and yellows – Packham's Triumph. Beurrebose, Winter Cole, Howell Josephine and Winter Nelis; apple varieties are Munro Favorite, Delicious, Northern Spy, New York pippin. Rome Beauty, Sturmer and Tasma being shown in addition to those already mentioned.[22]

As early as his time at Montavella, Freame produced beautiful displays of fruit. His connection to fruit and displays and presentation ran deep. For anyone who has wandered through the fruit displays of Tokyo's luxury fruit market Sembikiya, the connection to Freame's Japanese upbringing is clear, his displays a means of giving expression to the skills learnt growing up in a samurai household under the care of his single mother and later his stepfather, Magohiko Koba.

Harry Freame was a renaissance man. He turned his hand to most things, but not always successfully. With the advent of private ownership of motor vehicles, it was typical that Freame was one of the first settlers in the New England area to purchase one. However, it would be fair to say that as a driver he made a great infantry scout.

Reflecting the novelty of car ownership at the time, one paper reported jauntily on an accident involving Harry in 1927 under the headline 'Excitement'. 'Mr Harry Freame of Kentucky experienced an epic few moments on Monday last when his Whippet suddenly took the bit between her teeth and bolted off the roadway.'[23] Harry's car careened into another vehicle and bumped off the trunks of a few trees before finally coming to rest in a neighbour's galvanised fence. The paper reported that 'Mr Freame had a couple of passengers with him. All escaped without the proverbial scratch, but they were evidently pleased when the bolter had done stopping.'[24]

Unfortunately, it wasn't to be Harry's last accident. The following year while driving a fruit-packed truck to market, he flipped the vehicle over. Young Harry, aged just seven at the time, was travelling with him, and both father and son were pinned beneath the vehicle but somehow escaped serious injury.

Cricket proved to be a facet of Australian life that Harry's Japanese upbringing had failed to adequately prepare him for. It didn't stop him from being an active participant; he just wasn't very good. A match report from 1932 showed that Harry, batting down the order, made a pair of ducks. However, his fielding was commended, with the match report noting that 'Harry Freame, at silly point saved many runs, stopping some hot ones'.²⁵ Cook, cowboy, soldier, sailor, silly point. Most of the 'hot ones' were flying from the bats of the game's top scorers, Martha Rixon and Josie Murray, who finished with 25 and 23 respectively for the Kentucky Women's XI, who eventually defeated the Kentucky Men.

While throughout the late 1920s Harry's standing within the Kentucky community only grew, his private life became more complicated. Edith May had been away since 1924, and in that time Harry's relationship with Josephine Collins grew closer. On 27 October 1927 that relationship resulted in the birth of Harry and Josephine's second child, Josephine Grace Freame, who would be known as Gracie.

In 1931 Edith May returned to the Kentucky settlement. We can only imagine the shock she endured when she arrived. Not only had her husband fathered a daughter, who by then was almost four years old, but Josephine Collins had also brought her son, Chappie Collins, to live with her and Harry at Kentucky.

Whatever anger or hurt that Edith May harboured over Harry's actions, she and Harry adopted Gracie as their own daughter in February of 1931. Amazingly, considering the social mores of the day, the three adults and three children all remained under the same roof of the Kentucky cottage for a further three years. Eventually the strain of this arrangement became too much, and in 1934 Josephine and Chappie left for Sydney. It seems that Harry never saw either of them again. Throughout her life Gracie referred to Edith May as Aunty May, but it was only later in her life, well after the passing of Harry, Edith May and Josephine, that Gracie would finally learn the identity of her mother.

~

On 30 September 1931 when old soldiers received their edition of the Returned Soldiers League magazine *Reveille*, staring back at them from the cover was the serious face of Sergeant Harry Freame. The crayon with brush and ink sketch of Freame, completed by Sergeant David Barker in 1930, filled the front cover. The headline ran 'A Famous Anzac Scout'. Inside, the magazine dedicated three pages to the story of Harry Freame, in a section titled 'AIF Celebrities'.

The article, written under the pseudonym 'Assembly', recounted the tales of Harry's prewar career in Mexico and Africa and told of his days as a sailor. Unlike other press articles, it gave a more or less accurate account of Harry's upbringing, noting his Japanese birth and mixed-race parentage. This is probably an indication that within the AIF, Harry's Japanese ancestry was less of an issue than among the general public (in 1931 fearmongering about the Japanese was beginning all over again).

But most column inches, naturally, were reserved for Harry's exploits on Gallipoli, his remarkable powers as a scout and the importance of the work he was assigned to complete. 'Possessed of an uncanny sense of direction, Freame was never more in his element than when, wriggling like an eel, across the divide of no-man's-land, picking up information, and more information, to satisfy the voracious demands of the intelligence officer.'[26] Harry's capture and escape from the Turkish army and his rescue of Captain Jacob's group of men at Quinn's Post in the early days of the landing are retold in detail, with the article noting that 'His courage and resource during the landing operations were so outstanding as to attract the immediate attention of the divisional command and was rewarded with one of the first D.C.Ms given to an Australian soldier at Gallipoli.'[27] Interestingly, and as a measure of the uniqueness of Harry's war decoration, the writer observed that 'At Gallipoli decorations were awarded sparingly, in marked contrast to later days, in France, where some of the senior officers developed a high degree of skill in pressing for the award of decorations to officers and men serving under them.'[28]

Quotes from Charles Bean and Eric Longfield Lloyd, attesting to the bravery and skill of this famous Anzac, completed the article and two photos accompanied it. These were taken by Charles Bean and showed Harry peering through the loophole at the top of Wire Gully, from where he would sally forth each night into the roulette wheel of no-man's-land.

The article also mentioned that the walls of Harry's house were 'adorned with fine paintings and sketches reminiscent of scenes and incidents of wartime Anzac and France'. Later, as the legend of Harry Freame grew, other writers would speculate that these pictures were painted by Harry himself, but they were not. They were prints of watercolours by New Zealand war artist Horace Moore-Jones. At the outbreak of the war, Moore-Jones falsified his age, dyed his hair and joined the New Zealand Expeditionary Force. He landed at Gallipoli on the afternoon of 25 April 1915. His signature is clearly visible on each watercolour.

Remembrances of the war were clearly important to Harry, and the *Reveille* article, written in 1931, just twelve years after the end of the war, notes:

> To most of those who took no part in it, memories of the Great War have disappeared into the mists of time, but to Freame – and he typifies the spirit of the average Australian soldier – the war will ever remain a vivid and turbulent picture.[29]

At the going down of the sun, and in the morning, Harry never forgot.

To be fully understood, Harry's leading role in the Kentucky Soldier Settlement must be seen through this lens. Harry Freame, the man, the Marvel of Gallipoli, was born from the AIF and the Gallipoli landing. The Great War gave Harry Freame an identity, one that he could embrace wholeheartedly and which afforded him greater social status. No longer was he the half-Anglo child growing up in a Japanese society or, as he became later, the half-Japanese man in an Anglo society, never reconciling the two halves of his being with the social and political norms of the time no matter where he found himself.

Breezy Harry's wanderings can be interpreted as an attempt to find his place in the world. In the Dardanelles, in the killing field that was no-man's-land, he found it. There he became Harry Freame, Anzac, digger, the most trusted scout at Gallipoli. Within his soldier identity his samurai upbringing could be expressed rather than repressed. As Charles Bean would write, Harry's upbringings in the samurai tradition and his subsequent life experience made him unique among the Australian soldiers and enabled him to excel, and to stand out.

Those days at Anzac must have been exhilarating for the young man who, up until that point in his life, was always on the outside of whatever side there was. But whatever identity Harry forged for himself at Gallipoli, it existed only in the minds of the men who had served with him, only for as long as they remembered the war, because you couldn't remember the war and not remember Harry Freame.

Harry never forgot his treatment at the Weymouth soldiers' depot, where, without his colleagues from Anzac to vouch for him, he was just a bloke with dark skin who spoke funny. A strange-looking fellow who nobody believed. And so Harry fought with all he had to keep together that little band of returned soldiers at Kentucky, to keep alive the camaraderie and memories of that brutal war. By doing so, he was keeping alive Harry Freame. That is why he lined his walls with memories of those Turkish killing fields. Why he chose never to forget them. To forget them was to consign himself to history.

The tragedy for Harry Freame was that many of the returning men were determined to forget the war.

Chapter 10

Goodwill Mission

In 1934, a mere thirty-three years after Federation, the Australian Government decided it was the right time to launch its first international diplomatic mission. Until that point Australia had relied on the United Kingdom to manage its diplomacy, considering that what was good for the Empire was good for the dominion. It was a position that had significant cost savings for the Australian Government. Why pay to duplicate what the British were already doing? But by 1934 that view had shifted.

In April 1934 the Australian Eastern Mission set sail from Sydney. The itinerary would take the small party of Australia's pioneering diplomats to the Dutch East Indies, Malaya, French Indochina, Hong Kong, China, Japan and the Philippines. John Latham, who at the time held the positions of both attorney-general and minister for external affairs, led the mission.

A lawyer by training, and a keen fly-fisherman and lacrosse player, during the Great War Latham had been named head of naval intelligence, with the honorary rank of lieutenant-commander. He served as adviser to Prime Minster Billy Hughes at the Paris Peace Conference in 1919, an experience that left him with a deep dislike of Hughes, though he agreed with the need to defeat Japan's proposal for racial equality. Before the war Latham had run a successful law practice, but he was drawn to politics. In 1922 he ran as an independent in the seat of Kooyong and won. His campaign slogan was 'Hughes Must Go'. He rose rapidly in the field of politics and in the 1930s, then a member of the United Australia Party, he served as attorney-general, minister for external affairs and deputy prime minister in the Lyons Government.

Publicly, the Australian Eastern Mission was termed a goodwill mission. Upon his return from the mission, Latham explained to parliament why this was necessary:

> At the outset it was difficult for some to understand that any object would be served by sending a Mission of friendship to our neighbours. Hitherto, the general intercourse of Australia with these countries has been almost purely economical in character and it required some effort of the imagination to understand that the psychological effect of such a Mission might be very real and valuable. The Western mind does not always realize that in the East there are many people who appreciate a compliment even more highly than a bargain, and who see a genuine significance in a sincere act of courtesy.

Further stressing the goodwill element of the mission, Latham reiterated to parliament that 'it was not the object of the Mission to deal with trade matters'.[1]

But of course it was. In the grips of the Great Depression, Australia was desperate not only to increase trade with its Eastern neighbours but to secure existing trade in the face of pressure from South American and South African competitors, particularly in the wool and wheat sectors.

Australian politicians and trade officials had started to notice that British trade policy benefitted British interests more than it did Australian interests. A feeling took hold that Australia needed to start looking out for its own trade interests. That meant sending its own people abroad to build relationships and gather commercial and diplomatic intelligence.

Japan was a key focus and already a significant trading partner as a major buyer of Australian wool. It did not escape Latham's attention that Japan was also the country most displeased by Australia's strict adherence to the White Australia policy, an adherence that continued despite Japan's ongoing protests and proclamations of the affront that this policy caused its people.

Latham's insistence on calling the mission a goodwill mission was preferable to calling it a trade mission. A trade mission would be viewed as akin to going cap in hand to a people the Australian Government had been offending for thirty-three years and asking to increase trade because Australia's economic position was dire.

Latham received a lavish reception in Japan. Travelling with both his wife and daughter and a small staff, he dined with the Japanese emperor and empress, and held meetings with Japanese Prime Minister Saitō Makoto and Minister for Foreign Affairs Hachirō Hirota. The Japanese press provided extensive coverage of Latham's mission, with one paper, the Osaka *Mainichi*, dedicating twelve pages of coverage to the visit.[2]

When Latham returned to Australia, he tabled an official report to the Australian Parliament that outlined the results of the goodwill mission. But he also wrote several secret reports dealing with trade and the strategic position of Japan.

While in Japan Latham made the commitment that Australia would soon appoint a trade commissioner to Japan to facilitate the expanding trade relationship between the two countries. The Australian states had a history of embedding trade commissioners into overseas markets, but what Latham was promising would be the first trade commissioner appointed at a Commonwealth level. Though the position was never advertised, when it became public knowledge that Australia was to appoint a trade commissioner for Japan, Latham's office was flooded with applications from people with cultural and commercial knowledge of Japan and the East. They need not have bothered.

Latham had a very clear idea of the attributes that an incoming trade commissioner would need to have if he were to be successful in Japan, and also what he need not have. Latham wrote that the appointed trade commissioner would 'need not have any specialized commercial knowledge or business experience' and that according to sources he spoke to, a man with business knowledge 'would prejudice Australian interests' if appointed to the position of trade commissioner. Latham, while agreeing this may be hard to understand from an Australian point of view, argued that 'Both the Japanese officials and business men are more likely to give their confidence to a trade commissioner who has no present or has had no past direct connection to trade.'[3]

Latham's report also suggested that the trade commissioner appointed should be a middle-aged or elderly man, given the Japanese respect for age, and that the man should have knowledge of the Japanese language. Even more specifically, Latham's report advised that the trade commissioner for Japan should have a military background. A middle-aged to elderly man with a military background who spoke Japanese. It was clear that Latham was not recruiting for a trade representative in Japan; he was recruiting for an intelligence asset. It was also clear that Latham had someone in mind for the position. And that man was Eric Longfield Lloyd.

When Longfield Lloyd was confirmed in the position in June 1935, the press received the news favourably. On 2 August *The Sydney Morning Herald* gushed:

> Mr. Lloyd has been for nearly 20 years a student of Japan and the Japanese language; he was political adviser to Sir John Latham on the Eastern Mission last year; he has had considerable experience on the semi-diplomatic side of the Australian Government service. His qualifications to represent this country in Japan are unequalled.[4]

Of course there was another man whose qualifications more than equalled Longfield Lloyd's. But he was otherwise engaged on a small plot of land in Kentucky, New South Wales, battling frost and drought and moths and parrots, working to ward off starvation and feed his family. But it could never have been a job for Harry Freame, because Harry was never admitted into the officers' club that emerged post–World War I. And the first rule of the officers' club was to look after your own. As academic Bruce Bennett writes of Harry Freame, 'To officers and men, he was an Australian with special talents and skills, though never quite perhaps "one of them".'[5]

After Eric Longfield Lloyd did his time with Edmund Piesse and the Pacific Branch, largely spent chasing camera-wielding Japanese sailors around Newcastle, he transferred to the investigation branch of the Attorney-General's Department. There he spent his time tracking communists, fascists and Nazis. He was also appointed as a militia major in the Intelligence Corps. When he joined the ranks of the reservist officers in the late 1920s, he gained the honorary rank of lieutenant-colonel.

When John Latham set sail from Australia on his Australian Eastern Mission, Longfield Lloyd was at his side. For the duration of the goodwill mission, Longfield Lloyd accompanied Latham as his political adviser. In this role he demonstrated to Latham that he was the man to act as Australia's representative in Japan.

The business community did not receive the news of Longfield Lloyd's appointment as enthusiastically as the newspapers. The chairman of the Victorian Chamber of Manufacturers wrote to the deputy prime minister, Earle Page:

> Dear Sir, With the reference of Title Australian Trade Commissioner in Japan give to Mr. E.E. Longfield Lloyd it appears to my council to be a misnomer likely to prove embarrassing as trade matters are unlikely to come within his function.[6]

The letter is a clear nod to the intended strategic, or intelligence, functions that Longfield Lloyd was being deployed to pursue under the cover of the trade commissioner title. For not only had Australia come to the realisation that British diplomacy was not robust enough in advancing Australia's trade agenda, what Latham found on his tour of Japan was that Britain's appreciation of Japan's modernisation and its capabilities was out of step with what he observed personally on his tour. While the British intelligence reports described Japan as 'second rate and inefficient', Latham found the Japanese to possess 'vigorous efficiency in the affairs of every day life and in their commercial and industrial enterprises'.[7] However, Latham still failed to appreciate the military threat that Japan represented and reported that 'On the whole I think that the ambitions of Japan are at present confined to trade on the mainland of Asia, and the protection of Japan against attack from Russia probably by seizing the maritime provinces if an opportunity should present itself.'[8]

Latham's report on his Far East mission gained very little attention or traction within government circles. Parliament showed more interest in the cost of the mission than Latham's learnings. And Latham was unable to further promote his findings because soon after arriving home, in August 1934, he retired from politics and chose to return to his first love, the law. His on-the-ground learnings from his time spent in Japan went largely unheeded.

Within government circles the decision-makers continued to rely on the intelligence reports gathered and provided by the British Government, despite their irregularity and questionable quality. That intelligence in 1934 was describing Japan as a 'third rate power that could do no more than harass Australia with cruiser raids'.[9] One interested observer who did not believe this for an instant was Edmund Piesse, the man who had spent the early part of the 1920s arguing that Japan was no threat. Always a man to rest his opinions on the firmness of fact, by the mid-1930s Piesse had changed his mind.

~

In late 1935, frustrated by Australia's complacent policy towards Japan, Piesse published a small book titled *Japan and the Defence of Australia*. In it, Piesse argued that the international situation had changed drastically since the early 1920s and that the chance to enjoy peaceful relations with Japan had now passed.

By this time Nazi Germany had removed itself from the League of Nations, Italy clearly coveted Abyssinia and Japan had invaded and possessed Manchuria in China. Japan had subsequently removed itself from the League of Nations after that body sanctioned Japan for its belligerent actions in China.

Piesse pointed out that since World War I, British naval power had decreased, the United States had pursued an isolationist policy, the Anglo–Japanese Alliance was no longer in effect and inside Japan imperialists were achieving greater influence over Japanese policy and would look to expand the Japanese empire into Australia.[10]

The imperialists in Japan only needed the opportunity and any excuse. 'Japan and Australia might have a major difference,' wrote Piesse. He went on:

> In that case the possibility of war with Japan must be faced – a war perhaps brought about by the Japanese Navy and aided by a state of patriotic fury in Japan connected with the White Australia policy. Seemingly, such a war would be the product of

the Japanese Navy's imperial ambitions. White Australia would merely be a means of marshalling public opinion behind this expansionist policy.[11]

John Latham had already reported to the Australian Parliament that Japan's civilian government faced difficulties controlling the expansionist tendencies of the imperialists in the Japanese army and navy. However, he also reported, following discussions with Japanese foreign minister Hirota, 'I had no difficulty on the subject of the restriction of immigration as soon as it was realised that I knew that Japan prohibited by law immigration from China and Korea. The Japanese cannot live in their own country in competition with Chinese and Koreans.'[12] Latham, like so many before him, had failed to realise the true nature and extent of the offence caused to Japan's national psyche by the White Australia policy.

In the face of Japanese aggression, Piesse argued that Australia could rely on neither Great Britain nor the United States to come to its aid. Furthermore, the actions of Germany and Italy made it increasingly likely that Great Britain would soon be embroiled in a European war, leaving Australia as an attractively unguarded prospect for Japanese intentions in the Pacific.

Piesse's position flew in the face of the dominant thinking of the time in Australian defence circles, which subscribed to the theory of imperial defence. That theory posited that any attack on Australia would come from the sea, but as Australia could never hope to match the naval power of first-rate powers, it must align its defences with the British navy and contribute as much as possible to the empire's naval forces.[13]

The proponents of imperial defence argued that Australia would only be in danger if Britain itself was conquered. Piesse argued that rather than be conquered, Britain would only need to be tied up in European wars for Australia to be threatened and that Australia should not contribute to the British Empire's navy but instead concentrate on building up a land-based defence that could repel any aggression. Assurances from a British admiral that 'though Australia might be lost in the early stages of a war, if the Empire's navy defeated the enemy in the main battle Great Britain could reconquer Australia at her leisure'[14] did nothing to calm Piesse's concerns.

When in 1935 Britain deployed its fleet to the Mediterranean in an effort to curb fascist Italy's plans in Africa, Piesse saw a nightmare scenario unfolding for Australia. The following year the international situation only worsened, with Germany remilitarising the Rhineland, Germany and Italy declaring the Rome–Berlin Axis and Japan joining Germany in the Anti-Comintern Pact.

War in Europe, a war that would leave Australia increasingly exposed to Japanese aggression, was creeping ever closer. And as it crept, the British Government started to drop hints that in the event of a war in Europe, it would be difficult to send a British naval fleet to the Pacific that could match the power of the Japanese. The hint was taken, and in the 1937 Australian Budget, defence spending was increased by almost £25 million.[15] Significantly, it was increased mostly in army and air-force spending, indicating that Piesse's view of a land-based defence, or deterrent of Australia's enemy, was a more logical defence policy to purse rather than contributing more to the Empire's navy.

In addition to building up land defences, Piesse was also adamant that

Australia should do nothing to antagonise the Japanese and instead look to build friendly relations. The man best placed to do so was Lieutenant-Colonel Eric Longfield Lloyd, Australia's top man in Tokyo. But rather than improving Japanese–Australian relations, Longfield Lloyd did just the opposite.

In 1935 a Japanese-operated company, HA Brassert & Co., secured a fifty-year lease for an iron-ore mining operation at the Yampi Sound mines located in Western Australia. They immediately set about investing and developing the mines for production. Three years later, the Australian Government, with no warning, announced an embargo on the export of iron ore from Australia. The government justified the decision by referring to a report stating that the iron-ore reserves held in Australia were in fact a lot less than previously estimated and that whatever reserves Australia held would be needed domestically.

The Japanese protested the decision and applied diplomatic pressure to the government through the Japanese consul-general, Torao Wakamatsu. Wakamatsu argued that HA Brassert & Co. had already invested large amounts into developing the mines and that they should be allowed to export iron ore from their current project. However, the Australian Government was not for turning. Later it would be revealed that the report the embargo decision was based on was a lie, a fabricated excuse to stop the Japanese project.

The strategic importance of Yampi Sound to the Japanese was first flagged by Eric Longfield Lloyd from his position in Tokyo. In 1937, a year before the embargo was announced, Longfield Lloyd visited the Nagoya Pan-Pacific Peace Exposition. There he was surprised to see a map of northern Australia that included Yampi Sound marked as a Japanese expansion zone. Longfield Lloyd immediately reported this, along with a warning that the Japanese strategy of penetration, as seen in China, was through the establishment of seemingly innocent economic projects, much like that being developed at Yampi Sound. Longfield Lloyd believed that the Yampi Sound project would 'only result in the occupation and exclusive right over a portion of Australian Territory by Japanese interests and personnel'.[16] His recommendation was that 'the project be cancelled by any means whatsoever'.[17] So that is what happened.

Throughout 1937 and 1938, Longfield Lloyd closely monitored Japanese activity well outside the range of what could be considered trade-related matters. He reported on the creation of a southwards expansion movement, a project of Japanese imperialists. He raised concerns at what he saw as efforts to move the Japanese economy to a war footing, noting the increase in the manufacturing of war materials and the mobilisation of the general population.[18]

Longfield Lloyd's reporting was contrary to the assessments being supplied by British intelligence at the time, though it appeared that his word held greater sway in Australia than that of his British counterparts. Through Longfield Lloyd's network of contacts and reporting, the Australian Government was relatively well informed of developments in Japan. There could be no doubt that Japan was preparing for an extended military action in the Pacific and that Australia would be targeted. What the Australian Government lacked was knowledge of if and how the Japanese community in Australia would support such a move. What the nation needed was a man with unquestionable loyalty who could be inserted into the Japanese community in Australia. That man was Harry Freame.

In December 1938, as the world moved towards inevitable war, Harry Freame prepared himself for court. A finding against him for an unpaid debt had been upheld, and he was required to submit himself for examination. In court the examining prosecutor, Mr Edwards, asked that Harry turn over his bookkeeping. Harry informed the prosecutor that he had not brought the books but that he knew he owed money, and others owed him money, and any information that Edwards needed Harry could provide from memory.

Edwards then asked Harry if he knew the names of the people who owed him money and how much was owed. Harry again confirmed that he did.

'Would you like to give them to me?' Edwards asked.

'I would not like to do that,'[19] Harry replied, loyal to a fault.

Edwards pressed and Harry continued to refuse, until finally a compromise was struck. Harry agreed to write the names and amounts down rather than say them. All the men who owed Harry money were ex-diggers from Kentucky. Having obtained the names and amounts, Edwards then asked, 'Have you anything to collect from fruit sold?'[20]

Harry replied, 'I had no fruit to sell. I only had 480 cases against the 6000 usually. I grow apples and pears. I have no fruit in the packing shed.'[21]

Harry's story at Kentucky was not unique. The whole project had turned out to be a busted flush, no matter how hard the men worked. A Fruit Commission Inquiry that was held at Kentucky in early 1938 revealed the extent of their troubles. When soldier settler Walter Bayliss appeared before the commission, he was asked, 'What type of soil is your holding?' 'Cement, I would say,' replied Bayliss.[22] Bayliss's comment was typical of most of the ex-diggers who felt that the farms they had been given, and were still paying off, were duds.

When Harry did have fruit to sell, it was highly prized. He travelled extensively around New South Wales and Queensland, attracting favourable comment for both the fruit and his elaborate displays. The problem was there was just never enough.

By the time of his court appearance, Harry had spent almost twenty years on the land at Kentucky, trying to make ends meet, feed his family and pay off his debts. There must have been times during those decades when Harry Freame sat in his cottage in Kentucky and looked out over his orchards and wondered if he had used up a lifetime's allotment of luck at Gallipoli. To be wounded eighteen times and come out the other side was a good measure of luck in anybody's book. But still Harry could have used a little more.

Season after season his fruit crops had failed. If his trees escaped the frost, they were hit by the hail. If they avoided the codling moth, they were devoured by parrots. But there was nothing Harry could do; he was stuck there, indebted to the government. In many ways his situation, and that of the other returned diggers, was not unlike that which they had faced in the Dardanelles. No way forward and no way back, the only option to dig in and hope for a change of fortune.

If his business continued to struggle, at least Harry's family life was the happiest it had been in many years. Edith May's health had improved, though she still struggled with the heat of the Australian summer. After the departure of Josephine Collins, Edith May enjoyed taking back control of her domestic affairs, writing to family in England, 'I'm glad to say I have been able to manage it so far with a little assistance from Henry when he has not been too busy and I much prefer having my home my own again.'[23]

Young Harry had grown into an exceptional young man and proved himself adept both in the classroom and on the sporting field, excelling in tennis, rugby, cricket and athletics, his name a regular in the *Uralla News* sports columns for outstanding performances.

Gracie was also growing up, a darling of her father. In later years, when recalling her childhood, she would remember Harry stopping whatever work he was doing in the orchard to wander down to the primary school to meet her at the gate in the afternoon and carry her home, raised high on his shoulders. Harry would tell Gracie that his prize-winning Josephine pears were named after her. It was only many years later as a grown woman that she would discover that Josephine pears had in fact been around since the early 1800s.

But Kentucky was not immune to the news, and prejudices, of the world. For a new generation of Kentucky residents, the sons and daughters of the original Kentucky soldier settlers, as Japan's rise and aggression became more prominent, so the memories of Anzac and the heroic deeds of Sergeant Harry Freame faded. Both Young Harry and Gracie suffered the taunts of school colleagues who called out to them, 'Hally Fleame', a reference to their father's speech and ancestry. While Young Harry had success and popularity at school and on the sporting field, he confided to a friend that his only disappointment in life 'was the shape of his eyes'.[24]

For a man with the skills of Harry Freame, the outbreak of World War II in September 1939 may have seemed like a stroke of good fortune. Here was a chance to get back to work he knew, work that paid the bills, work that didn't rely on the fortune or favour of Mother Nature, work that would once again put food on his family's table. If there was one thing that war needed, indeed demanded, it was men, and as Harry had learnt at Gallipoli, it didn't matter what colour their skin was or how they spoke. All that mattered was that a man could shoot straight and wouldn't let his mates down.

But if the war did seem like a lucky break, there was more bad news to come first. On 7 September, just four days after Australia's declaration of war, Edith May Freame died. Young Harry described her last days in a letter back to Edith May's family in England:

> Of the letters I have written to you I am afraid this is the hardest ... my dear mother, and your sister, passed peacefully to eternal rest at 6:45 pm on Thursday evening September 7th ... ever since the cold snap in June she has been ill and after fighting to keep going she eventually broke down on the morning of August 24th when she had two heart attacks. Although she was fairly ill that day, she insisted that dad keep a delayed appointment in Sydney on that day and so he left Kentucky on the Wednesday night before to meet a lady friend and missionary from Japan who knew and worked with his sister Grace so that he was in Sydney with me at the time. Apparently mother got up to get Grace away to school and just after she had left mother suffered the two attacks while alone and it was not until a salesman called that she was able to get help ... dad left for home immediately and doctor told him that it was a matter of days. The real trouble was that mother was suffering from the worst form of sugar

diabetes which naturally affected the heart besides other severe complications ... she put up a gallant fight ... she passed on after being semi-conscious for a long period ... The main trouble was that mother never realised she was so ill ... as she would have nothing to do with doctors and was afraid of having to go to hospital.[25]

Harry was a man accustomed to death and dying, but now it was in his own home. Edith May's death hit him hard. Continuing his letter, Young Harry wrote:

I am sorry to have to tell you although because I am young I have been able to stand the shock fairly well such is not the case with dad, who after all the worrying months while mother was ill has been completely broken up, so much that ever since her death he has been extremely ill being confined to his bed after a painful heart attack on the following Sunday.[26]

In his letter Young Harry seems philosophical about his mother's death, an attitude no doubt inculcated by his Church of England upbringing. Somewhat presciently he wrote, 'all this is very sad but we must realize that although we please ourselves what we do while we live, we have no power to dictate how long we are to live.'[27]

For his distant family, Young Harry outlined his plans. At the time of Edith May's death, having finished high school the year before and holding a bursary for further study, Harry had been living in Sydney, where he worked part-time while studying. But upon his mother's death, he decided to give up the city life and move back to Kentucky to help his father on the farm. He felt that this was his filial duty, writing:

> my ideas are these – although dad never ever said much he always thought a lot and he has suffered a terrible blow with mother's death and is ever so lonely, so that with Grace going away to school next year I know I must try and fill the empty place to a certain extent and keep his time occupied. I realize that I cannot entirely fill the empty place – none can – but I do think in time I might help him forget a little.[28]

This letter provides a fascinating insight into Harry's character. The father who never said much but thought a lot, broken by the death of his wife of thirty-three years. The letter is also a window into the soul of the outstanding young man that Young Harry Freame, just eighteen at the time, was growing into.

Whatever tides of grief swept over Harry Freame, they did not drag him under for long. On 1 November he sent off a letter enquiring about a role in the Second AIF. His reply was soon coming:

> My dear Freame, I wish to acknowledge your letter of 1st November, and note that you have engaged a married couple to manage your farm; also that you have found a school at which to place your daughter. I only wish that the situation overseas had developed sufficiently to allow me to bring you down to Sydney to work for my section. As I have already told you, if the war does commence you can be quite sure I will send for you immediately.[29]

The letter was signed, 'With kind regards, Yours truly, WJR Scott'. Walter John Rendall Scott. War hero, insurance broker and one of the most mysterious operatives in the history of Australian intelligence.

This letter would signal a new chapter in the story of Harry Freame.

Part III

They Got Me

Chapter 11

An Agent Revealed

When Walter John Rendall Scott first wrote to Harry Freame on 1 November 1939, there was no role available for Harry. But just a month later the situation changed, and on 4 December 1939 Harry Freame was hired by Scott to perform 'defence work of a highly secret nature'. Walter John Rendall Scott, known to all as simply Jack Scott, was to be Harry's handler.

Born in the NSW town of Bingara in 1888, Scott, known by all as Jack Scott, was working in insurance when World War I broke out. He signed up in May 1915 and served with distinction in the 19th and 20th battalions. He was twice mentioned in dispatches and was awarded the Distinguished Service Order. Scott was related to the famous Street family, a legal dynasty in New South Wales. Scott's uncle, Sir Philip Street, would become lieutenant-governor and chief justice of New South Wales. Geoffrey Street, Scott's cousin and Harry Freame's old friend from the trenches in Gallipoli, would eventually serve as the minister for defence. Jack could not be better connected and became 'a man whose influence outstripped his nominal rank'.[1] At the close of the war Scott was involved in repatriating Australian troops from Europe. Back in Sydney he was described as a ladies' man, a popular invitee on Sydney's party circuit, known for his singing ability and his love of gambling and fast cars.

There is a possibility that Jack Scott was the inspiration for Jack Calcott, a key character in DH Lawrence's 1923 book *Kangaroo*, written in Thirroul on the south coast of New South Wales when Lawrence visited in the early 1920s. For years *Kangaroo*'s plot, dealing as it does with secret armies populated by Australian diggers returned from World War I, was written off by academics as the fantastical imaginings of a writer at the height of his creative powers. More recently scholars have considered the possibility that Lawrence's plot was lifted directly from contemporaneous events. And at the centre of those events was Jack Scott.

After returning to Australia, Jack Scott became involved with the King and Empire Alliance, a quasi-militia organisation that had as its objective the 'welfare of the British Empire and the counteracting of attempts to introduce and encourage disloyal doctrines'.[2] At its peak, the alliance had almost 3000 members, mostly returned diggers concerned at the creep of bolshevism in Australia.

It seems that Scott, despite going back into insurance after the war, never lost his predilection for service, and throughout the 1920s was involved in various right-wing counter-revolutionary militia organisations, mostly clandestine but at times with close links to the government and security forces of the time. Chief among these was the Old Guard, and in 1931 Scott held the rank of chief of staff in this organisation. The Old Guard, an ultra-secretive group whose membership again consisted mainly of returned diggers resident in New South Wales, had a membership of 30,000 men, all sworn to uphold law and order if the civilian government collapsed, which was a real possibility during the premiership of Jack Lang in the early 1930s.

In fact, Lang was eventually removed from office by the governor-general, avoiding a crisis. This also removed the immediate need for the Old Guard, which from 1932 onwards started to disband and fade into obscurity. Many of its members joined the United Country Party, one of those being Harry Freame, who worked as a local party organiser throughout the 1930s. It may have been through the Old Guard that Harry Freame first met Jack Scott.

Around the same time as the Old Guard dissipated, Jack Scott developed an infatuation with Japan. Over a period of three years from 1932 to 1935, Scott wrote thirty-one pro-Japanese letters and articles for the Sydney papers. His writings supported Japan's actions in Manchuria, praised Japan's modern advances and reassured Australian readers that Japan was no threat to Australia and deserved better treatment from the Australian Government. Speaking at a Legacy Club event in Sydney in March 1933, an organisation that Scott helped to found, Scott told his audience that the future of Manchuria:

> was assured under the tutelage of Japan whose task however would occupy her fully for many years. Japan with England's friendship would help to maintain peace in the East ... It was ludicrous to think that for the next fifty years Japan would have even the spare time to look towards Australia.[3]

At the time of writing these articles, Scott was in constant contact with the Japanese consulate in Sydney, even receiving reports from the consulate from which to base his writings on. He was also advising the consul-general on how to respond to anti-Japanese press in Australia. Scott regularly dined with Japanese consular officers and reciprocated the invitations for dinner at his own house.

Scott was also a prominent member of the Japan–Australia Society, which in the 1930s, in addition to promoting friendlier relations between Japan and Australia, also functioned as a mouthpiece of Japanese propaganda. It was through this society that Scott first met Ken Sato, a key Japanese propagandist and spy who was active in Australia at the time. We will soon come back to Sato.

Scott's writings were keenly received by the Japanese consul-general and were forwarded to the Japanese foreign minister, Hachirō Hirota. In 1934 Japan rewarded Scott's support and advocacy by inviting and paying for him to visit both Japan and Manchuria. Scott accepted, his trip neatly coinciding with John Latham's goodwill mission to Japan. The consulate advised Scott to publicly refer to his trip as a holiday, but it was nothing of the sort, as he was introduced to Japan's leading political, business and military figures.

Scott's reporting on what he saw in Japan was much more effusive and pro-Japanese than Latham's impressions gleaned at the same time. Scott's articles were pure pro-Japanese propaganda, with one newspaper quoting Scott in saying that 'Japanese industrialists worked under the happiest of conditions and factories were well equipped with up-to-date machinery. In his visits to the factories in Japan and Manchukuo he did not see one unhappy employee.'[4]

However, in 1935 Scott's writing suddenly ceased. It was at this time that military intelligence recruited Scott on the recommendation of another friend, Eric Longfield Lloyd, who by then was the director of

An Agent Revealed

the Sydney office of the Commonwealth Investigation Branch. Scott's knowledge of Japan was obviously a desirable asset in an intelligence service that increasingly saw Japanese invasion as a growing threat. As well as keeping an eye on Japanese citizens in Sydney, Scott was involved in the surveillance and monitoring of both fascist and Nazi elements in the German and Italian communities. But if anyone had any doubts about the wisdom of recruiting a man with such obvious and public sympathies for the Japanese cause to spy on Japan, none were expressed at the time.

In the lead-up to World War II, the Japanese consulate in Sydney directed and oversaw all Japanese espionage activity in Australia. An undated Australian intelligence report written sometime after the end of World War II found that Japanese:

> intelligence activity in a foreign country revolved around the Consulate, the directing headquarters for subversive activity which was always staffed beyond normal consular needs. Apart from ordinary staff and agents working under cover, special agents were sometimes attached to the diplomatic staff solely for espionage purposes.[5]

It should have come as no shock. Eric Longfield Lloyd as Australian trade commissioner in Tokyo fulfilled a similar role.

This report also provides an insight into how Australian intelligence agencies viewed Japan's espionage efforts:

> Any discussion of activities by Japanese abroad should be prefaced by a clear statement of their unique concept of espionage. Where

we would define espionage as activities aimed at secretly collecting information from an actual or potential enemy on his capabilities in war and plans for attack or defence, to the Japanese, espionage and fifth column are almost indivisible. Espionage and fifth column, including such subversive components as economic, political, and psychological penetration and propaganda, form one aspect of Total War.[6]

The Australian intelligence community had a basic understanding of the means and methods employed by Japanese intelligence, but they were no closer to being able to distinguish what was espionage and what was the benign collection of information for commercial and political purposes. The result was that nearly all activity by Japan's consular officers was considered espionage. No doubt there was actual espionage taking place – indeed, the consul received yearly funds for 'Secret Service Work' – but at other times the consulate's activities were so overt that if they were to be considered espionage, it would be espionage of the most inept kind.

In 1937 the Japanese consul-general wrote to the minister of the interior requesting information on the 'Communist Party and Pro-Russian Associations'.[7] In 1940 the Public Library of New South Wales received a request from the Japanese consulate for the 'title, size, scale, publishers of the latest land maps and air charts on Australia'.[8] A Japanese vice-consul made a request to the Commonwealth Government for a report on the ideological leanings of the state and federal governments. The consulate was also a large purchaser of books, buying up titles such as *British Fighter Planes*, *New Zealand from the Air*, *Mechanisation in Australian Industries* and *Grenade Training* from Sydney bookshops.[9]

It may well be that the Japanese believed that overt action was less likely to draw suspicion to their activities. More likely they thought very little of Australia's counterintelligence capabilities. In 1938 a Japanese artist, Rokuo Arai, was commissioned by Osaka Shosen Kaisha Shipping Line to paint a picture commemorating the role of the Japanese warship *Ibuki* in escorting Anzac troops to the Middle East in 1914. For the composition of his painting Arai had settled upon a scene of the *Ibuki* 'co-operating with the HMAS *Melbourne*'.[10] When Arai arrived in Australia, he applied for permission to paint Australian warships at Garden Island, Sydney, claiming that he needed some 'local colour'[11] and that the HMAS *Penguin*, then docked at Garden Island, was the same colour that the HMAS *Melbourne* had been in 1914. Arai's request was refused.

He then applied for permission to visit Garden Island. That too was refused. Finally Arai resorted to the tried-and-true Japanese espionage technique, employed so successfully up and down the Australian coast in the early part of the 1900s, and simply 'went fishing' – posing with a fishing rod he never used and taking his easel with him. In all, Arai made around forty sketches of the Garden Island buildings and vessels, the nerve centre of the Australian navy. The pictures were completed from the residence of an employee of the Japanese company Mitsui, who had an apartment at Potts Point with a clear view of Garden Island. To be fair, Arai did complete the commissioned work of the *Ibuki* and HMAS *Melbourne* and returned to Australia in 1939 to present the picture to Prime Minister Robert Menzies. It is unclear where the other pictures painted in 1938 ended up, though it is highly likely they were handed to Japanese intelligence.

In addition to monitoring Japanese spies, Australian intelligence agents were also trying to identify and monitor Australian citizens considered to be pro-Japanese. These ranged from deluded crackpots to far-right sympathisers. But just as it was difficult to differentiate Japanese espionage from benign information collection, so it was difficult to distinguish between Australian citizens with an interest in Japan and Japanese culture and Australian citizens who were spying for Japan or who would happily collaborate with a Japanese invasion force.

Highlighting this difficulty is a postwar intelligence report that named Australian artist Norman Lindsay as a Japanese agent. The report stated that Lindsay 'developed a strange and sudden affection for Japanese art and drew many Pro-Axis and Anti-Soviet (pictures). Lindsay's art is typical of bourgeois degeneracy. His house used to be lavishly decorated with "art" gifts from the Japanese consular officials and business people in Australia.'[12]

A key Japanese agent in identifying and cultivating persons friendly to Japan's cause throughout the 1930s was Ken Sato, a journalist by trade who had been educated in the United States. An intelligence report made by Eric Longfield Lloyd described Sato as:

> of alert type – alert beyond the usual run of Japanese. He is – or used to be – very fluent in the English language and is usually smartly dressed and invariably 'going somewhere in a hurry' or engaged apparently in doing several things at once at high speed. Although much of his journalistic capacity and general air of smartness in the past was clearly attributable to American training along 'hustle' lines, he was at no time other than entirely Japanese in underlying sentiment ... and it was noticed that the veneer of modernism and often expressed devotion to 'foreign' ways and

An Agent Revealed

aspects of things generally rapidly diminished to give place to marked Japanese nationalism in the year or two preceding the war. He had, like other Japanese at the time, an ambition to further Japan to no less than world domination.[13]

If Sato did envision world domination for Japan, during the 1930s he tried to bring it about through propaganda. In 1935, backed by his employer the news agency Osaka *Mainichi*, he produced an Australia–Japan goodwill publication that was widely circulated in both countries. This allowed him to visit Australia, where over a period of five months he not only gained an understanding of that nation but also befriended prominent Australians including Charles Kingsford Smith and John Latham.[14]

Sato's knowledge of Australia would eventually be put to use by Japanese authorities during the war, when he was employed at the Ōfuna prisoner-of-war camp to interrogate Australian prisoners.

Despite the best efforts of Australian intelligence agencies, the darkest spot in Australia's intelligence capabilities in the late 1930s centred around the sentiment and actions of the Japanese community in Australia. Where did their loyalties lie? To Australia or their homeland? What would be their response if Japan invaded Australia? Would they resist or collaborate?

~

Operating out of Victoria Barracks in Sydney, Jack Scott headed up a group that combined intelligence agents from both military intelligence and NSW police. In July 1939 his team compiled a list of all Japanese consular staff, including Australians. These people and who they interacted with were closely monitored. By 1940 this hybrid unit had expanded this list to include every Japanese citizen in New South Wales and had even mapped where they were living. Scott and his team conducted investigations into almost one hundred Japanese citizens then residing in Sydney.[15] These investigations included the shadowing of Japanese people as they went about their daily business. The national archives hold the files of the reports submitted by field agents. It was laborious, painstaking and boring work.

An entry made by Constable John Cross in the file of Kenichiro Yoneda, manager of the shipping firm Yamashita, provides an insight into the typical day of an agent tasked with tailing Japanese nationals:

> I beg to report that on the 6th February, 1941 I took up duty in the vicinity of Macquarie Place. At 1pm I followed three Japanese from Sirius House to the Florentino restaurant, next to the Prince Edward Theatre in Elizabeth Street. At 130pm I saw two Japanese enter the Japanese Club, No. 3 Bond street.[16]

Apart from the fact that the Japanese enjoyed Italian lunches and frequented the Japanese Club – hardly revelatory results – a review of the archives shows that surveillance of Japanese citizens failed to reveal much to the watchers.

When not following their own leads, agents followed up on tips from the public, which were rarely helpful. After observing suspicious behaviour, William Davies was moved to write to the NSW premier:

> Sir, I have recently left my employment at Royal Naval House, Sydney owing to my health. For years I have been writing about the Liar and Thief The Jap; telling various people in High places we wanted defence and more defence. I now propose that drastic steps should be taken, as I am convinced after a recent observation that Japs are about posing as Chinese. I have been taking stock. On Sunday last while people were strolling around Hyde Park and other places I saw Japs taking stock. There seems to be quite a lot of 'Chinese' about. The Jap will go in rags to gain his information. Last Sunday's fellows were all well groomed.[17]

It was not only William Davies who was concerned about Japanese intelligence agents posing as Chinese nationals. Later, security services would compile a list of every Chinese-owned or Chinese-run restaurant in Sydney, along with detailed lists of their employees.

From his country farm at Kentucky, this was the world that Harry Freame was thrown into in December 1939. With no training, just his knowledge of Japanese language and culture, he was set loose among the Japanese community of Sydney, his role known only to his right-wing-leaning handler, Jack Scott, and a few select members of the General Staff of Military Intelligence.

From Freame's surviving pocketbook we see that his counterespionage activities were aimed at the higher end of the Japanese community. The names Kuematau Murai and Kisuki Toyoda are written neatly on the yellowed pages in Freame's hand, along with their addresses. Murai was the Japanese consul during this period and Kisuki headed up the Domei News Agency. Both men were considered key parts of the Japanese intelligence and propaganda network in Australia.

Unsurprisingly Harry's Japanese language skills soon came to the attention of other Australian Government departments charged with monitoring Japanese activity in Australia. In mid-1940 the Censorship Staff approached Harry. Would he be interested in a job?

At the same time as approaching Harry, through a man named Burdekin, Censorship checked in with their Military Intelligence colleagues to see if they had heard of a man called Harry Freame, no doubt wanting to make sure of his credentials before employing him. Reg Powell of Military Intelligence told Burdekin that he would look into it and that Burdekin should not do anything until he had investigated further.[18]

Powell then discussed the offer from Censorship with Harry, who assured him that a role with Censorship would not upset his existing relationships with the Japanese community in Sydney. Without disclosing what it was, Harry assured Powell that he had a watertight cover story for his presence among the Japanese and that Censorship had promised him that he could conduct his work in a way that guaranteed the Japanese never knew about it. Thus assured, Powell then went back to Burdekin and told him he had no issue with Censorship employing Harry Freame. However, he did not reveal to Burdekin that Harry was already working for Military Intelligence.

While Australia's military and intelligence agencies were working out how best to utilise Harry Freame's unique skills, Harry met and fell in love with divorcee and mother of two Harriet Brainwood. The pair became acquainted through Harriet's sister Adeline, who lodged at the same boarding house as Harry in Sydney. Described as 'trim and shapely' with 'an air of sophistication about her',[19] Harriet had worked as a nurse. She was also known among her friends for having certain psychic abilities, and later in life she appeared on an ABC program demonstrating her abilities.

Harry and Harriet enjoyed a whirlwind romance, the two marrying in St John's Anglican Church at Milsons Point, Sydney, on 16 August 1940. Harriet's family was not immune to the prejudices of the day and immediately ostracised her for marrying a Japanese man. The wedding came not much less than a year after the death of Edith May Freame, and Harry's haste may possibly be explained by his desire to look after Harriet in case anything was to happen to him in the course of his espionage work.

On the day after his marriage, 17 August, Harry joined the staff of the Censorship office. Here he would assist in the collection and analysis of Japanese material. The war was proving to be a boon to his personal finances, and if he was happy about this, he would be even happier the following month, when the Department of External Affairs approached him with yet another job offer.

After five years of service in Japan, Eric Longfield Lloyd returned to Australia in 1940 and immediately took up the role of deputy director in the Commonwealth Investigation Branch, highlighting the fluid lines between diplomacy and spying. Longfield Lloyd's return left Australia without high-ranking representation in Japan at a time when it was becoming ever more critical. War with Japan was now widely considered inevitable, but the Australian Government decided to send diplomatic representation to Japan in the hope of delaying any aggressive action on Japan's behalf. It was a major decision for the Australian Government to take, for up to that point in time, almost four decades after Federation, Australia had still not had permanent diplomatic representation in any country. Japan would be Australia's first full diplomatic posting.

Equally amazing was the fact that despite Japan dominating Australia's security, economic and political thinking for the past four decades, there were very few Australians with a suitable background to fill the role of Australian Minister to Japan. Eventually the job was given to John Latham. After retiring from politics in 1934, Latham had been made Chief Justice in October 1935. To clear the way for Latham's appointment in Japan, in early 1940 the Australian Parliament passed legislation allowing Latham to hold the dual posts of Chief Justice and Australia's first minister to Japan, essentially a modern-day ambassador's role.

Although Latham had made a successful tour of Japan in the 1934 goodwill mission and, according to newspaper reports, had for many years displayed an appreciation of Japanese art and culture,[20] he did not speak Japanese. He would need an interpreter – who else but Harry Freame.

It is not clear how the name Harry Freame found its way to Latham, but a likely connection would have been through Harry's old 1st Battalion comrade Eric Longfield Lloyd. They had remained in contact and sometimes met up for Anzac Day in Sydney, a red-letter day in Harry's year, one not to be missed.

However, after hearing that Harry Freame was a possible interpreter, Latham had a hard time locating the man himself now that Harry had sunk into the murky world of counterespionage. On 30 September 1940 the secretary of the Department of External Affairs, Lieutenant-Colonel William Roy Hodgson, sent a telegram to Jack Scott on the general staff of the Department of Defence.

An Agent Revealed

'I have been unable to locate Mr. Harry Freame, and Military Intelligence, Sydney, inform me he is quite unknown to them. Can you assist please?'[21]

Hodgson, like Harry, had served and been badly wounded at Gallipoli, but unlike Harry he continued in the army and returned to serve in France. When Jack Scott received Hodgson's telegram, he immediately phoned Hodgson and explained that the work Harry was currently engaged in was so secret that nobody at Military Intelligence was even aware Harry Freame existed. Then, in an act that flew completely in the face of that secrecy, Jack Scott provided Hodgson with Harry Freame's personal address and telephone number. That a secret agent's personal details could be handed out so freely over a telephone line seems remarkable. And negligent.

Two weeks after the interaction between Scott and Hodgson, news of Harry's appointment was announced in the major newspapers and syndicated through the regional newspapers:

Interpreter Appointed For Tokio Legation

Canberra, Thursday. – The Commonwealth Government has appointed Mr. Harry Freame, of Sydney, interpreter to the Australian Legation in Tokio.

Mr. Freame, who was born in Japan, speaks and writes Japanese fluently. He is at present engaged on special defence work.[22]

This last line sparked a panic that reverberated throughout the Department of Defence. In an internal hand-scrawled memo accompanying the clipping from the Melbourne *Sun* newspaper, Jack

Scott demanded to know 'what the special defence work is & who supplied this information'.[23]

Philip McBride, Minister for Defence, sent off a strongly worded letter to his ministerial counterpart at External Affairs, 'Black Jack' John McEwen. It began: 'I wish to invite your attention to an announcement which appeared in the Melbourne "Sun" newspaper of 13th September 1940.' After providing an extract from the article, McBride continued:

> The published statement from Canberra that Freame 'is at present engaged on special defence work' has caused considerable embarrassment to the Army, and the possibility cannot be overlooked that this appointment may now be viewed with suspicion in Tokio.
>
> Furthermore, the protection of special agents is an Army responsibility and any action, as in this case, which discloses such an agent, is regarded as a serious matter with possibly far reaching consequences. That Freame was engaged on secret work and known only to one officer was given as confidential information to Lieutenant-Colonel Hodgson.
>
> That such leakage of information from Canberra is possible is disturbing and it would be appreciated if your Department would make enquiries as to the source of the 'Sun' newspaper information.
>
> I would be glad to receive your assurance that suitable action has been taken to ensure that no breach of secrecy precautions is possible in future.[24]

An Agent Revealed

But Black Jack was in no mood to give assurances or even allow his department to take the blame for the leakage of secret army information. 'My dear minister,' McEwen wrote on 2 October 1940:

> In reply to your letter of 30th September, about Mr. Harry Freame, I desire to inform you that the Secretary of my Department, Lieut.-Col. W. R. Hodgson, whose name is mentioned in your letter, assures me that there has been no disclosure of any confidential information to the press about the activities of Mr. Freame.
>
> Mr. Freame has been engaged in defence work for some time and this was well known to the Japanese authorities here, including the Consul-General.
>
> Mr. Freame has been acting as interpreter and translator in connection with the censorship in New South Wales, in regard to which there is no secrecy. It was this which was mentioned to the press, and no reference was made to any special defence work, as was actually reported. The fact of Mr. Freame's work with the censorship was unknown yesterday to Major Scott of the Intelligence Section of the General Staff.
>
> Knowing that Mr. Freame had been freely intermingling with the Japanese community in Sydney, my Secretary specially raised the question of his appointment to the staff of the Tokyo Legation with the Consul General of Japan, with a view to ascertaining his attitude towards the appointment. The response was that it was an excellent one, as Mr. Freame had created a very favourable impression.
>
> Had the matter not been mentioned, there might well have

been cause for Japanese suspicion, as I gather the Japanese are well aware of the connection of both Mr. Freame and Mr. Donnelly with the Defence Department in the capacity mentioned.[25]

After reading McEwen's reply, Jack Scott sent his own memo to his minister on 9 October:

It is quite incorrect to say that Freame's association with Censorship was not secret ... The suggestion that the Japanese community 'are well aware of the connection of both Mr. Freame and Mr. Donnelly with the Defence Department in the capacity mentioned', is one which must be viewed with concern.

It denotes a leakage of information connected with a secret appointment. A request should be addressed to the Minister for External Affairs asking that all the facts to substantiate such a suggestion should now be made available to allow of the further necessary enquiry being carried out.[26]

Importantly, Scott finishes his memo by highlighting 'The advisability of Eastern Command being advised that Freame should no longer be employed as a secret and undercover agent must now be considered'.[27]

In his memo, Jack Scott also confirms what Black Jack McEwen had alleged, that he himself had no idea that Freame was also working for Censorship. And there was a very good reason for that. By the time Freame's name was being bandied around the press, Jack Scott was no longer Harry Freame's handler. In fact he was no longer working for Military Intelligence.

Though Scott had played a prominent role in rounding up suspected Nazis at the outbreak of World War II, speeding around Sydney 'like a motorized avenging angel',[28] by 1940 his police colleagues started to suspect Scott of having divided loyalties.

His prominent championing of Japan through the middle period of the 1930s, his role in the Japan–Australia Society and his close relationship with Japanese business interests and the Japanese consulate were well known in political and intelligence circles and not easily forgotten. Jack Scott understood his past defence of Japan would be viewed with suspicion by his colleagues. In a letter sent in 1937, Scott wrote to a commanding officer:

> I have been asked by the Japanese Community to give a lecture on the Japanese position of the Rotary Club here on Tuesday the 14th. I feel very uncomfortable about it as my feelings have undergone a complete change over in regard to them. On the other hand from the point of view of my job I think it better to appear otherwise or as before. What do you think? I hope you feel as I do that it's important to retain such confidence as they may have.[29]

Were these the words of a man who had sincerely had a change of heart, or a double agent trying to hide his true position? Scott's defenders in Military Intelligence attributed the rumours being put out against him as the result of professional jealousy.

Whatever the case, such was the suspicion of Scott and the seriousness of the divide it was driving between Military Intelligence and their NSW police colleagues that in early 1940 Scott was prohibited from accessing secret files, and in June 1940 he was removed from Military Intelligence and transferred to the general staff in Melbourne.[30]

If, as McEwen claims, the Japanese were already aware of Harry Freame's association with the defence department, could Jack Scott, Harry Freame's own handler, have been the leak? Scott's own subsequent behaviour in the war only tends to confuse the matter further.

After commanding the guerilla warfare training centre for independent companies at Wilsons Promontory in Victoria, in December 1941 Scott was moved back to Melbourne to take up the role of liaison officer for AIF troops stationed on the islands of Timor and Ambon. The troops on Ambon, known as Gull Force, were commanded by Leonard Roach. Throughout January 1942, with a significant increase in Japanese activity in the area making a landing on Ambon ever more likely, Roach made repeated pleas to Scott and other commanding officers for reinforcements. On 13 January Roach advised that 'Gull Force "could not hold out for more than one day" without additional firepower and adequate air and naval support' and recommended evacuating the 1131 Australian troops off the island.[31] Rather than back his officer on the ground, Scott approached his commanding officers and offered to immediately replace Roach, full well knowing that without further resources dedicated to the defence of Ambon, his mission had 'no hope of survival'.[32]

On 14 January Jack Scott arrived on Ambon and took over command of Gull Force. A force of 20,000 Japanese invaded two weeks later on 30 January. Scott surrendered himself and his men four days later. Interned as prisoners of war, first on Ambon and then afterwards on the island of Hainan, Jack Scott became infamous among the Australian prisoners for handing over Australian soldiers to be punished by Japanese guards. This included brutal beatings, which left one young soldier, Private George Roy, close to death.[33] Of the original 1131 members of Gull Force, 779 never came home. Scott's men never forgave him for his role at Ambon and Hainan, and he was ostracised from the Australian military community following the end of the war.

Jack Scott's behaviour at Ambon is strange. On the outer with Australian intelligence, did he volunteer for a suicide mission hoping to make himself useful to Japanese troops? Did he hope that his past support for Japan would be remembered and that he would be able to change sides? Or had he never recovered from the traumas of World War I, where he was badly wounded? This is possible, given that between the wars, family members remembered him walking into the family home waving around a revolver, threatening to shoot himself.[34] While they were prisoners of war, Australians under his command attempted to have him certified as insane.[35]

Historian Andrew Moore, the leading writer on far-right groups in New South Wales between the wars, retells a story in the book *Alien Justice* where another agent, Ken Cook, became suspicious of Jack Scott's Japanese connections after allegedly almost being killed by the Japanese vice-consul not long after sharing sensitive information with Jack Scott. Moore describes Cook as 'an outstanding agent'.[36] More recently, journalist Nick Hordern described Cook as a 'fraud and a shonk'.[37] The duelling historic views of Ken Cook highlight just how hard it is to assess the lives of intelligence agents with any real clarity.

From the distance of almost 100 years, looking back into the purposely opaque world of espionage and counterespionage, it is difficult to tell the good guys from the bad guys, those neat distinctions we all like to make, to find order within the disorder. The intelligence world has always had a facility for drawing in the chancers and fraudsters and fantasists to play their parts alongside the patriots and nationalists and quiet heroes, and often it is difficult, either at the time or with the benefit of hindsight, to tell the groups apart. This may forever remain the case with Jack Scott.

Whether Harry Freame's secret role was inadvertently leaked by Lieutenant-Colonel Hodgson of External Affairs or deliberately by Jack Scott at Military Intelligence will never be known. If an investigation was ever held, the results are lost to history: there is nothing in the archives. What is known is that when Harry saw his name and his role splashed across the pages of the newspapers, he was 'horrified' and confided to his family that the leak was going to 'cause him a lot of trouble'. He was right.

Chapter 12
Undercover Operations and an Underhand Attack

Throughout the spring of 1940, Japanese agents tailed Harry around Sydney, keeping a close watch on him before he left for Tokyo. But others were watching him too. On 19 September 1940 Mrs Thomas of Bellevue Street, Manly, wrote to the police inspector at Manly Police Station. She wrote:

> I know of a case which I think should be reported. It is of a man living at 53 Glen Street, Milsons Point. This house is a residential and when the man applied for a flat in the building he told the proprietor that he was in the secret service. He was a perfect stranger and had never seen the proprietor before. Some weeks ago he was 'shadowed' by a man he said looked like a Jap and he left the house by any way he could find so that the man watching the house would not see him. I may say I know the lady who keeps the house and she thinks he is quite genuine. She has just told me this man is going to Japan with the newly appointed Australian

Commissioner – one of the staff and will be leaving on Sep 26th. He gives me the impression he is a 5th Columnist. A Tall very dark thin man. He uses the house telephone which is XB2870. This is confidential. I do not want my name mentioned.[1]

Harry Freame, the Marvel of Gallipoli, the man employed by no fewer than three government departments in the fight against Japan, was being denounced as a fifth columnist, a term that originated in the Spanish Civil War and came to describe any small group of people who would undermine the defence of a nation from within in time of war.

The paranoia that Japanese fifth columnists might have been operating in Australia was ill-directed in Harry's case, but not as far-fetched as it may seem. In fact, at the time that Harry was trying to shake Japanese spies off his trail in Sydney, one such fifth columnist was already working for the Australian Government in Queensland.

In May 1938 the University of Queensland initiated a Japanese language program and brought out a Japanese man called Ryonosuke Seita to head up the program. In 1940 Seita was transferred to the Federal Government's censorship office in Brisbane, employed in a similar role to that which Harry held in Sydney. Seita, though, was a Japanese spy and had headed up Japanese intelligence operations in Queensland since his arrival in 1938. At the outbreak of war with Japan, Seita was arrested and interned. A search of his Brisbane property found propaganda materials and other objects linking him to a man named Mitsuru Tōyama, suspected of being the head of the ultranationalist, clandestine and much-feared Black Dragon Society.[2]

After investigating Harry Freame as a suspected fifth columnist, Manly police were able to confirm Freame's identity. A typewritten note on his file simply states, 'We beg to report having inquired into this matter, and have definitely established that Mr. Fream, 53 Glen St. Milsons Point, a half caste Japanese, has been selected by the Military Authorities to act as translator to the Australian Legation in Japan.'[3]

Harry had escaped suspicion, suspicion that other Japanese descendants loyal to Australia would not be able to dodge as tensions with Japan grew. Many Japanese people living in Australia were suspected of treason or espionage and denounced or harassed in public. Often with little to no evidence against them. And this overt public aggression and suspicion of Japanese people explains why Harry would recklessly reveal to a prospective landlord his role in the secret service: it was an attempt to prove his loyalty to a stranger who was suspicious of his dark skin and strange intonation of speech. Harry had been dealing with this all his life. But it also highlights Harry's complete lack of training in modern espionage.

Mrs Thomas's letter provides corroborative evidence that following the leaking of Harry's defence role in *The Sun*, Japanese agents had indeed begun to follow him in Sydney. Harry must have been under enormous pressure. Not only did he have the daily worries of avoiding Japanese intelligence agents on his own turf, he would have also been preoccupied with thoughts of what awaited him in Japan.

Ostensibly Harry's role in Japan was to travel ahead of the legation and set up the office before John Latham arrived. On Latham's arrival, Harry was to act as interpreter and translator for him and the rest of the legation. But that was only cover. Harry's true role, as a spy operating under diplomatic cover, was to gather information on Japanese activities and the Japanese Government's plans and attitudes towards Australia. Some of this would have been done by scanning the Japanese-language newspapers and by keeping an eye and an ear to the ground. But, most crucially and most dangerously, Harry would also have been tasked with collecting human intelligence by cultivating intelligence assets, men and women with knowledge of Japan's inner workings, assets who could forewarn Australia of Japanese aggression, who could share with Harry Freame Japan's innermost secrets. Assets who would betray their country.

And standing in Harry's way was an enemy who not only knew his identity but had publicly sworn to eliminate any foreign spies or any Japanese nationals who aided and abetted foreign spies in their work. Unfortunately, Harry was both foreign spy and Japanese national. His fate if caught would be that of the traitor, and Harry knew what that meant.

Harry would have read in the Sydney papers of an incident that had occurred in Japan a few months earlier. On 29 July the Japanese ministries of war and justice in Tokyo made a joint announcement advising that 'In view of the ever-increasing activities of foreign organs of espionage and conspiracy in this country of late, the military police, under the direction of prosecutors, arrested, as a first step on July 27, those constituting part of a British espionage network covering the entire country.'[4] In all, eleven British subjects were arrested in the sweep carried out by the feared Japanese military police, the Kempeitai. Among those arrested was Reuters correspondent James Melville Cox.

Two days later on 29 July, the Japanese press reported that Cox had died by suicide, jumping from a fourth-floor window while being questioned by the Kempeitai. The Japanese authorities released a note that he had allegedly left for his wife: 'I know what is best, Always my only love. I have been well treated, but there is no doubt how matters are going.'[5]

The Japanese released the note as proof that Cox had died by suicide. 'In the light of the above note, it seems that with the progress of the investigation, deceased became aware of the fact that he could not escape conviction.'[6] For the rest of the world, though, the note merely proved that Cox, a suspected British spy, had been murdered by the Kempeitai. This impression was backed up by an announcement made just a few days later, when Japan's minister of the army, General Tojo, told the Japanese cabinet, 'the Army would not hesitate to take drastic measures against Japanese caught assisting "foreign secret agents," also those who were pro-British.'[7] For Harry Freame, about to deploy to Japan, it was an ominous warning.

In the aftermath of the leaking of Harry's role to the press, Minister for Defence Philip McBride suggested to his ministerial counterpart at External Affairs, Black Jack McEwen, that considering the leak 'the possibility cannot be overlooked that this appointment may now be viewed with suspicion'.[8] Jack Scott in his internal memo went a step further and suggested that Eastern Command should be advised 'that Freame should no longer be employed as a secret and undercover agent'.[9] Despite the warnings, nothing was done. On 11 October 1940 Harry Freame boarded the SS *Tanda* and set sail for Tokyo.

For the duration of the cruise, the passengers of the SS *Tanda* could enjoy the extravagant (by wartime standards) onboard menu of potage Jacqueline, baked snapper and Hollandaise, ox tongue à la mode or roast stuffed turkey and bread sauce. But lest they fall into a false sense of security, at the bottom of the onboard dining menu was a stark warning: 'Smoking on deck after dark is strictly prohibited.'[10] Any light or glow would have made the ship a target for patrolling enemy boats and submarines. Harry would not have needed any warning. It was wartime and once again, as he had so many times during the Great War, he was heading into enemy territory.

A few days after departing Sydney, on 14 October Harry wrote to Gracie, whom he had been unable to farewell in person. At the time of his departure, Gracie had been in hospital in Armidale. On 13 November he again wrote to Gracie, not as the hardened intelligence officer and war veteran but the doting father concerned for his daughter's health and school marks. He signed off his letter by asking her to write to him as often as possible while he was away.

The letter gives us a sense of where Harry's mind was and what he was leaving behind. Young Harry was growing into a fine young man. He had finished high school and was now working on the farm but with plans to return to Sydney to start studying for an accounting degree. Harry would have had no worries about Young Harry's future. His mind would have been with his daughter, Gracie. She had had a hard time adapting to Harry's new wife, Harriet, a third motherly figure to adjust to in her short life. Gracie's stepsister, Alison, was also a problem; the two young girls never seemed to get along with each other. Rather than move to Sydney with Harriet and Alison, Gracie had stayed at a boarding school in Armidale. But she hadn't found that to her liking either and had run away a number of times. Adding to Harry's worries would have been the state of the farm's finances. Despite his various jobs in Sydney, he was in arrears on the payments to the Soldier Settlement Commission. The confiscation of his block and all that he had worked for the last twenty years was a very real possibility. But no matter how heavy Harry's domestic worries weighed upon him, they would have to wait until after he returned from Japan.

Arriving in Tokyo, Harry made contact with his Japanese family. His niece Cecelia, the daughter of Harry's sister Grace, came to live with him, possibly assisting in the running of Harry's household. Harriet would later consider this a mistake, seeming to suspect Cecelia of having some connection to what was to befall Harry.

His domestic affairs in order, Harry set to organising the office for the Australian legation, leasing office space, hiring servants and generally preparing the ground for the arrival of John Latham. But while attempting to perform the duties of his cover role, Harry was also aware of the need to gather intelligence for his other paymasters back in Sydney. This was proving much harder to achieve. At every turn Harry knew he was being shadowed by Japanese agents of the Kempeitai, who kept a close eye on the interpreter-cum-intelligence agent, following his every move, noting his every conversation. They were waiting for Harry to make a slip, waiting for a moment to make their move.

Adding to Harry's stress, or possibly because of it, not long after arriving in Japan he fell ill. Before leaving Australia he had had bouts of measles and pleurisy, which he'd only just recovered from before departing. The strain of travel and the stress of being under twenty-four-hour surveillance from a military police unit as feared and deadly as the German Gestapo only exacerbated his illness.

On 27 January the Kempeitai made their move. Harry Freame was attacked on the streets of Tokyo in an attempted garrotting – a method commonly used by the Kempeitai. They would have approached him from behind and thrown a piece of cord or wire around his neck, attempting to hold closed or even cut into his windpipe until he died of strangulation. It was a swift and efficient way to kill someone, preventing them from calling out and leaving behind no traceable evidence. With his one good arm, Harry fought as the chokehold tightened. In his desperate bid for life, he managed to injure or distract his attackers momentarily, enough to loosen the terrible grip of the garrotte and allow him to break free. He fled, and escaped with his life – just barely.

But the attack had left him seriously injured. He tried to recover from it quietly, unwilling to draw attention to himself or alarm other members of the Australian legation. But his injuries were too grave. A week later on 4 February, Harry admitted himself to St Luke's International Hospital in Tokyo. He would have felt safe choosing this hospital because it was known as the American hospital and staffed by American doctors and nurses, who he could assume were outside the sphere of influence of Kempeitai agents.

It was only after checking in that he learnt that, in response to the deteriorating diplomatic relationship between the United States and Japan, the US Government had evacuated all the American staff from the hospital only days earlier. This discovery may have caused Harry to hide his true condition, and the reason behind it, from the Japanese doctors, lest they hand him over to the Kempeitai to finish the job.

From his hospital bed, on letterhead from the Australian Tokyo Legation, he wrote to Gracie:

> I am sorry to say that I never felt good since I left home, but got worse day by day since arrived in Japan and now I am in inmate of this Hospital [St Luke's Hospital] so far I have gone through 3

Xray examinations and they (the expert doctors) does not know what is wrong with me yet. But I may be told this afternoon. I have lost 10lbs in weight and my voice I could only speak in a sort of whisper.[11]

A short time later Patrick Shaw of the Australian legation requested Freame's medical file from the attending doctor at St Luke's. In a surprising breach of patient confidentiality, the file was provided on 20 February by Dr Ikeda. Ikeda had conducted numerous tests on Harry and provided Shaw with a comprehensive report:

Mr. H.W. Freame came to see me on February 4th, 1941, complaining of his gradual loss of the body weight, gastro-intestinal troubles since his arrival in Japan two months ago. Four or five days before he came for the consultation, diarrhea developed, and it was still continuing when I saw him. At the same time he stated that he lost his voice suddenly on January 31st morning when he woke up, whereas he did not notice any trouble in his voice until the previous night. I have advised him to stay in the hospital for a thorough examination. The diarrhea was soon controlled by giving smooth diet and adstringents. The gastro-intestinal series were made but no positive findings. The X-ray of the lungs was essentially negative. A laryngoscopic examination showed a complete paralysis of the left nervus recurrence, and partial paralysis of the right musculus internus. To find out the cause of this paralysis of the vocal cords, careful study of the mediastinum with X-ray were made. The aorta shadow in both the anterior-posterior and lateral positions was wider than normal but not to the extent we can call it an aneurism. The X-ray of the oesophagus with barium balls and thick barium shows a certain stenosis at its second narrow point. There is a certain pathology in the mediastinum is suspected but not to the degree we can make any definite diagnosis. The further developments should be watched as regard to the nature of the paralysis of the left recurrent nerve. In view of these findings and the nature of the disease I strongly feel it is advisable for him to return to his home country for further observation and treatment. The urinalysis and stool examinations were negative.[12]

Ikeda finished his report by providing Freame's blood count results, which were considered normal.

After receiving Ikeda's report, it was evident that Freame was in serious ill health and the Australian legation cabled home on 6 March:

We are writing to advise you that, though the matter is not quite certain yet, all the indications are that Mr. Freame will have to be invalided back to Australia. Some five weeks ago suddenly he completely lost his speech. He had not been looking well for some time, in any case, and had been feeling unwell. He went into hospital and they diagnosed the condition as one of paralysis of some of the vocal cords and recommended that, as treatment would be long and as his physical condition was not good and needed building up, he should go back to Australia ... We will be extremely sorry to lose Mr. Freame, for his assistance to us in the initial days of the Legation has been invaluable, and he has smoothed out many nitches and prevented many mistakes ... apart from his illness, there seems to be good reason for suggesting that Mr. Freame would be more useful in Australia on censorship and intelligence work than here ...[13]

On 10 March John Latham notified his bosses back in Canberra of his decision to send Harry back to Australia. 'Mr Freame having developed afflicted vocal cords which cannot be treated here has been recommended by medical authorities to return to Australia and is leaving by Kashima Maru Friday March 14th.'[14] Harry's Japanese sojourn was over. He was going home after just four months.

Dr Ikeda had found paralysis of the vocal cords and noted that Harry had told him of his sudden loss of voice, which Harry had also mentioned when writing to his daughter. It is quite clear from the note of 6 March and Latham's message of 10 March that the key question of Freame's health revolved around his vocal cords and his loss of speech, both seemingly attributable to the attempted garrotting – though Harry had of course not mentioned this, fearing it would only put him in further danger.

Harry claimed he did not know how he had lost his voice, but this was not true. He did know, but he would not reveal it until he was far from Japan and far from the reach of the feared Kempeitai military police.

Chapter 13

Deathbed Whispers

Harry Freame returned to Australia a broken man. When he set foot on land at Sydney on 12 April 1941, he was unable to dress himself. Indeed he could barely walk, and required assistance to disembark the *Kashima Maru*, which had carried him home from Japan.

He was interned at the Mater Hospital in North Sydney and placed under the care of doctors Stuart Allen and Justin Stormon. Showing no signs of improvement, Freame was then examined by Dr RJ Murphy, described as 'a throat specialist of Macquarie Street'.[1] But the medical team could not find what was wrong with Harry Freame. After a period of three weeks, doctors took Harriet Freame aside and told her that there was nothing they could do for her husband, that he was better off at home, surrounded by friends and family. Official reports show that Harry Freame was discharged from the care of the Mater Hospital with his condition as 'undiagnosed'.[2]

Having never fully regained his voice, Harry communicated in the barest of whispers. Harriet asked him repeatedly what had happened. Had he caught a cold or some other illness? With a shake of the head, at first Harry refused to answer, or if he did say anything he told Harriet to ask Young Harry, the father having confided in his son what had taken place in Japan.

As the days passed and the end drew nearer, Harry eventually disclosed the secret he had been keeping since January. 'They got me,' Harry told Harriet.[3] He later told friends who came to visit that on 27 January, while walking on the streets of Tokyo, agents of the Kempeitai attempted to strangle him. He had fought them off with his one good arm, but the damage was done.

'And why didn't you tell Sir John Latham about this?' Harriet asked her husband.

'He would have got the wind up,' Harry replied.[4]

It is unlikely that Sir John Latham was thinking about Harry or any of the men at External Affairs who had been sent with him to Japan at the time. On 21 May as Harry lay dying, the external affairs department fired Freame on the grounds that he was no longer useful to them, giving him his one-month notice. It was not unexpected. On 16 April, just a few days after Harry's return to Australia, External Affairs had written to their counterparts in Military Intelligence. 'It is not anticipated that this Department will continue to employ Mr. Freame. In the circumstances I would be glad to learn whether you desire to utilise his services.'[5]

Military Intelligence had no use for Harry either, and they in turn wrote to the Director of the Security Service and the Censorship Staff to see if they might have need of Freame. The Security Service didn't want to touch Freame either, but Censorship did:

> The District Censor is desirous of obtaining the services of the abovenamed [Harry Freame] at the earliest possible moment, and

it will be appreciated if he may be advised to contact the District Censor as soon as possible, with a view to retuning to the work upon which he was engaged prior to his departure for Japan.[6]

But there was no going back; Harry's wars were over.

Harry Freame's death was not an easy one. His final days were spent with family and friends, but he had great trouble swallowing: 'food and drink went down the wrong way and ... thick mucous kept coming up.'[7] A morphia pill went down his windpipe and lodged in his lungs. Finally on 27 May 1941 Hidetsugu Kitagawa, also known as Harry Freame, the Marvel of Gallipoli, died, choking in the arms of his wife Harriet.

Harriet sent a message to Gracie in Armidale, telling her to catch the train to Newcastle but not giving the reason why. When Gracie stepped onto the platform at Newcastle station, she was met by her stepsister, Alison. Alison gave Gracie the devastating news that her beloved father was dead, then turned and walked away. Gracie hopped on the same train that had brought her down from Armidale and returned home alone, no doubt devastated.

A few weeks later a letter arrived for Gracie. It was from Harry's Japanese niece Cecelia:

> Your father's death ... Your father's so hard life ... He was so lonely and had no friends. He wished to adopt me as his own child and bring me to Australia with him. Uncle Harry was the most brave and trustful soldier to his country. He never grieved and never murmured. He was always cheerful and kind to anybody.
>
> It is very sad that the awful matter seems to close us. If anything

happens on the Ocean, it may continue 5 years or 10 years. When you grow up, come to your father's born country.

I am with you at each steps on your hard life. Remember my praying and make yourself a nice and religious woman. I believe we can meet him again in some future day ... Pray for me too. From your ever loving sis,
Cecelia.[8]

Harry was laid to rest a few days later in the Church of England section of the Northern Suburbs Cemetery in an unmarked grave, Harriet being unable to afford anything more than a few flowers. In addition to a few friends and family, also at his graveside were grey-faced men from the departments of external affairs, defence and the attorney-general.

On 4 June an obituary appeared in the Sydney papers: 'The death of H.W Freame DCM ... leaves a gap in our national life it will not be easy to fill. He died as courageously as he lived.'[9] 'Life of Thrill and Incident Comes to a Close' ran the headline of another obituary. 'Life of Incident Strange but True' was yet another. But the most touching tribute, and no doubt one that would have meant most to Harry the old soldier, was that written by his former commanding officer, FJ Kindon, published in *Reveille* on 1 July. 'He was an outstanding figure on Gallipoli,' wrote Kindon. He continued:

Associated as he was, in most of his activities with Capt. A. J. Shout, he was the ideal scout. Both his temperament and his experience (he had served in irregular wars in various places including Mexico) made him invaluable in this capacity. He could move about No-man's Land as if he were invisible; he was a marvellous revolver shot and, above all, he had that cool calm brain without which these capacities would be of little use ... He was a great soldier and a good comrade. A wonderful welcome will be his when he enters the shades of Valhalla and is greeted by the brave men who have preceded him there.[10]

Harriet Freame and her young family were left destitute. But Harry's friends and the networks that he had so skilfully cultivated while alive would not forget their old comrade or his family.

On 3 June Ernest Etheridge, honorary treasurer of the North Sydney sub-branch of the Returned Soldiers League, wrote to Frederick Stewart, minister for external affairs. Stewart had replaced Black Jack McEwen in October 1940, just as Harry was setting out for Japan. Etheridge had been one of the men to visit Freame on his deathbed. 'There are circumstances contributing to the unfortunate early death of Mr. Freame that I think may be favourably considered in the interests of the widow and children,' Etheridge wrote.[11] What Etheridge was after was a pension or gratuity that would keep a roof over the heads of Harriet, her daughter, Alison, and stepdaughter, Gracie.

A few days later on 7 June, Military Intelligence initiated efforts to obtain a copy of Harry Freame's death certificate, which had been signed off by Dr Justin Stormon. However, as the certificate had not yet been registered, their attempts were unsuccessful.

If, as he lay dying in Harriet's arms, Harry had contented himself with the thought that he had died for a grateful country that would look after his young family, he was sadly mistaken. On 23 June 1941, almost a month after the passing of Harry Freame, Military Intelligence interviewed Ernest Etheridge, seemingly at the behest of Lieutenant-Colonel Eric Longfield Lloyd. Etheridge told the investigating officer that he had been at Harry's bedside and that Harry had told him that he had been garrotted in Japan. The officer asked him, why then Freame did not report the attack. To this Etheridge responded 'that it was quite in keeping with what he knew of Freame's character. He was a man who disliked fuss, or that his oriental blood might have accounted for it'.[12]

Etheridge also related how in Japan, while an intern of St Luke's, Harry had been under the care of Japanese doctors, the American staff having been evacuated earlier. This was significant. Japanese doctors would have been reluctant to report an attempted strangulation lest they themselves come under the observation of the Kempeitai: they likely thought it best to keep this secret to themselves. Similarly, Harry would quite likely have suspected that the doctors were under the watch of the Kempeitai, and therefore would have been reluctant to make an accusation of garrotting: best wait until he was safely back in Australia.

A few days after the Etheridge interview, Military Intelligence next called in Harriet Freame and conducted an interview with her. Harriet reiterated her belief that Harry had been garrotted in Japan. She also revealed that she had been trying to sell some of Harry's clothes to make ends meet.[13] Harriet wasn't asking for a gratuity or even a pension; all she asked was that Military Intelligence help her find work as a nurse.

Interestingly the record of this interview mentions that the investigating officer had also been in contact with Dr Justin Stormon, and that as of 26 June the Department of External Affairs had called him twice to discuss Harry's death, although the record doesn't indicate what they spoke about. The investigating officer had stumbled upon the fact that External Affairs were also conducting their own discreet enquiries into Harry's death. Two separate investigations by two different government departments is surely an unusual amount of departmental interest in the death of an interpreter – but of course Harry had never been just an interpreter.

A curious thing happened between Harry's death and his burial. A curious thing that would have a lasting impact. When Dr Stormon signed Harry's death certificate, he gave as cause of death 'carcinoma of the gall bladder': gallbladder cancer. Why is this curious? First, because gallbladder cancer is extremely rare. The Australian Cancer Council defines a rare cancer as one that has an incidence rate of less than six cases in 100,000 Australians per annum. Gallbladder cancer has an incidence rate of just 1.9 cases per 100,000 people per annum. In 2022 400 people were diagnosed in Australia. So it does happen, but it is uncommon.

One way of diagnosing gallbladder cancer is through blood tests. Harry underwent a full range of blood tests in Tokyo, but no sign of cancer was found. Is it likely that just three months later the disease would claim his life?

Another curious thing: prior to his death, no diagnosis of gallbladder cancer was given to the family, and as far as we know, Harry never received this diagnosis. The first the family knew of the cancer diagnosis was when they saw it on Harry's death certificate.

Could it be that an autopsy had found a cancer that had previously gone undetected? The answer there is a definitive no, because no autopsy was performed.

A final curiosity: Harry's death certificate states that he suffered from gallbladder cancer for three months prior to his death. The medical records from both Japan and the Mater show this to be untrue.

Roger Byard, emeritus professor and a senior specialist forensic pathologist at Forensic Science South Australia, after reviewing Harry's surviving medical files, said that without an autopsy the assertion that Harry died of gallbladder cancer is 'highly conjectural'.[14]

Johan Duflou, a consulting forensic pathologist and clinical professor at the University of Sydney, also examined Harry's medical files. His expert opinion was that there was 'no convincing evidence' to support the conclusion that gallbladder cancer was the cause of death, and that attributing Harry's death to gallbladder cancer appeared 'to be not more than an educated guess, but in my view the death has absolutely not been explained'.[15] Duflou said that there did appear to be an existing condition that Harry suffered from, an 'apparent mass in the mediastinum'. He explained:

> What can happen is that a physical event can suddenly bring it to the fore, and maybe that's what happened here. In other words, this mass which also affected the nerve was damaged to some extent and in some way as a result of the garrotting, and the combined result was to cause the paralysis of the vocal cord.[16]

Managing the investigation for External Affairs in 1941 was none other than Lieutenant-Colonel Hodgson, the man who Military Intelligence suspected had leaked the nature of Harry's intelligence work in the first place. A conflict of interest? Most likely, but for now let's give Hodgson a pass.

Hodgson instructed his private secretary, R Rowe, to interview Harriet Freame on 20 June, six days before Military Intelligence would do so.

Rowe focused on the fact that Harry's death certificate was at odds with Harriet's claims about how Harry had died. After acknowledging that Harriet was a trained nurse of some standing in the Sydney nursing community, Rowe reported to Hodgson:

> She nursed her husband through his recent illness, and strongly discounts any suggestion that his death was caused by cancer. When I suggested that the medical opinion appeared to support the view that cancer was the cause of death, she said there was no conclusive evidence of this and that x-ray plates taken did not reveal any sign of cancer.[17]

Rowe then reported on his conversation with Dr Stormon, the man who signed off on Freame's death certificate:

> As advised previously, I telephoned Dr. Stormon, who treated Mr. Freame on his return to Sydney, and he stated that while no post mortem had been made to establish the cause of death, following a consultation between himself, Dr. L. Dunlop and Dr. Stuart Allen, of Macquarie Street, Sydney, it was concluded that cancer was the cause of death, and this was accordingly stated on the death certificate.[18]

Stormon doesn't elaborate on how the three doctors came to this conclusion in the absence of an autopsy. But without an autopsy, the assertion that Harry died of gallbladder cancer was dubious, and Stormon knew as much. 'I have had a further telephone conversation with Dr. Stormon,' Rowe reported. 'He expressed some regret that a postmortem was not held, but re-affirms that Drs. Stuart Allen, Dunlop and himself were satisfied that the cause of death was carcinoma of the gall bladder.'[19]

Rowe then went on to report:

> In reply to a question by me, Dr. Stormon stated that Mr. Freame had almost completely lost his voice, his throat condition was such that, in his, Dr. Stormon's opinion, it could have been caused by attempted strangulation; and further, if strangulation had been attempted to a serious degree, the resultant injury to the throat and organs could reasonably be considered to have hastened Freame's death. Incidentally, he mentioned that soon after his return from Japan, Mr. Freame was examined by Dr. R.J. Murphy, throat specialist of Macquarie Street, who was 'unable to connect Freame's throat condition with cancer'.[20]

Here we have the consulting doctor's opinion that Harry suffered from an injury to the throat, consistent with attempted strangulation that was unconnected to cancer and that this had hastened Freame's death. It seemed conclusive. But it wasn't.

On 3 July External Affairs sent a telegram to Sir John Latham in Tokyo, requesting more information on Freame's time in Japan:

Death certificate Freame states cause of death was cancer but widow and family insist owing to nature of throat injury that he was garrotted in Japan, quoting in support statement of Freame that 'they got me.' Have you any information which might indicate that he probably attacked. Widow left destitute and we are confronted with question as to whether contributing factor in death was his service in Japan involving moral obligation to offer some compensation.[21]

And here we now approach the reason behind the external affairs department's investigation: liability and, by extension, compensation. In short, money.

Latham was quick to respond. 'Freame began to show symptoms of illness soon after arrival and illness gradually increased. He never suggested to staff and to doctors that he had been attacked by anybody.'[22]

By early July, the government had still not provided any support to Harriet Freame and Harry's family. But Freame's friends would not let the matter rest. On 10 July member of Federal Parliament Charles Morgan, prompted by a letter from Charles Donnelly, who had worked with Harry at Censorship, wrote to Frederick Stewart, minister for external affairs, again raising the suspicious nature of Harry's throat injury 'contracted in the course of his official duties'[23] and pleading for government assistance to be provided to Harriet and the younger children (Young Harry was about twenty by now). Stewart was quick to reply that he had the Freame case in hand and assured Morgan that 'the most sympathetic consideration possible'[24] would be extended to Harriet.

At the same time, the minister for home security, Joseph Abbott, was also being lobbied by the Uralla sub-branch of the Returned Soldiers League, Harry's home league.

Abbott immediately took up Harry's cause and wrote to the Prime Minister's Department. 'Sgt. Freame was a man who rendered very distinguished service in the last war,' Abbott wrote. 'He was again serving his country in this war in the capacity of interpreter to the Australian Minister ... I would appreciate it very much if this case could be investigated, and if possible a pension or compassionate grant made to the late Sgt. Freame's widow.'[25]

Having realised that the Harry Freame issue was not going to go away quietly, Lieutenant-Colonel Hodgson of External Affairs started to apply pressure to the slow-turning wheels of bureaucracy. His dilemma was how to make a payment to Mrs Freame without the government admitting any liability in Harry's untimely death. It was an issue that would occupy Hodgson, External Affairs, the Prime Minister's Department and the Attorney-General's Department for the better part of the next three months. Again, a lot of ministerial attention for an interpreter supposedly struck down by cancer.

On 21 July the Attorney-General's Department provided a reply to Hodgson, advising him on how to proceed: 'There appears to be no legal liability on the Commonwealth to Mrs. Freame in respect of the death of her late husband,' the internal memo begins.[26] This opinion must have been based on the investigation carried out by Hodgson, after the interviews with Mrs Freame and Dr Stormon conducted by Hodgson's personal secretary.

The memo then helpfully provides the wording that could be used to pay off Mrs. Freame and avoid any liability for Harry's death:

To amount paid to me by the Commonwealth of Australia as an act of grace and without in any way admitting any liability so to do as a solatium for the death of my husband, Henry Wykeham Freame [*sic* – this should be Wykeham Henry Freame] who died on the 27th May 1941 while in the employ of the Commonwealth. £50.[27]

Solatium. It's a word you don't hear very often, but it means a consolation. A consolation of £50 for a dead husband. Of course £50 doesn't sound like much these days, but it wasn't much in 1941 either.

Happy with this elegant, if miserly, solution, Hodgson drafted a paper for his minister to approve the payment. Hodgson helpfully set out the particulars for the case:

Mr. Freame while in Japan, developed an illness necessitating his return to Australia. It is understood that his widow has been left practically destitute. Although a suggestion that Mr. Freame's illness might possibly have been due to garrotting in Japan based upon the opinion of Mrs Freame, who was a trained nurse, and a statement by Mr. Freame that 'they got me', was not borne out by the medical evidence or by enquiries made at the Legation in Tokyo, it is felt that having regard to the fact that before his engagement Mr. Freame was assisting the department of the Army in security matters and had been under severe strain, some ex-gratia payment might be made to Mrs Freame in all the circumstances.[28]

Hodgson here appears to be fudging the medical evidence of Dr Stormon. No mention is made of Stormon's concerns around the lack of autopsy or Stormon's comment that Freame's throat condition 'could have been caused by attempted strangulation; and further, if strangulation had been attempted to a serious degree, the resultant injury to the throat and organs could reasonably be considered to have hastened Freame's death.' Nor is any mention made of the fact that the severe stress Freame was under prior to his departure to Japan was caused directly by the leaking of his name as a secret agent to the local press by government officials.

Of course attempting to get at the truth was no longer the aim of the process, if it ever had been. The true aim was made clear by Minister Stewart's scrawled handwritten note at the bottom of Hodgson's paper: 'Approved subject to full discharge of Commonwealth liability being obtained.'[29]

~

During his final days, Harry wrote a moving farewell to Lieutenant-Colonel Longfield Lloyd, his old comrade from the 1st Battalion. In one of the last surviving photos of Harry, he is pictured with Longfield Lloyd, strolling the streets of Sydney on Anzac Day 1940. Both men wear suits and hats. Harry carries a rolled-up newspaper in his left hand. Two old soldiers reminiscing, yes, but no doubt also discussing the new war.

After Harry's death Longfield Lloyd wrote a letter of condolence to Harriet. We do not have that correspondence, but we do have Harriet's reply. Of Harry's death Harriet wrote:

> It was indeed dreadful. I would love to be able to tell you all about it. I know it was as you say, but I don't know if Sir John Latham is even aware, for Harry would probably not to worry him, try to

attribute it to other causes ... he was so shadowed here and then after those silly people of the *Sun* office printing that about him, we were horrified at the time.[30]

After detailing her personal situation, Harriet ends her letter by telling Longfield Lloyd, 'It was leaving myself and little girl and the two at Armidale so destitute that worried Harry so. I am sorry to tell all this but it is what he went through.'[31]

Though Longfield Lloyd's original letter to Harriet is lost to history, we can safely infer from Harriet's reply – in particular her line 'I know it was as you say' – that Longfield Lloyd also believed that Harry had been garrotted by Japanese agents in Tokyo. Unfortunately nobody else in the corridors of powers would countenance this possibility. In death, the most trusted scout at Gallipoli would not be believed.

At some point in July 1941, Lieutenant-Colonel Longfield Lloyd finished his investigation into the death of his old comrade. He sent his findings directly to the Department of External Affairs. The report, labelled 'Secret', is dated only as July, so it is unclear if Lieutenant-Colonel Hodgson was in receipt of Longfield Lloyd's report before he wrote his paper for Minister Stewart. None of the information contained in Longfield Lloyd's report is evident in Hodgson's report, which suggests he did not receive it until after he made his own report. Perhaps he rushed the job for some reason, or maybe he did write it after he had received Longfield Lloyd's findings but chose not to include them, indicating something more nefarious.

One of the key concerns in Harry's story is why he did not tell anybody in Japan of the attack. Longfield Lloyd leads his report by addressing this mystery: 'knowing the late Mr. Freame's reserved nature and his intense pride in his ability to take care of himself, combined with certain characteristics attributable to Japanese blood strain, he would not have mentioned any such incident to the legation and that, in any case, if it had been evidenced in the medical sense, a Japanese-staffed hospital (in which he was, it seems, a patient) would not have disclosed it, out of fear of reprisals by the Japanese authorities.'[32]

Longfield Lloyd is correct in saying that not reporting the attack is entirely consistent with Harry's character. There are echoes in this incident of another event from Harry's past: his capture and subsequent escape from Turkish troops during the fighting at Gallipoli.

In 1958 Charles Bean was preparing to write about the life and service of Harry Freame. During his research Bean received a copy of the 1931 issue of *Reveille* that featured Harry Freame as one of the celebrities of the AIF. Bean was astounded to read the story of Harry Freame's sojourn behind enemy lines, his capture and remarkable escape. Bean had never heard the story. It is strange that it wasn't until 1958 that Bean first read of this incident. The first newspaper report of Freame's capture and escape was published in 1916, the story told not by Freame but by a soldier who had been with Freame in hospital in London.

Upon learning of the story, Bean immediately set out to confirm it, writing to his two lifelong collaborators, Johnnie Balfour and Arthur Bazley, who had both contributed articles to *Reveille* in the past. Bazley informed Bean that he had met Freame a few times and at one point had questioned him about the escape because 'the exploit did not appear in your second volume. I think he told me that the story was true, but I wondered why, and I still wonder, how it was that he did not tell you about it at Anzac, or that Shout did not mention it.'[33]

For his part Johnnie Balfour also remembered meeting Freame on two occasions and, though he had not heard the story of the escape from Turkish troops, he did confirm that Freame carried a pistol under his armpit and remembered Freame telling him that 'he never fired at a Turkish head – rather at the buttons of his tunic, two or three from the stomach to chest'.[34]

Bean never did get around to publishing anything on Harry Freame, but his private letters reveal what he made of Harry and his story. 'I never knew Freame to tell me anything which, so far as I could check it, was not literally true,' Bean recorded in his private papers. And to Johnnie Balfour, Bean wrote:

> The incident was never mentioned to me, but of course it may have happened before the main events of which he spoke to me. If it came from a reliable source I have little doubt that it was true, for I never knew Freame to exaggerate – at least as far as I could judge of his statements.[35]

It is no surprise that Freame didn't mention this exploit to Bean or his commanding officers at Gallipoli, just as it is no surprise that he did not mention the attack he suffered in Japan to John Latham. Freame was even reluctant to tell his wife Harriet what happened to him. Longfield Lloyd is closest to the reason why, when he speaks in outdated terms of something in Freame 'attributable to Japanese blood strain'. Not blood, but education. Harry was raised and educated in the Bushido code, and this learning never left him.

Deathbed Whispers

Honour is a key tenet of the Bushido code, and the flipside of honour is shame. This concept is embedded in the young Japanese samurai from the earliest age, as Inazō Nitobe explains:

> A good name – one's reputation, the immortal part of one's self ... any infringement upon its integrity was felt as shame, and the sense of shame (*Ren-chi-shin*) was one of the earliest to be cherished in juvenile education. 'You will be laughed at,' 'It will disgrace you,' 'Are you not ashamed?' were the last appeal to correct behavior on the part of a youthful delinquent. Such a recourse to his honor touched the most sensitive spot in the child's heart, as though it had been nursed on honor while it was in its mother's womb.[36]

For Harry, capture by the enemy, or being attacked and bested by the enemy, was not a war story to be shared with an inquisitive journalist or even reported to your commanding officers. It was an event that infringed Harry's honour, as a man who took great pride in his soldiering, in 'his ability to take care of himself' as Longfield Lloyd wrote. Being subject to attack or capture was a great shame for Harry.

But to return to Lieutenant-Colonel Longfield Lloyd's secret report on the death of Harry Freame in the winter of 1941, he continues:

> Further it was to be gathered from other remarks within the late Mr. Freame's family circle, that they had felt misgiving by reason of some newspaper remark about his reported activities in Australia prior to departure whereby Japanese attention might

have been attracted to him in a hostile fashion.

Any such assumption by those close to him, upon the premises indicated in paragraph 2 above [the garrotting], possibly could find a parallel in happenings which have by no means been unknown in Japan, since there has long existed there a category of persons who bear the cognomen 'Garotsuki' – and the dying man's own reported words were strongly suggestive of injury received perhaps in that way.[37]

Longfield Lloyd completes his report by suggesting that:

The possibility of Mr. Freame having received injury in Japan is not a remote one – and it has often been considered significant, through many years past, that more than a few people who have served there in varying official capacities, have shown strange deteriorations in health, some even with quite noticeable rapidity and in the face of previous medical history of perfect condition.

Whatever the original or contributing cause of the loss of one who was a very gallant soldier in war and who must have been a devoted member of the Australian Legation establishment, the case of those who were dependent upon the late Mr. Freame is one which, I sincerely suggest, calls for the best consideration.[38]

In the mealy-mouthed wording typical of bureaucracy, then and now, Longfield Lloyd's report is supportive overall of the case that Harry was garrotted in Japan. Of all the people involved at the time, Longfield Lloyd may have been best placed to judge the case. He knew Freame personally and he had also served in Japan for five years. He was familiar with the cut and thrust of intelligence work. Regardless, Longfield Lloyd's report was never to see the light of day, just another testament to wasted bureaucratic energies, a yellowing paper lying in the National Archives.

Because by the time Longfield Lloyd made his report, Treasury had already arrived at its decision. Harriet Freame was to get £50 to compensate for the death of her husband. But of course, only if she agreed to indemnify the Commonwealth of any liability.

When the minister for home security found out about the payment, he immediately wrote to his counterpart at External Affairs:

> It seems to me, in view as I am informed of the very difficult position in which the late Sergeant's widow was left that 50 pounds is a very small amount to grant her ... I am writing to you, therefore, to ask would it be possible to have this amount of 50 pounds increased to what I would think was a more adequate sum, at the very least 100 pounds. I must say that I had in my mind in the beginning an amount of somewhere about 200 pounds.[39]

After receiving Abbott's request, the minister for external affairs relayed it to Treasury. On 14 October 1941 the Department of the Treasury advised 'that after full consideration, the Minister is of the opinion that payment of any further amount cannot be justified in the absence of any new factors supporting the request'.[40]

Fifty pounds. For giving your life for your country. In comparison, the widow of James Melville Cox – the Reuters correspondent and British spy who the Kempeitai threw from a fourth-storey window in Tokyo – received £5000 from the British Government.

It might be tempting to think that Harry's treatment was due to the colour of his skin, the intonation of his speech, his Japanese birth. But a story from 1946, five years after Harry's murder and a year after the war had finished, points to a different theory, one that paints the Commonwealth as nothing more than miserly bean counters.

It is the story of Norman Wootton, described as a 'likeable and overloaded Commercial Secretary and Assistant Trade Commissioner'.[41] Wootton was also a part-time spy for Australian intelligence. In 1942 he was based in Singapore. As the Japanese closed in, he set about helping expatriate Australians find a way out of Singapore and back to the safety of Australia. He himself did not manage to leave and was captured by the Japanese. Wootton spent three years as a prisoner of war. During his internment he sold a few personal items to purchase extra food. He also borrowed money, signing postwar promissory notes. He was recorded as saying 'only those who borrowed survived'.[42]

Wootton survived his internment, and when he returned to Australia he put in a claim for entertainment and living allowances for the period 1942 to 1945 in an effort to pay back the money he had borrowed to survive. The claim was compliant with his salary entitlement. After ten months of deliberation, Treasury provided their response: 'It seems clear that the officers who were detained by the enemy were not involved in expenses overseas during the period of detention.'[43]

Among Harry Freame's surviving papers there is one very interesting sheet of lined paper. It seems to have been torn from an exercise book.

Deathbed Whispers

What came before it and what comes after it is unknown, but what is there is a word for word copy, written out in Harry's unique hand, of a passage from a book titled *Strange Intelligence: Memoirs of Naval Secret Service*:

> the work itself was thankless, perilous and distinctly unremunerative, and those engaged in it too often found themselves caught in a web of intrigue and misunderstanding that has outlasted the war, and from which some may never hope to escape. It is safe to say that none of the survivors would ever dream of taking up Intelligence work again, under any consideration whatsoever. The romantic associations of secret service exist largely in the imagination of writers who have had no experience of the real thing.
>
> For reasons that to me are inexplicable, intelligence work, however hazardous it might be, and however valuable the results, was never sufficiently recognised by our home authorities as deserving of reward. It may be that this pointed neglect is due to an inherent prejudice against the whole business of espionage. If that be the attitude of the authorities, it is both illogical and unfair, in the view of the fact already stated that ...[44]

The words must have resonated deeply for Harry as his hand moved across the page, copying them into his exercise book. He knew firsthand the 'perilous and distinctly unremunerative' nature of intelligence work. He had experienced the ignominy of having his service go unrewarded and unrecognised. Reading this note, it is easy to speculate that at the end of a life of service, these words gave voice to a deep regret that Harry felt at the illogical and unfair treatment he had received from his country in return for a life of dedicated service. Harry Freame knew how he died. I am not sure he ever knew what he died *for*.

Chapter 14

Young Harry

As Harry lay choking on his own mucus, maybe he gained a modicum of solace knowing that at least Young Harry had the farm at Kentucky, the piece of land that Harry had spent twenty years trying to improve, trying to make it yield something approaching a living. But if he did console himself with that thought, once again Harry would be let down in death as he had been so often in life.

On 10 October 1941 the secretary for lands confiscated the full 43 acres of Harry's farm at Kentucky. The public humiliation in the paper read, 'Reason for forfeiture, non-payment of instalments of purchase money'.[1] No consideration was given to the fact that Harry had been dead for five months. Perhaps it says something about the priorities of bureaucracies that the government was able to take back 43 acres of unproductive land faster than it took to pay Harry's widow £50.

Young Harry was working on the farm at the time. Such was the shame he felt that he never told his stepmother or Gracie what had happened. Here you can see shadows of his father in Young Harry: not wanting to worry others, not wanting to bring shame to the family. Gracie would not learn that the family farm had been confiscated until many years later, when she turned twenty-one and attempted to claim the land as her own.

Having given up his career and studies in Sydney to return to the farm to help his father following Edith May's death, Young Harry was now at a loose end. But there was a war on, and if there was one thing the Freame men knew how to do, it was to fight. And Young Harry had a better reason than most for fighting the Japanese. Unlike the Commonwealth Government, Young Harry was convinced that the Japanese had killed his father. So on 31 October 1941, twenty days after his farm was confiscated, he enlisted in the Australian Army.

In a letter to his uncles and aunties in England, Harry would later write:

> I don't know whether I mentioned it in the graph or not, but as well as being in the AIF, I am also a permanent soldier as I chose to make it my profession. I did my course through the Royal Military College Duntroon, which is the equivalent of Britain's Sandhurst and am now a member of the Australian Staff Corps.[2]

Here Young Harry is being a bit modest. Nicknamed 'Maori' because of his olive skin and dashing looks, he excelled at Duntroon, winning the King's Medal, which is awarded to the cadet that tops their class academically. On the sporting field, whether it be cricket or rugby, he was an unstoppable force. A rugby match report from May 1943 described Freame 'as one of the best college centres for years'.[3] In July Freame set the Royal Military College try-scoring record against the RAAF School of Technical Training, crossing the line seven times. The newspapers described him as 'big, well-built, fast and has a strong fend'.[4]

But whatever sporting future Freame had ahead of him would have to wait, for now his mind was set on army life. As he wrote of the army to his relatives in England, 'I like the life – perhaps it is in the blood Dad was pretty keen on the army.' He then writes of his father:

> To give you the details of Dad's death – after mother died dad once again entered the army in the Intelligence Corps and held a captain's rank. When the Australian Government decided to send a Minister to Japan, Dad was transferred to the Diplomatic Corps ostensibly as an interpreter for the Minister. He was the first to arrive in Japan and hired the servants, fixed up offices and quarters etc ready for the Minister's arrival. He spent about five months there doing intelligence work, but unfortunately, through a mistake on somebody's part before he left Australia, the Japanese were able to guess this was what he really went to Japan for and they kept a very close watch on him ... We have reason to believe his death was not natural as he came home a broken man, and as he told me, so that he would be at home to die. However, the Japs are now paying in kind and reaping what they sowed.[5]

In another letter to relatives, Young Harry wrote that his father was 'officially sent as an interpreter to Latham but was really in an intelligence role'. Writing of the leaking of Harry's identity, Young Harry wrote, 'Dad said before he went that it would cause him a lot of trouble but he still went. He was under very strict surveillance by the Japanese intelligence people from the time he landed.'[6] Of his father's death, Harry writes,

'Of course nothing could be done about it at the time but they shall be paid back in kind.'⁷ He is speaking here of the Japanese, whom he held responsible – and he would soon confront Japanese soldiers in the jungles of Borneo.

After graduating in April 1944, Young Harry was keen for action. He was made a lieutenant and attached to the 2/24th Battalion. Freame was present when the battalion landed on Tarakan on 1 May 1945, a reserve force for the 2/48th and 2/23rd battalions, part of Operation Oboe, which had as its objective the retaking of Borneo from the Japanese.

After a successful landing, on 2 May Young Harry and the 2/24th were ordered to push forward and capture the airfield. Intense fighting ensued, with the Japanese holding onto heavily fortified defences. One Japanese position, an impregnable pillbox nicknamed Wills, was holding up the advance. The pillbox was dug into the ground with Japanese troops firing from the loopholes on the advancing Australians. Some Australian troops got close enough to lob grenades through the open slits, but the Japanese soldiers simply threw them back out. Unable to move forward until the position was cleared of enemy forces, the battalion called up a flamethrower, and when it arrived Young Harry took hold of it. What he had in mind was to pay the Japanese back in kind for the death of his father.

Covered by small arms fire, he moved out into the open and then jumped on top of the pillbox. Waiting for his moment, he leapt down and aimed a squirt of flame deep into the pillbox. The screams of the incinerated Japanese soldiers could be heard coming from deep within the bowels of the pillbox, the stench of their burning flesh filling the air. Freame waited a moment and then sent another deadly spurt into the

Japanese position. An explosion followed as ammunition supplies held within the pillbox detonated.

Young Harry scrambled to safety. The pillbox burned for four days. It was Harry's first taste of combat and his coolness and courage under fire did not go unnoticed. His commanding officer described his action as 'one of the riskiest pieces of work I've ever seen' and 'one of the finest in the Division's history'.[8] High praise considering the 2/24th had also fought at Tobruk.

Back home in Australia, Gracie's thoughts were often with her older brother. For one so young she had suffered terrible losses in her life. At twelve she had lost her stepmother, and then two years later, at fourteen, her beloved father. Gracie had had a hard time since. She had spent time at an Armidale boarding school for girls but had run away three times. When Young Harry enlisted, he gave as his next of kin Josephine Grace Freame.

By 1945, when Harry was proving himself in battle in faraway Tarakan, Gracie was living in Sydney and working at the Martin Place office of Blue Metal and Gravel, the Kiama-based quarry company. On 6 April, while on holiday in Newcastle, Gracie sent a six-page letter to Harry. She told him of her lunches with friends from the office and games of tennis on the weekends at Cremorne. She had been to see *For Whom the Bell Tolls* for a second time and enjoyed it greatly. Somewhat portentously she wrote, 'I will have to go to the dentist soon, my teeth are aching sometimes lately.'[9]

But like many young Australians, Gracie's mind was occupied by thoughts of when the war might be over. Berlin had fallen in Europe, a feat celebrated with the ringing of church bells in Australia, but for Gracie the war would not be over until the young Australians fighting in the north, her brother included, were all safely back home. Then it would be time to celebrate. US President Roosevelt had not long died, and Gracie reflected on how unfair it was that he died so close to the end of the war. 'I suppose if he had died earlier it would have been worse when the war was at its peak but still with the end approaching it's a pity he didn't see his goal.'[10]

Gracie finished her letter: 'Well Harry, I shall have to close now and get ready to go to Church. I hope you are keeping well and looking after yourself and will write later again. Lots and lots and lots of love. Grace.'[11]

A month later, on 12 May, Gracie received a reply by telegram:

> It is with deep regret that I have to inform you that NX177991 Lieutenant Henry Wykeham Freame was killed in action on 8th May 1945 and desire to convey to you the profound sympathy of the Minister for the Army – Minister for the Army.[12]

After clearing the pillbox on 5 May, Harry's 2/24th Battalion had continued inland, but Young Harry had not. On 7 May, suffering from an abscess in his tooth, Harry was medically evacuated from the front and sent back to the military hospital for dental treatment. The war diary of the 2/24th Battalion coldly records what happened. 'Lt. Freame who was evacuated to hospital the day before was killed this morning by enemy action. The enemy had infiltrated to the CCS [Casualty Clearing Station] area and threw a fuzed 75mm shell.'[13]

Harry Freame died on 8 May, the day the Allies declared victory in Europe. But Europe was a long way from the blood and jungle of Tarakan.

Later, at a ceremony at Armidale High School to honour alumni who had fallen in World War II, Young Harry was singled out for special attention. Gracie summed up the eulogy later in a letter: 'Harry Freame had served his country with distinction and gave his life in the cause. Who knows what, in another time free from war, Harry Freame might have become?'[14]

Chapter 15

A Hero Forgotten

The years passed. Those who remained grew old. But for Harriet Freame it was hard to let go of the way her country had treated her husband. In December 1963, more than two decades after Harry Freame's death, Harriet took up her pen and wrote directly to the prime minister of Australia, Robert Menzies.

The letter is a long, rambling affair, roving from one thought to the next, but her account of the events leading up to Harry's death had not changed in twenty years. She told Menzies how her husband had come home from Japan a broken man, barely able to walk off the ship. She described how Harry's 'throat was twisted and food went down the windpipe instead of the gullet'. And she wrote of her undying conviction that Harry had been garrotted in Japan:

> It was generally supposed by the staff and friends that his was a natural illness. It was not so and I have proof. Five people in my presence asked him what happened on the 27th. January, 1941. He said he had been garrotted ... asked why he had not told Sir John Latham, he said – if he had known 'he would have got the

wind up', his words, and been in danger, which situation was bad enough at the time.¹

Harriet had no doubt what the root cause of the trouble had been. 'You see,' she wrote, 'he was on the intelligence staff, just prior to his Japan trip, and was in a very dangerous position.'²

In support of her argument, a few days later Harriet also forwarded to Menzies a handwritten letter from Mr HA Jenkins, one of the five witnesses who had been at Harry's bedside. Jenkins wrote:

> I have no hesitation in stating that what she [Harriet Freame] has written to you about her late husband Henry Wykeham Freame [*sic*] after his return from Japan on Good Friday 1941 from service in the Intelligence Dept of Australia. His manner at the Mater Hospital North Sydney when I called to visit him he could not speak distinctly, his voice very weak and throat twisted. I knew him personally before he went to Japan and thought highly of him. He did give me to understand that in Japan he was garrotted.³

Harriet had just one request of Menzies:

> I think my husband died for his country just as surely as he could have in his career of the first war ... I would like a headstone on his grave at Northern Suburbs. It has taken every effort to keep going by me so have had no money for fares, flowers etc so it has been sorely neglected.⁴

In a postscript she adds, 'I wish to inform you that I have not had one penny from the Intelligence Dept or any other Government Department on account of his death, and I think that the least that could be done for his memory would be a decent grave and headstone.'[5]

The Prime Minister's Department responded in April 1964:

> Enquiries have disclosed that the late Henry Wykeham Freame Snr. [sic] was engaged as Interpreter, Translator and Controller for the Australian Legation at Tokyo, from 26th September, 1940 and that he had previously been employed by the Defence Department on work connected with Intelligence, Censorship and Translation of Japanese.[6]

The letter then goes on to recount how Harry was sent home from Japan after:

> his condition was diagnosed as paralysis of the vocal chords [sic] ... He died in Sydney on 27th May, 1941, and the death certificate showed 'Carcinoma of the Gall Bladder' as the cause of death.
>
> A Repatriation Board and the Repatriation Commission have each decided after carefully considering all the evidence, that the cause of his death was not due to his war service. The Commonwealth War Graves Commission may only provide a headstone for the grave of an ex-serviceman whose death has been accepted as due to war service ... The Commission may also erect a 'non-war grave' headstone over the grave of a person who was attached to the Armed Forces of any Member country of the

British Commonwealth of Nations during the 1939–1945 War.

In the circumstances, I regret to inform you that a headstone may not be erected over the grave of your late husband at the Commonwealth's expense.[7]

In a fine example of bureaucratic pettiness, the letter ended with 'You mentioned that you had not received compensation from any government department on account of the late Mr. Freame's death. You may not have remembered that you received a special payment of 50 pounds on 13th October, 1941.'[8]

In fact there is room to doubt that Harriet had even received this meagre amount. On the relevant file regarding payment to Harriet Freame, there is a hand-scrawled note admitting that it was possible that after Treasury refused the request for the payment to be increased to £100, the file had simply died. There is a reference to a receipt in the file but not the receipt itself.

This new rebuff must have been a bitter blow for Harriet.

Previously unseen archives that I accessed as part of my research for this book show that the Repatriation Commission's investigation was flawed from the beginning. Harriet Freame had written to Menzies insisting that Harry did not die of gallbladder cancer. She claimed his death was from a garrotting that occurred during the course of his intelligence work. The Repatriation Commission did not investigate whether Harry really did die of gallbladder cancer; they investigated whether or not gallbladder cancer could be linked to Harry's war service. The question should not have been whether the cancer was linked to war service; it should have been whether Harry even had cancer. But this was never looked at.

Further complicating the Repatriation Commission's investigation was advice received from the defence department stating that Harry 'was not employed as a soldier during the Second War, either with Intelligence or elsewhere'.[9]

There is so much evidence, so many internal documents from government files, that clearly shows that Harry Freame was employed in the intelligence services during World War II that I can only conclude that by 1964 the Australian Government was attempting to cover up the circumstances surrounding the death of Harry Freame.

What did the government have to fear?

In 1935 an Australian man, James Mackenzie, working in Korea, was detained by the Japanese Kempeitai. He was charged with spying after the Kempeitai found photos in his possession. A confession was forced from him, and the Japanese newspapers gleefully reported the capture of an international spy. Mackenzie was no spy; he was a seventy-year-old reverend who worked as a Presbyterian missionary. In a diplomatic note advising of the incident, the British Government stated that at the time the Kempeitai was 'unfortunately independent of civil government and … very much a law unto itself'.[10]

Fuelled by what many in Japan saw as the West's refusal to allow Japan a seat at the international table as an equal, militarism in Japan increased during the second half of the 1930s. And as militarism increased, so did the strength and power of the Kempeitai.

The Australian Government was aware of how the increasingly uncontrollable Japanese military establishment were dealing with international spies. They had seen how James Cox had been dealt with: an open window and a four-storey drop.

By October 1940 when Harry set sail for Tokyo, Japan had already signed the Tripartite Pact, or Berlin Pact as it was sometimes known, a military alliance with Germany and Italy, with whom Australia was at war. The Australian Government was, for all intents and purposes, sending Harry Freame, a publicly exposed undercover agent, behind enemy lines.

This was of course a familiar experience for Harry – he had made his name sneaking around behind enemy lines. He knew the dangers. But this time it was different, because this time his name had been leaked by the Australian Government. His role in special defence work was widely circulated before his departure. He was followed in Sydney by Japanese agents. Not only was Harry's name leaked, but Australian officials even raised it directly with Japanese intelligence agents at the Japanese consul in Australia before he left.

Of course the consulate would have been delighted with Harry's appointment. They must not have been able to believe their luck. Here was the Australian Government coming to them and asking what they thought of sending to Japan a man who had been outed as an undercover agent. It beggars belief. Did the Australian Government really believe that Harry's official role as interpreter would provide him any protection? That the Japanese, who had declared their intent to pursue foreign spies and any Japanese who helped them, would pose no threat to Harry?

In denying Harry a war grave, the government hid behind the fact that he was officially employed as an interpreter. There can be no doubt, as evidenced by the testimonies of Harry's family and friends, that Harry was employed in an intelligence role in Japan, under the cover of being an interpreter. It was common to embed spies in Australia's overseas missions. As far back as 1916 New South Wales's commercial commissioner in

Kobe, John Suttor, was providing intelligence and conducting clandestine activities in Japan on behalf of Edmund Piesse.[11] Eric Longfield Lloyd was another who had filled the dual role of diplomat and spy, as was the ill-fated Norman Wootton in Singapore. The practice of blurring the lines between diplomats and trade commissioners and spies is still common today.

Whatever state of advanced naivety afflicted the Australian officials before Harry's departure, once he had returned to Australia to die, they must have been crystal clear about their role and liability in his attack and imminent death. How else to explain the extreme interest in Harry's death in the weeks following his demise? Public servants from the intelligence agencies and External Affairs were calling Freame's doctors, attempting to attain a death certificate. Were they attempting to change the doctor's opinion? Were they pushing for a cause of death that was not strangulation? Something hard to prove? Something uncommon? Gallbladder cancer, for example? The doctors themselves expressed concern at a lack of autopsy, but nobody gave a reason as to why no autopsy was performed. Was there an official interest in not wanting to know how Harry Freame really died?

And why were the Prime Minister's Department and the Attorney-General's Department so concerned with the death of a sixty-year-old interpreter twenty years after the event if it was really from natural causes?

Why wasn't Harry's version of his own death believed? There can only be one conclusion. The Australian Government sent Harry Freame to a near-certain death and then covered up their role in it.

At the headquarters of the US Central Intelligence Agency in Langley, Virginia, a star is placed on the Memorial Wall every time a

US intelligence agent is killed in the line of duty. The wall holds 140 stars. As academic Bruce Bennet notes, 'Australia has almost no record of honouring, or even remembering its secret agents.'[12]

Harry Freame was the first Australian intelligence agent to lose his life while serving the nation. Harry didn't get a star. He didn't even get a headstone.

Chapter 16

Answers in the Archives

In chasing answers to why Harry Freame's heroic role at Gallipoli has been forgotten – and why the government was unwilling to acknowledge that his life ended in the service of his country as a spy, I found that there was much to be learnt from the archives.

Harry Freame left behind a treasure trove of personal possessions: seaman's logbooks, Spanish and French dictionaries, a lapel pin of Inca design, Freemasonry labels and badges sent from his grandmother to his father in Tokyo in the 1800s, letters of recommendation from generals and commanders of the Anzac troops, Harry's letters to his wife Edith May, a souvenir bullet attached to a tiny echidna engraved with the word 'Dardanelles'. There is Harry's address book from his time as an Australian spy in Sydney, his diplomatic passport and his business card: 'Mr. H. W. Freame, Attache'. Clear plastic folders hold family photos – some from Japan, others from Harry's seafaring days. There is one of Harry in uniform standing out the front of the hospital where he had recovered in London, at ease among Australian soldiers who all wear the look of young men who have seen enough of war. Another black-and-white photo shows a small monkey clinging to a human hand. On the back are written the words 'Harry's Marmoset'.

There are Harry's final letters to his daughter, Gracie, written from his sickbed in St Luke's Hospital, asking his young daughter what she would like him to bring her from his trip to Japan.

I wanted to understand why Harry Freame sailed for Japan as an undercover agent after his cover had been blown in Sydney. Even before leaving he was being tailed by Japanese agents in Sydney, and he expressed concern to those closest to him about the leaking of his name by the press. Yet still he went. Why?

Harry's possessions offer a possible explanation. They reveal a man who absorbed an identity at Anzac, that of the Australian digger, but also a man who never renounced his Japanese identity. Among his belongings there are a large Japanese print of a tiger stalking through bamboo, ornamental boxes engraved with Japanese characters, photos of Harry's mother and sister in Japanese kimonos, and Harry's own kimono, bright orange and green, a flash of colour and Japanese elegance. He harboured his Japanese identity, nurtured it, hid it when he felt he had to, but always maintained it, even if secretly. It must have been difficult at times for Harry to carry within himself two identities that in the wider world were in constant and outright conflict with each other. To be Harry Freame, the Anzac digger, born in Japan, living in a country that excluded men who looked and spoke just like him. Could it be that when he was appointed interpreter to the Tokyo legation, he saw an opportunity for his first identity, that of a man born in Japan, to be valued in its own right at last? *The Bulletin* described the appointment as a 'link in friendly relations'.[1] A similar tone was struck by Johnnie Balfour, replying to Charles Bean's letter in 1959. After bumping into him before he left for Japan, Balfour writes that Harry 'was looking forward to his projected stay in Japan with great keenness and felt that he could be of some help to Latham in guiding him in the way he should deal with Japanese officials'.[2]

Did Harry see his role as one of peacemaker between Japan and Australia? A position in which he could influence Australia's engagement with Japan even at this late stage, with war all but inevitable? In striving for friendly relations between Australia and Japan, did he see a potential healing of an internal conflict that he had carried within himself for twenty-five years? It's certainly possible. But his decision may also have been driven less by internal idealism and more by external pragmatism.

By the late 1930s Australian intelligence agencies were already keeping lists of Japanese citizens in Australia. At the outbreak of war these would be the first people rounded up and interned. As we have seen, in September 1940, a month before leaving for Japan, Harry himself was denounced by an overzealous neighbour as a Japanese fifth columnist. Did Harry fear arrest if war with Japan did start? At the time the thinking in government and intelligence circles was that Japanese citizens could not be trusted, no matter how long they had lived in Australia, that their loyalty was solely to Japan. Indeed in January 1942 Young Harry Freame would come to the attention of Uralla police as a possible Japanese sympathiser.

Did Harry feel the need to prove again his loyalty to his adopted country? Did he feel that no matter what he had done in the past, it was never enough, was never going to be enough to counter suspicions about people from his birthplace? Did Harry feel that suspicious eyes were falling on him and the only way to dispel any shadow of doubt about where his loyalties lay was to once again venture into the dangers of no-man's-land? To win the trust of those who wouldn't or couldn't do what he himself was prepared to do? It is possible. But I think Harry had enough friends in high places, including the intelligence services, to keep him out of the sights of those who wished to lock up every Japanese citizen in Australia.

There is a temptation to attribute Harry's actions to what Longfield Lloyd would refer to as Harry's Japanese 'blood strain': what he really meant was his Japanese upbringing, his education in the Bushido code. It's a romantic picture: the Japanese warrior, loyal to his master, returning to certain death. That Harry was returning to his country of birth only adds to the poignancy.

But in returning to Japan, Harry's actions were not those of one who follows the code of Bushido. In his seminal book on the Bushido code, Inazō Nitobe quotes a prince of Mito saying, 'To rush into the thick of battle and to be slain in it, is easy enough, and the merest churl is equal to the task; but, it is true courage to live when it is right to live, and to die only when it is right to die.'[3] Harry Freame was not ready to die. He still had too much to live for. His was a life cut short.

When Harry left Australia, he had in his mind his young family. Gracie was then thirteen, his stepdaughter a year older. He had a new wife to care and provide for. Young Harry was a grown man but still only twenty years of age. Harry felt the weight of familial responsibilities on his sixty-year-old shoulders. His only concern on his deathbed was that he would leave his family with nothing. And he did. For sadly, after a lifetime of the most courageous service, first in the AIF at Gallipoli and then in his soldier settler communities at Montavella and Kentucky, Harry Freame by 1940 had nothing to show for it. He was broke. He was being dragged before the courts for unpaid debts. For twenty years he had lived on the edge of starvation on his soldier settler block, never complaining, never quitting, holding onto that little flame of hope that next season would be better, next season there would be no frost, or moth, or hail or heat.

When war within Europe broke out in 1939, just a few weeks before his first wife, Edith May, died, Harry tried to sign up for the army but was rejected because of his advanced age. He protested publicly that a man who was capable of fighting for his country should be allowed to, regardless of the years he dragged behind him. It was the same story as World War I all over again. Harry wanted to fight, but his country wouldn't let him. Nevertheless, in the intelligence world he found a place and the work came in. It must have been a great relief. Food once again graced the family table. So when Harry was asked to go to Japan, what could he say? What choice does a broke man have when offered work? Very little, regardless of the potential dangers it holds.

When the Australian Government covered up its role in Harry's death, it covered up the memory of Harry, his legacy. Each day, at the going down of the sun, if we do not remember Harry, we consign him further to history. The fact that this occurred before, during and after a war with Japan, only made things easier for those who wished to forget Harry Freame. There was little appetite for remembering the life of a Japanese-Australian in the aftermath of the brutal Pacific War, a time when Australia's fear and hatred of all things Japanese peaked, fuelled by the atrocities the Japanese committed against Australian prisoners of war.

But postwar there was one man who was willing to speak up not just on behalf of Harry Freame, but on behalf of all the Japanese and Chinese people who had made Australia home. Charles Bean was an unlikely spokesman for the benefits of multiculturalism, as for many years of his life he was an ardent supporter of the White Australia policy, a believer that Asian peoples could not successfully live side by side with white British citizens. But by 1949 after witnessing two world wars that cared nothing for racial stereotypes, where heroes came in all different skin colours and death cared not a jot for theories of racial superiority, Bean, to his credit, had changed his mind.

Bean never forgot his meeting with Harry Freame on 7 June 1915, as Turkish shrapnel whizzed and banged around their heads. After returning from the war and starting work on his *Official History*, it was to Harry Freame that Bean wrote when he required detailed sketches and plans of the Turkish entrenchments at Gallipoli. Harry had left an impression on Charles Bean that never faded.

In 1949 Australia's Asian population was coming under the scrutiny of those still clinging to a White Australia policy. Bean made his views on this clear in the pages of *The Sydney Morning Herald*.

> The talk of the evils due to cross breeding is, in this case, sheer trash, and very like the kind of trash that Hitler spoke ... It was a half-Japanese who was the finest scout in the first AIF, Harry Freame, a man who devoted himself to Australia; who won the first DCM at Anzac – it should have been a VC; who headed a soldier settlement through the peace years until just before his death he was chosen by Sir John Latham as part of our legation to Tokio; whose son, as fine a citizen as we ever had, died a hero's death in the Second AIF.[4]

Bean does well here to draw attention to one of the great undiscussed hypocrisies of modern Australia. That as a nation we could send troops to fight a German enemy that espoused a theory of racial superiority while maintaining at home, as a central tenet of our national identity, the White Australia policy, an instrument of racial exclusion founded in a belief of racial superiority.

Also of interest in Bean's defence of Freame is the line that Harry's DCM should really have been a Victoria Cross. There is enough evidence to suggest that Harry never gained an officer's commission because of the colour of his skin and the general belief that he was Mexican. Bean's observation raises the spectre that these considerations of race also denied Harry a VC.

Charles Bean travelled to World War I with a clear idea of the Australian soldier and his characteristics, and much of his journalism, at least in the early part of the war, was determined to confirm his pre-existing beliefs in the superiority of Australian troops. It was also an attempt to confirm his belief in the superiority of the British race. Bean felt that the Australian soldier's egalitarianism, resourcefulness, commitment to the fair go and his undying sense of mateship would shine through, and his extensive writings helped cement these characteristics as national traits for generations to come.

When the first, somewhat exaggerated, accounts of the performance of the Australian soldiers were published, there was relief in Australia that the digger had proved himself, had not been found wanting. It was confirmation of the superiority of that distinct strain of the British race, the white Australian. And this sense of superiority ran through the most important policy of the young country, the White Australia policy.

But the reality was a little more complex. While there were undoubtedly numerous acts of bravery and courage in those first weeks of Gallipoli, there were also many incidents of Australian troops who refused to fight, some who returned too quickly from the front line, others who refused to set out for it. And understandably so. These were young, poorly trained men, thrown into a hellfire of Turkish shrapnel and bombs.

Bean's dilemma in reporting these acts by Australian soldiers, which did not align with his pre-existing opinions, are neatly demonstrated in his retelling of the incident of Freame's attack on German Officers' Trench. In his diary Bean recorded Freame calling the Australian soldiers who refused to go with him on his night raid 'cowards'. And yet when this anecdote is retold in the *Official History*, the cowards remark is not included. Bean couldn't bring himself to relay anyone calling the Australian soldiers cowards, or to indicate that a man of Japanese birth may have been braver than the Australians. Of course Bean paints himself into a corner by dealing with absolutes. A much more nuanced approach would have allowed him scope to recognise the faults and strengths in individuals rather than attempt to fit every soldier into the straitjacket of caricature. But indulgence of nuance is not how myths are made.

Given the tightly bound concepts of national identity and racial purity that dominated Australian policy at the time, would it be reasonable to think that in 1915 a Japanese man would receive the very first Victoria Cross to be awarded to an Australian? It seems highly unlikely.

In any event, Albert Jacka won the first Victoria Cross for Australia. The citation reads:

Lance-Corporal Jacka, while holding a portion of our trench with four other men, was heavily attacked. When all except himself were killed or wounded, the trench was rushed and occupied by seven Turks. Lance-Corporal Jacka at once most gallantly attacked them single-handed, and killed the whole party, five by rifle fire and two with the bayonet.[5]

The awarding of the VC conferred national hero status upon Albert Jacka. He was given £500 and a gold watch by Australian businessman John Wren, gifts that Wren had promised to whoever won the first VC for Australia. When Jacka returned from the war, his ship was met by the governor-general at the head of a large crowd, and Jacka was driven to a town-hall reception in an eighty-five-car convoy. When Jacka passed away in 1932, he was given a state funeral. Six thousand mourners filed past his coffin; his funeral procession counted over a thousand returned soldiers among it.

If you would like to read more about Albert Jacka, you could pick up a copy of *Hard Jacka*, or *Jacka VC: Australian Hero*, or *Jacka, VC: Australia's Finest Fighting Soldier*, or *In Search of Jacka, VC*, or *Return of the Gallipoli Legend: Jacka VC*. No doubt there will be more books about Jacka on the way, written by that peculiar class of Australian historian who still sees Australian history as white history, those who continue to ignore the colour of true Australian history.

Harry Freame had ten people at his funeral and some nice words from his old comrade FJ Kindon: 'He could move about No-man's Land as if he were invisible; he was a marvelous [sic] revolver shot ... He was a great soldier and a good comrade.'[6] He also referred to his 'cool, calm brain without which these capacities would be of little use'. There, Kindon's words recall those of Inazō Nitobe describing an adherent of the Bushido code:

> The spiritual aspect of valor is evidenced by composure – calm presence of mind. Tranquillity is courage in repose. It is a statical manifestation of valor, as daring deeds are a dynamical. A truly brave man is ever serene; he is never taken by surprise; nothing ruffles the equanimity of his spirit. In the heat of battle he remains cool; in the midst of catastrophes he keeps level his mind. Earthquakes do not shake him, he laughs at storms. We admire him as truly great, who, in the menacing presence of danger or death, retains his self-possession.[7]

Albert Jacka won the VC and other military honours for his daring acts of courage. But he won his VC because he was white. Awarding Jacka the first VC confirmed for a young nation that its belief in the superiority of the white British race was well held; it confirmed the nobleness and value of mateship, resourcefulness, the fair go and egalitarianism.

Harry could never have won the first VC. Because awarding Harry that honour would have been a repudiation of all that the young nation of Australia held dear. Harry's fighting prowess and bravery did not come from any sense of Australian mateship or an abiding belief in the fair go. It came from his education in the Bushido code, the code of the samurai warrior.

But even Harry's fighting courage has been doubted by modern writers. Writing of Harry's time in Gallipoli in *Australia's First Spies*, John Fahey argues:

> The evidence suggests that he [Freame] was most likely reckless. The fact Freame dressed up as a Wild West scout wearing a bandana and two pistols (one on each hip), sporting a shoulder holster and carrying a bowie knife, betrays a look at me element in his character that would make him a dangerous man to be around on a battlefield.[8]

Such a conclusion flies in the face of the evidence that Harry was an exceptional scout precisely because of his ability to avoid being seen. Rather than being a 'look at me element', the way Harry dressed in Gallipoli was a rational response to the unique work he was required to undertake. Journalists who interviewed Harry described him as modest, a man who said little. Fahey's conclusion that Harry was a dangerous man to be around also runs contrary to the testimony of his digger comrades. Lieutenant-Colonel Longfield Lloyd, writing in 1931, described Harry as a man who 'combined sincerity with an inflexible determination and a fierce but cool courage; he was one whom anyone would be glad to have at his side either in War or Peace – I know that I would.'[9]

To this we can add the glowing recommendations of Harry's 1st Battalion commanders. From Major Sasse: 'During the whole of the fighting, Sergt. Freame was under my command and proved himself to be the most reliable & capable man I had. He is a splendid fighter, excellent disciplinarian and always had the confidence of the men under him.' From Lieutenant-General Walker: 'I shall always remember your splendid service.'[10]

And from Charles Bean himself, who described Freame as 'probably the most trusted scout at Anzac'.[11] Or from Lieutenant-Colonel Dobbin, writing in 1918 after witnessing three years of fighting with the AIF:

> I regard him as one of the finest of the men I had with me. I saw a great deal of him and some of his wounds were received while actually in my company. I strongly recommend him as a conscientious, keen and capable soldier whose superior it would be difficult to find.[12]

Fahey dismisses this support for Freame from Charles Bean and members of the AIF as being irrelevant, as 'Charles Bean and the AIF that landed at Gallipoli in 1915 were barely trained and had no experience of war fighting'.[13] In Fahey's mind neither Bean's nor Harry's colleagues were in any place to make a judgement of Harry's fighting talents, a position that ignores the fact that these accounts of Harry came after the war, when all the men had seen their fair share of fighting and were in a position to distinguish the courageous from the cowardly.

Maybe even now Harry Freame just doesn't fit the mould of what most people consider an Australian hero should be. Chris Masters, in his book about the defamation case brought by Australian VC recipient Ben Roberts-Smith against him and fellow journalist Nick McKenzie, writes that part of what allowed Roberts-Smith to act as he did for so long and get away with it was the nation's belief in the Anzac myth: 'When Ben Roberts-Smith left the Army, the legend came alive. The myth of the classic Anzac, seven-foot-tall and bulletproof, found human form.'[14]

But what if the classic Anzac wasn't seven-foot tall and bulletproof? What if the classic Anzac was dark-skinned, spoke English as a second language and was born Hidetsugu Kitagawa? It is hard to write the story of Harry Freame's life and not imagine a different outcome. We need only to look at the life of Albert Jacka to see what may have awaited officer Harry Freame VC. Jacka returned to a hero's reception and went into business with powerful associates. When he died, a public appeal raised £1195 towards a plaque and sculpture for his grave and a house for his widow. There was no unmarked grave and a destitute widow for Albert Jacka VC. Today his portrait hangs in the Australian War Memorial.

And what if Harry had been given the officer's commission that he so desired and had so obviously earned? Well, how did the other officers of this story fair? Longfield Lloyd returned from the war and bounced around from one intelligence position to the next before receiving his diplomatic appointment to Japan. Geoffrey Street, who had spent a short, terrifying time in a trench in no-man's-land with Harry, came home to resume his place in his family's judicial dynasty, eventually going into politics and rising to minister for defence before his life was tragically cut short in an aviation accident in 1940. Jack Scott, William Roy Hodgson and Edmund Piesse all transitioned from the war into a relatively comfortable postwar life supported by cosy government positions. Not for them the tilling of the barren fields of a soldier settlement, the pangs of hunger in an empty belly, the eternal prayer for rain or respite or just a little bit of luck.

It could be argued that Harry failed to make officer not because he was a 'Mexican', but because he was injured and he could no longer hold a rifle. But that argument fails to recognise that Harry had never used a rifle; he did his work with two revolvers, one on each hip. Nor did many other officers use a rifle, content to marshal their troops from the back, well out of danger and in no need of firing a shot. Brigadier-General Walker was sure there was a position for an officer that did not require the use of a rifle.

Nor was a wound an obstacle to returning to duty or even advancement. Major Jack Scott was only promoted to major after being wounded. Brigadier-General Walker was evacuated from Gallipoli after two rounds from a Turkish machine gun badly wounded him in the arm and hip; he returned to command troops in France.

But none of these precedents really matter for Harry Freame. Harry could only ever have become a commissioned officer if Australia truly was a land of the fair go, where egalitarianism reigned and a man was judged by his resourcefulness and his willingness to have a go.

Epilogue

After spending a year looking into the remarkable life of Harry Freame, one mystery remained. Who had placed the headstone on Harry's grave? I would eventually solve that too, but in a very roundabout way.

In 2019 author Brian Tate raised the matter of Harry's unmarked grave with the then acting minister for veterans in the NSW Government, Dr Geoff Lee. Dr Lee in turn raised the matter with his Commonwealth counterpart, Minister Darren Chester. Chester's response to Tate was that 'Mr. Freame is not eligible for Official Commemoration given that he died from cancer of the gall bladder, which is a condition that cannot be linked to his war service.'[1] It was a repeat of the reply that Prime Minister Robert Menzies sent to Harriet Freame in 1964.

On 26 June 2023 I took it upon myself to write to Prime Minister Anthony Albanese and the minister for veterans' affairs, Matt Keogh, on behalf of Harry Freame:

> I am writing to raise with you both the case of Wykeham Henry Koba Freame, known in his time simply as Harry Freame. Freame served in World War 1 in 1st Battalion AIF. He landed on Gallipoli on the morning of 25 April and distinguished himself during those first days of fighting, winning the first Distinguished

Epilogue

Conduct Medal (DCM) for an Australian soldier. Official historian Charles Bean wrote that over the course of those first few days, no Australian soldier was more ubiquitous than Freame as he took water to comrades, reinforced firing lines and rounded up stragglers, despite himself being shot twice by snipers. Bean expressed the opinion that Harry's DCM should really have been a Victoria Cross. All up Freame was wounded 18 times at Gallipoli, a shell through the right arm during the battle of Lone Pine, finally forcing his evacuation back to Australia.

... Harry Freame currently lies in an unmarked grave in North Sydney. It seems an affront to a man who served so courageously. Newspaper reports of the day state that Freame was a household word on Anzac and Charles Bean, described him as 'the most trusted scout on Anzac.' Over the years, a few other petitioners have requested that the government right this wrong by providing a headstone with Harry's service badge for his grave but they have always been answered that Harry did not die in service of his country but of cancer and therefore was not eligible.

I am hopeful, that now is the time that as a country and as Government, we can do the right thing by Harry Freame by honouring his service and sacrifice by placing a headstone complete with his service badge upon his final resting place ... Every 25 April we make a promise that at the going down of the sun, and in the morning, we will remember them. It is time that we honoured that promise. It is time that we remembered Harry Freame.[2]

I was soon contacted by the Department of Veterans' Affairs. The crux of the matter was that for Harry Freame's grave to be eligible for a headstone, I would have to prove that Freame was employed as either a soldier or intelligence agent during World War II, and that his death was due to that service. I sent the department the evidence I had collected, feeling confident that I had satisfied both points. Whether they would listen to me was another matter.

My answer came at the beginning of October 2023 in the form of a letter from the Department of Veterans' Affairs: 'Thank you for your request relating to War Grave eligibility for the above veteran Mr Harry Freame. The application has been considered, and is accepted for War Graves purposes.'

But it was not that simple. The bureaucracy of the Australian Government wasn't about to let Harry go that easily. The letter continued:

> on consideration of the evidence including the official cause of the veteran's passing, I consider it a reasonable hypothesis that the following factor from Statement of Principles 89 of 2015 is met and can be related to the veteran's World War 1 service:
>
> Smoking at least ten pack-years of cigarettes, or the equivalent thereof in other tobacco products, before the clinical onset of malignant neoplasm of the gallbladder, and:
>
> (a) smoking commenced at least five years before the clinical onset of malignant neoplasm of the gallbladder; and
>
> (b) where smoking has ceased, the clinical onset of malignant neoplasm of the gallbladder has occurred within 20 years of cessation.[3]

Epilogue

Harry would get his headstone, but the government was still sticking to the line that he died from gallbladder cancer, and arguing that the cancer was caused by smoking cigarettes, which formed part of the ration packs of all Anzacs at Gallipoli. While smoking does increase your risk of gallbladder cancer, the link between the two is far more tenuous than that of smoking and lung or throat cancer. The department's response left me satisfied and dissatisfied at the same time. And it placed me in a dilemma. Should I insist on overturning Harry's official cause of death and risk losing his headstone? Or should I say nothing and allow an eighty-year-old lie to go on?

I called the department. I explained that while I was grateful for their decision, I didn't believe that Harry died of gallbladder cancer at all, given all the evidence I'd seen.

Luckily I got an honest official on the call. 'Look, mate,' he told me. 'We have an official cause of death on his death certificate and we can link that to his war service. Harry will get the headstone he deserves.'

I left it at that. There was no sense in pushing it any further. Harry will get the headstone he deserves, but I still think he deserves the truth; he deserves to be believed. And I am left with the feeling that the Australian Government has still not taken responsibility for sending Harry Freame to his death.

A few days later I received a letter from the Commonwealth War Graves Commission. Once a veteran has been deemed eligible for a headstone by the Department of Veterans' Affairs, it is the responsibility of the War Graves Commission to place the headstone. But they have some conditions. And one of those is that 'an official commemoration can only be placed at the gravesite of an eligible veteran if the gravesite remains completely unmarked, i.e. bare earth/lawn'.[4]

I had a problem. Harry's grave had remained unmarked for eighty years. His unmarked grave was the reason I had started writing this book. But when I had visited the grave, it was no longer unmarked. A mysterious headstone had appeared. The War Graves Commission didn't care if the details of that headstone were correct or not. The fact it was there was enough to stop them proceeding with their headstone. It now became important to find out who had placed that headstone. Only they would be able to remove it.

I called the cemetery and received the same answer that I had been given almost twelve months earlier when I had visited Harry's grave. They had no record of the grave ever being marked with a headstone. But they promised to investigate. A week passed. And then another. Finally the cemetery got back to me. It was good news. They had located a permit that had been issued giving permission for a stone to be laid on the gravesite of Harry Freame. The name on the permit: Malcolm Freame.

When I finally tracked down Malcolm, he told me that he was the great-grandson of Harry Freame's half-brother, William Henry George Freame, the boy born to Ellen Jane Coker and William Henry Freame in 1867, months after William Henry had absconded to his new life in Japan. In 2021 after learning of the life of his distant relative Harry Freame, Malcolm felt it was his familial duty to mark Harry's grave.

Finding Malcolm, a descendant of William Henry Freame, made me feel as if I had come full circle in the Freame story. But more importantly, Harry Freame would get his official headstone, complete with the Australian Defence Force badge. The digger from the land of the rising sun could now rest below the rising sun that he had lived and died for.

Acknowledgements

Writing a book obliges the author to incur an enormous number of debts. Publishing the book allows them to discharge some of those debts, if only those of gratitude.

In retelling the life of Harry Freame, I owe thanks to many people who in big and small ways contributed to the final book. First of all to Brian Tate. Brian attempted to bring Harry's story to the Australian public in the 1990s but was told at the time that Australian readers weren't interested in biography. I hope that has changed. Before the time of the internet and digital archives, Brian spent years piecing together Harry's life. The result of that work was a self-published book titled *The Gallipoli Samurai*. Brian and his book were important guides for this work, pointing me down the trail of where Harry had been. I also came to know Brian as a friend with whom I would have long conversations about Harry's life and share my latest discoveries. His enthusiasm and passion for telling this story were guiding lights.

Susan McGregor also played an instrumental part in the writing of this book. Susan was a friend of Harry's daughter Gracie and made available to me the personal collection of letters and photos and objects of the Freame family. Susan was another welcome source of encouragement, inspiration and friendship.

Sheila Goodyear, who married into the family of Harry's first wife, Edith May, was another who provided me with access to personal letters, photos and objects of the Freame family held in England, for which I am very grateful.

Other people I would like to mention for their support and encouragement and assistance are Sharon Collins, granddaughter of John Chappie Collins, Kana Thorpe, Koyama Noburu, Hana Hanamoto, Jeff O'Brien, Susan Mason, Judith Grieve, Peter Hoare, Professor Melanie Oppenheimer, Constance Thurleyhart, Johan Duflou, Roger Byard, Romain Caillaud, Malcolm Freame and Carolyn Morrow for her uncanny ability to decipher cursive writing. Also a thank you to Greg Cormack, Matt Crichton, Sandra Barron, Shaun Butta and Michael Quinn for always being around to bounce ideas off. Special thanks to my office assistant Maria Canela.

We are so lucky in Australia to have access to archives that hold our nation's stories, and I would like to acknowledge the assistance provided by the staff of the Australian War Memorial – including Jennifer King, for image assistance – the National Library, the NSW State Library, the NSW State Archives Collection and the National Archives of Australia in both Sydney and Canberra.

Thank you to Martin Hughes and the whole Affirm Press team for believing in Harry's story and helping to bring it to the world in the best possible shape.

And, finally, thank you to my wife, Carolina, for bearing with dignity and grace and eternal patience the insufferable fate of having married a writer.

References

Chapter 1: Hell on Earth
1. David Fallon, *The Big Fight*, WJ Watt & Company, 1918.
2. BV Stacy, FJ Kindon & HV Chedgey, *1st Battalion: History of the First Battalion AIF 1914–1919*, 1931.
3. Ibid.
4. John Masefield, *Gallipoli*, The MacMillan Company, 1916.
5. Phillip Schuler, *Australia in Arms*, T Fisher Unwin, 1916, p. 113.
6. CEW Bean, *Official History of Australia in the War 1914–1918*, Vol. 1, p. 309
7. Ibid. p. 333.
8. CEW Bean, manuscript regarding Harry Freame DCM, NAA: AWM38, 3DRL 6673/893.
9. Australian War Memorial, 'A Difficult Landing', www.awm.gov.au/visit/exhibitions/anzac-voices/landing, accessed 8 March 2024.
10. Bean, manuscript regarding Harry Freame DCM.
11. Australian War Memorial, 'Honours and Awards (Recommendation) HW Freame', www.awm.gov.au/collection/R1605921, accessed 8 March 2024.
12. Bean, manuscript regarding Harry Freame DCM.
13. Stacy, Kindon & Chedgey, *1st Battalion*, p. 31.
14. Eric Ward, War Diary, 6 October 1914 – 28 July 1915, Mitchell Library, State Library of New South Wales, acms.sl.nsw.gov.au/_transcript/2014/D14312/a4633.html, accessed 8 March 2024.

Chapter 2: Born Between Worlds
1. Britannica: https://www.britannica.com/event/Charter-Oath.
2. Edward R. Beauchamp, 'Griffis in Japan: The Fukui Interlude, 1871', *Monumenta*

Nipponica, Winter, 1975, Vol. 30, No. 4, pp. 423–52, Sophia University.
3   Ernest Satow, *A Diplomat in Japan*, Seeley, Service & Co Limited, 1921.
4   Edward R. Beauchamp, 'Griffis in Japan', pp. 423–452.
5   Author correspondence with Japanese academic Koyama Noburu.
6   Ibid.
7   Ibid.
8   Ibid.
9   Yvette Tan, 'The Japanese Christians forced to trample on Christ', BBC, www.bbc.com/news/world-asia-50414472.
10 Nitobe, Inazō, *Bushido, the Soul of Japan*, G.P. Putnam's Sons, 1905.
11 Ibid.
12 CEW Bean, Notes on W H and H W Freame, NAA: AWM38, 3DRL 8042/110E.
13 FJ Kindon, 'Sgt. W.H. Freame, DCM', *Reveille*, July 1941.
14 H Hesketh-Prichard, *Sniping in France*, EP Dutton and Company, 1920.
15 Brian Tate, *Gallipoli Samurai*, Dragonwick Publishing, 2011.
16 John Fahey, *Australia's First Spies: The Remarkable Story of Australia's Intelligence Operations, 1901–45*, Allen & Unwin, 2018.
17 John Collins, *Who are we?: Our Collins family history*, John Collins, 2010.

Chapter 3: The 'Mexican' Scout

1   FREAME, Wykeham Henry – Service Number – 764 [box 1731], NAA: C138, C19352.
2   'AIF Celebrities', *Reveille*, vol. 5, no. 1, September 1931.
3   FJ Kindon, 'Sgt. W.H. Freame, DCM'.
4   CEW Bean, Diaries and Notebooks, June 1915, AWM38, 3DRL606/9/1.
5   'AIF Original', *The Sun*, 27 April 1935, p. 8.
6   'AIF Celebrities'.
7   Harry Freame, 'New Recruits: Gruelling Work', *Reveille*, 1 August 1932.
8   Schuler, *Australia in Arms*, p. 113.
9   'Amazing Scout', *The Evening News*, 25 April 1922, p. 8.
10 Ibid.
11 Ibid., p. 241.
12 Bean, *Official History of Australia in the War 1914–1918*, p. 326.
13 'Amazing Scout', p. 8.

References

14 Bean, Diaries and Notebooks, June 1915.
15 HART Harry Oliver [ELART Edward]: Service Number – 103, NAA: B2455, HART H O.
16 John Gammage, 'Typed transcript of diary of John Kingsley Gammage, 1915–1916', Australian War Memorial, www.awm.gov.au/collection/C1304839?image=11, accessed 8 March 2024.
17 Bean, Diaries and Notebooks, June 1915.
18 Ibid.
19 CEW Bean, 'The Real Significance of the White Australia Question', *The Spectator*, 13 July 1907, p. 13.
20 Ibid.
21 Bean, Diaries and Notebooks, June 1915.

Chapter 4: In Search of a Commission
1   Private letters of Harry Freame held by Susan McGregor.
2   Stacy, Kindon & Chedgey, *1st Battalion*.
3   Freame, 'New Recruits: Gruelling Work'.
4   Stacy, Kindon & Chedgey, *1st Battalion*.
5   Schuler, *Australia in Arms*, p. 113.
6   John Vial, Vial war diary, 6 August – 19 November 1915, Mitchell Library, State Library of New South Wales.
7   Ibid.
8   Fallon, *The Big Fight*, 1918.
9   Vial, Vial war diary.
10 Gammage, 'Typed transcript of diary'.
11 Rhys Crawley, 'Lone Pine: Worth the Cost?', *Wartime Magazine*, Autumn 2007.
12 Freame, 'New Recruits: Gruelling Work'.
13 Ibid.
14 Schuler, *Australia in Arms*, p. 113.
15 Bean, *Official History of Australia in the War 1914–1918*, p. 565.
16 'Victoria Cross: Captain AJ Shout, 1 Battalion, AIF', Australian War Memorial, www.awm.gov.au/collection/C1160952, accessed 8 March 2024.
17 CEW Bean, 'Brave Commander', *The Tamworth Daily Observer*, 26 October 1915, p. 2.
18 Ibid.

19 Personal papers of Harry Freame.
20 Ibid.
21 Ibid.
22 Ibid.
23 Ibid.
24 Ibid.
25 Ibid.
26 FREAME, Wykeham Henry – Service Number – 764.
27 CEW Bean, Notes, n.d.; on W H and H W Freame, NAA: AWM38, 3DRL 8042/110E.
28 Ibid.
29 Ibid.
30 FREAME, Wykeham Henry – Service Number – 764.
31 Hesketh-Prichard, *Sniping in France*.
32 Bean, manuscript regarding Harry Freame DCM.
33 Cameron Hazlehurst, *Ten Journeys to Cameron's Farm: An Australian Tragedy*, Australian National University Press, 2013.
34 Eligibility of Candidates – Mr: Abdul Wade, NAA: MP84/1, 1862/5/983.

Chapter 5: A Hero's Return
1 'Invalids Return', *The Daily Telegraph*, 29 July 1916, p. 5.
2 'Sidelights of War', *The Northern Star*, 29 September 1915, p. 8.
3 'Saved Their Lives', *The Sun*, 28 July 1916, p. 8.
4 'A DCM Hero from Glen Innes', *The Northern Star*, 13 September 1916, p. 7.
5 'Invalids Return', p. 5.
6 Ibid.
7 Ibid.

Chapter 6: Japan and Australia
1 Correspondence with H Eitaki; Acting Consul General for Japan, with reference to the Immigration Restriction Act, and admission of Japanese Subjects, NAA: A8, 1901/203/1.
2 Commonwealth of Australia 1901, Parliamentary debates, Senate, 13 November 1901, *Historic Hansard*, historichansard.net/senate/1901/19011113_senate_1_6/#subdebate-8-0-s2, accessed 8 March 2024.

References

3 Ibid.
4 Commonwealth of Australia 1901, Parliamentary debates, House of Representatives, 12 September 1901, *Historic Hansard*, historichansard.net/hofreps/1901/19010912_REPS_1_4_c1/#debate-6, accessed 8 March 2024.
5 Ibid.
6 Ibid.
7 Ibid.
8 'Japan and Australia', *The Argus*, 17 March 1904, p. 5.
9 Commonwealth of Australia 1905, Parliamentary debates, House of Representatives, 6 December 1905, *Historic Hansard*, historichansard.net/hofreps/1905/19051206_reps_2_30/#debate-6, accessed 8 March 2024.
10 Lieut JG Fearnley re Japanese Espionage and a Secret Service, NAA: MP84/1, 1877/5/5.

Chapter 7: A Mis-start at Montavella

1 Tomoko Horikawa, *Japanese-Australian Clash over the White Australia Policy, 1894–1919*, Doctoral thesis, University of Sydney, 2022.
2 Ibid.
3 EL Piesse, 'Japan and Australia', *Foreign Affairs*, April 1926, vol. 4, no. 3, Council on Foreign Relations.
4 Commonwealth of Australia 1916, Parliamentary debates, House of Representatives, 14 September 1916, *Historic Hansard*, historichansard.net/hofreps/1916/19160914_reps_6_79/#subdebate-12-0-s1, accessed 8 March 2024.
5 Ken Fry, 'Soldier Settlement and the Australian Agrarian Myth after the First World War', *Labour History*, May 1985, Liverpool University Press.
6 'Soldiers' Settlements', *Construction and Local Government Journal*, 15 January 1917.
7 'Group Settlement', *The Farmer and Settler*, 3 May 1918, p. 3.
8 'Soldier Settlers', *The National Advocate*, 26 March 1918, p. 2.
9 'Dissatisfaction at Montavella', *Australian Town and Country Journal*, 10 April 1918, p. 5.
10 'Soldier Settlers', p. 2.
11 Ibid.
12 Bruce Scates & Melanie Oppenheimer, *The Last Battle: Soldier Settlement in*

Australia, 1916–1939, Cambridge University Press, 2016.
13 'Group Settlement', p. 3.
14 'Settlement Upon a Grandmotherly Plan', *The Farmer and Settler*, 9 April 1918, p. 1.
15 Ibid.
16 'At Last', *The National Advocate*, 14 January 1919, p. 2.
17 Ibid.
18 'Personal', *The National Advocate*, 7 December 1918, p. 2

Chapter 8: 'Repugnant Restrictions' and Corruption at Kentucky
1 'Australia's First DCM', *Cootamundra Herald*, 7 November 1919, p. 3.
2 NK Meaney, *Fears and Phobias: E.L. Piesse and the Problem of Japan, 1909–39*, National Library of Australia, 1996.
3 Ibid.
4 Ibid.
5 Ibid.
6 Ibid.
7 Photographs and letters from or about Professor Murdoch, NAA: A4311, 774/15.
8 Far East – Enquiries by Major E L Piesse, NAA: A6661, 1402.
9 Horikawa, *Japanese-Australian Clash over the White Australia Policy, 1894–1919*.
10 Japan relations with Australia, NAA: A981, JAP101 PART 1.
11 'Race Equality', *Tweed Daily News*, 21 March 1919, p. 3.
12 'Japan and the Peace Conference', *The Mercury*, 25 February 1919, p. 4.
13 Photographs and letters from or about Professor Murdoch.
14 Fahey, *Australia's First Spies*.
15 'On the Land', *The Sydney Morning Herald*, 16 February 1920, p. 5.
16 Fallon, *The Big Fight*.
17 'From Cowboy to Sea-cook', *The Armidale Express and New England General Advertiser*, 8 Oct 1920, p. 6.
18 Ibid.

Chapter 9: Slim Pickings
1 'Kentucky Notes', *The Armidale Chronicle*, 17 November 1920, p. 2.

References

2 'Who's Who in Sydney', *Everyones*, 6 October 1920, p. 15.
3 Private letters of Edith May Freame.
4 Ibid.
5 Ibid.
6 'Killing Kentucky', *The Evening News*, 11 September 1922, p. 10.
7 Ibid.
8 Ibid.
9 Japanese Espionage – General, NAA: A981, JAP 55.
10 Ibid.
11 Ibid.
12 'Sinister Purchases', *The Herald*, 15 December 1922, p. 3.
13 Private letters of Harry Freame.
14 Private letters of Edith May Freame.
15 Tate, *Gallipoli Samurai*.
16 'Kentucky', *The Uralla Times*, 30 June 1924, p. 2.
17 'Kentucky News', *The Uralla Times*, 6 October 1924, p. 2.
18 'Kentucky', *The Armidale Chronicle*, 25 October 1922, p. 2.
19 'District News', *The Armidale Express and New England General Advertiser*, 1 June 1920, p. 8.
20 'Kentucky', *The Uralla Times*, 29 November 1923, p. 3.
21 'Grand Masonic Ball', *The Uralla Times*, 25 August 1927, p. 2.
22 'Kentucky Fruit', *The Uralla Times*, 25 March 1929, p. 2.
23 'Excitement', *The Uralla Times*, 14 April 1927, p. 2.
24 Ibid.
25 'Ladies Trounce the Old Hands', *The Uralla Times*, 14 January 1932, p. 1.
26 'AIF Celebrities', *Reveille*, vol. 5, no. 1, September 1931.
27 Ibid.
28 Ibid.
29 'AIF Celebrities'.

Chapter 10: Goodwill Mission

1 Far East. Report presented to Parliament of the Australian Eastern Mission, 1934, by the Right Hon J.G. Latham, NAA: A981, FAR 5 PART 17.
2 Ibid.
3 Far East. Australian Eastern Mission 1934. Reports. 1. Printed report. 2. Secret

report on international position in Far East. 3. Conf. report on Appointment of trade commissioners. 4. Conf. report on trade between Australia and Japan. 5. Conf. report on Australian wool in the East. 6. Press Cuttings from Japanese newspapers, NAA: A981, FAR 5 PART 16.
4 'Trade Commissioner', *The Sydney Morning Herald*, 2 August 1935, p. 10.
5 Bruce Bennett, 'Traditional Myths and Problematic Heroes: The Case of Harry Freame', *Asiatic*, vol. 4, no. 2, December 2010.
6 Wayne Gobert, *The Origins of Australian Diplomatic Intelligence Reporting in Asia 1933–1941*, Masters thesis, University of New South Wales, 1989.
7 Far East. Report presented to Parliament of the Australian Eastern Mission, 1934, by the Right Hon J.G. Latham.
8 Ibid.
9 Gobert, *The Origins of Australian Diplomatic Intelligence Reporting in Asia 1933–1941*.
10 Meaney, *Fears and Phobias*.
11 Ibid.
12 Far East. Report presented to Parliament of the Australian Eastern Mission, 1934, by the Right Hon J.G. Latham.
13 'Sea Power', *The Argus*, 2 August 1935, p. 9.
14 Meaney, *Fears and Phobias*.
15 Honae Cuffe, *The Genesis of a Policy: Defining and Defending Australia's National Interest in the Asia-Pacific, 1921–57*, Australian National University Press, 2021.
16 Ibid.
17 Ibid.
18 Gobert, *The Origins of Australian Diplomatic Intelligence Reporting in Asia 1933–1941*.
19 'Kentucky Resident Examined', *The Uralla Times*, 8 December 1938, p. 5.
20 Ibid.
21 Ibid.
22 'Fruit Commission at Kentucky', *The Armidale Express and New England General Advertiser*, 14 January 1938, p. 3.
23 Private letters of Edith May Freame.
24 Tate, *Gallipoli Samurai*.
25 Private letters of Young Harry Freame.
26 Ibid.

27 Ibid.
28 Ibid.
29 Private letters of Harry Freame.

Chapter 11: An Agent Revealed

1 Hazlehurst, *Ten Journeys to Cameron's Farm*.
2 'For Empire', *The Sydney Morning Herald*, 20 July 1920, p. 7.
3 'Japan and Australia', *The Sydney Morning Herald*, 31 March 1933, p. 16.
4 'Relations with Japan', *The Kalgoorlie Miner*, 20 July 1934, p. 7.
5 Japanese Intelligence and its operation in Australia – Wartime, NAA: A8911, 2.
6 Ibid.
7 Ibid.
8 Ibid.
9 Ibid.
10 Rokuo Arai, Painting of Japanese warship 'Ibuki', NAA: A461, 748/1/522.
11 Japanese Intelligence and its operation in Australia – Wartime, NAA: A8911, 2.
12 Papers of Professor K.H. Bailey related to Royal Commission on Espionage, NAA: M1507, 35.
13 Request by Australian Commercial Counsellor, Tokyo, for information concerning a Mr Ken Sato, NAA: A432, 1949/544.
14 Espionage (Japanese) [includes Report of Japanese Associations and Activities], NAA: A8911, 11.
15 Pam Oliver, 'Interpreting "Japanese activities" in Australia, 1888–1945', Australian War Memorial, www.awm.gov.au/articles/journal/j36/oliver, accessed 8 March 2024.
16 Yoneda, Kenichiro (Japanese), NAA: C123, 9997.
17 Japanese – Associations and activities, NAA: A373, 5190.
18 Mr Harry Freame – Interpreter Australian Legation to Japan, NAA: MP729/6, 15/403/16.
19 Tate, *Gallipoli Samurai*.
20 'Sir John Latham: Minister to Japan', *The Dubbo Liberal and Macquarie Advocate*, 24 August 1940, p. 3.
21 Mr Harry Freame – Interpreter Australian Legation to Japan.
22 Ibid.
23 Ibid.

24 Ibid.
25 Ibid.
26 Ibid.
27 Ibid.
28 Andrew Moore, '"… When the Caretaker's Busy Taking Care"? Crosscurrents in Australian Political Surveillance and Internment, 1935–1941', in *Alien Justice: Wartime Internment in Australia and North America*, edited by Kay Saunders & Roger Daniels, University of Queensland Press, 2000.
29 NSW Security Service file – Activities of Japanese consular officers, NAA: C320, J20.
30 Andrew Moore, 'Scott, William John (1888–1956)', *Australian Dictionary of Biography*, National Centre of Biography, Australian National University, adb.anu.edu.au/biography/scott-william-john-8373/text14695, first published in hardcopy, 1988, accessed 13 November 2023.
31 Michael Evans, *Developing Australia's Maritime Concept of Strategy: Lessons from the Ambon Disaster of 1942*, Land Warfare Studies Centre, 2000.
32 Ibid.
33 Tony Wright, '"You Just Have to Go On": Talking to the Last Survivor of Ambon', *The Age*, 15 August 2020.
34 Moore, '"… When the Caretaker's Busy Taking Care"?'.
35 Moore, 'Scott, William John (1888–1956)'.
36 Moore, '"… When the Caretaker's Busy Taking Care"?'.
37 Nick Hordern, 'The Man Who Never Was (Easton-Cook's War): Part 1, Hero or Fraud?' *A Rich Life*, 27 March 2020, arichlife.com.au/the-man-who-never-was-easton-cooks-war-part-1-hero-or-fraud/, accessed 8 March 2024.

Chapter 12: Undercover Operations and an Underhand Attack

1 Mr Harry Freame – Interpreter Australian Legation to Japan.
2 Espionage (Japanese) [includes Report of Japanese Associations and Activities].
3 Mr Harry Freame – Interpreter Australian Legation to Japan NAA: MP729/6.
4 His Majesty's Government 1940, Parliamentary debates, House of Lords, 30 July 1940, vol. 117 cc1–3, https://api.parliament.uk/historic-hansard/lords/1940/jul/30/arrest-of-british-subjects-in-japan, accessed 8 March 2024.
5 'Japanese Army Will Take "Drastic Measures"', *The Queensland Times*, 31 July 1940, p. 5.

References

6 Ibid.
7 Ibid.
8 Mr Harry Freame – Interpreter Australian Legation to Japan.
9 Ibid.
10 Ship's menu from the personal letters of Harry Freame.
11 Personal papers of Harry Freame.
12 Ex Gratia – Payments for widow of Harry Freame, NAA: A1838, 1255/43.
13 Ibid.
14 Ibid.

Chapter 13: Deathbed Whispers

1 Australian Minister in Tokyo – H.W. Freame – Question of Compensation for Widow of ..., NAA: A981, AUS 186.
2 FREAME, Wykeham Henry – Service Number – 764.
3 Mr Harry Freame – Interpreter Australian Legation to Japan.
4 Ibid.
5 Ibid.
6 Ibid.
7 Freame, Henry Wykeham (Japanese) [born in Australia], NAA: C123, 10067.
8 John Ryan, 'The Earlier Life of Wykeham Henry Freame', *Armidale and District Historical Society, Journal and Proceedings*, March 1984.
9 Australian Minister in Tokyo – H.W. Freame – Question of Compensation for Widow of ....
10 Kindon, 'Sgt. W.H. Freame, DCM'.
11 Australian Minister in Tokyo – H.W. Freame – Question of Compensation for Widow of ....
12 Freame, Henry Wykeham (Japanese) [born in Australia].
13 Ibid.
14 Personal correspondence with author.
15 Personal correspondence with author.
16 Ibid.
17 Australian Minister in Tokyo – H.W. Freame – Question of Compensation for Widow of ....
18 Ibid.
19 Ibid.

20 Ibid.
21 Ex Gratia – Payments for widow of Harry Freame.
22 Ibid.
23 Australian Minister in Tokyo – H.W. Freame – Question of Compensation for Widow of … .
24 Ibid.
25 Ibid.
26 Ibid.
27 Ibid.
28 Ibid.
29 Ibid.
30 Freame, Henry Wykeham (Japanese) [born in Australia].
31 Ibid.
32 Australian Minister in Tokyo – H.W. Freame – Question of Compensation for Widow of … .
33 Bean, Notes, n.d.; on W H and H W Freame.
34 Ibid.
35 Ibid.
36 Nitobe, *Bushido*.
37 Australian Minister in Tokyo – H.W. Freame – Question of Compensation for Widow of … .
38 Ibid.
39 Ibid.
40 Ibid.
41 Colin Fraser, 'The Friendly Spy Who Died Alone', *Quadrant*, 7 December 2008.
42 Ibid.
43 Ibid.
44 Personal papers of Harry Freame.

Chapter 14: Young Harry

1 'Forfeited Soldiers Group Purchases', *Government Gazette of the State of New South Wales*, 10 October 1941.
2 Personal papers of Young Harry Freame.
3 'Star Game at Duntroon', *The Canberra Times*, 29 May 1943, p. 4.
4 'Freame's Record', *The Canberra Times*, 19 July 1943, p. 3.

5   Personal papers of Young Harry Freame.
6   Ibid.
7   Ibid.
8   'Australians Capture Airstrip on Tarakan', *The Age*, 7 May 1945, p. 3; 'AIF Uses Flame to Clear Jap on Tarakan', *The Courier-Mail*, 7 May 1945, p. 3.
9   Personal papers of Gracie Freame.
10 Ibid.
11 Ibid.
12 Ibid.
13 2nd Australian Imperial Force and Commonwealth Military Forces Unit War Diaries 1939–45, 2/24th Infantry Battalion April-May 1945, AWM52, 8/3/24.
14 Personal papers of Gracie Freame.

Chapter 15: A Hero Forgotten
1   Ex Gratia – Payments for widow of Harry Freame.
2   Ibid.
3   Ibid.
4   Ibid.
5   Ibid.
6   Ibid.
7   Ibid.
8   Ibid.
9   Ibid.
10 Japan – Espionage – Rev. J.N. McKenzie, NAA: A981, JAP 56.
11 Fahey, *Australia's First Spies*.
12 Bennett, 'Traditional Myths and Problematic Heroes'.

Chapter 16: Answers in the Archives
1   Personal Items, *The Bulletin*, Vol. 61, No. 3163, 25 September 1940, p. 1.
2   Bean, Notes, n.d.; on W H and H W Freame.
3   Nitobe, *Bushido*.
4   'Names Chinese Jap. as Austn. Heroes', *The News* (Adelaide), 30 August 1949, p. 7.
5   Australian War Memorial, 'Victoria Cross: Lance Corporal Albert Jacka, 14 Battalion, AIF', www.awm.gov.au/collection/C94174, accessed 8 March 2024.

6 Kindon, 'Sgt. W.H. Freame, DCM'.
7 Nitobe, *Bushido*.
8 Fahey, *Australia's First Spies*.
9 'AIF Celebrities', *Reveille*, Vol. 5, No. 1, September 1931.
10 Letter from Sasse to Freame from private letters of Harry Freame, held by Susan McGregor.
11 Bean, *Official History of Australia in the War 1914–1918*.
12 Letter from Dobbin to Freame from private letters of Harry Freame, held by Susan McGregor.
13 Fahey, *Australia's First Spies*.
14 Chris Masters, *Flawed Hero: Truth, Lies and War Crimes*, Allen & Unwin, 2023.

Epilogue
1 Personal correspondence of Brian Tate, sighted by the author.
2 Author's personal correspondence.
3 Letter from Department of Veterans' Affairs to author
4 Personal correspondence between author and Office of Australian War Graves.